POLITICS & RELIGION IN
SEVENTEENTH-CENTURY FRANCE

W. J. Stankiewicz

POLITICS & RELIGION IN SEVENTEENTH-CENTURY FRANCE

A Study of Political Ideas from the Monarchomachs to Bayle, as Reflected in the Toleration Controversy

GREENWOOD PRESS, PUBLISHERS
WESTPORT, CONNECTICUT

Library of Congress Cataloging in Publication Data

Stankiewicz, W   J
    Politics & religion in seventeenth-century France.

    Reprint of the ed. published by the University of
California Press, Berkeley.
    Bibliography: p.
    Includes index.
    1. France--Politics and government--17th century.
2. Edict of Nantes. 3. Religious liberty--France.
I. Title.
[DC121.3.S8 1976]   944'.03   76-2075
ISBN 0-8371-8770-2

© 1960 by The Regents of The University of California

Originally published in 1960 by University of California Press,
Berkeley

Reprinted with the permission of University of California Press

Reprinted in 1976 by Greenwood Press,
a division of Williamhouse-Regency Inc.

Library of Congress Catalog Card Number 76-2075

ISBN 0-8371-8770-2

Printed in the United States of America

To My Mother and Father

PREFACE

The work on this book—which was originally submitted as a Ph.D. thesis at the University of London—began at the instigation of the late Professor Harold Laski, who at one time intended to write a study covering similar grounds. His profound knowledge of the period and his inimitable gift of imparting enthusiasm for scholarly pursuits are very well known to those whom he had helped to discover obscure texts and clarify their own ideas. The research continued under Mr. William Pickles, of the London School of Economics and Political Science, who gave much of his time, providing invaluable criticism and direction in the crucial period during which the essay was being molded.

I am grateful to my friends Professor Peter Brock, of the University of Alberta; Mrs. Carol Maclure, of London; Dr. Marketa C. Goetz, of the University of British Columbia; Mme Jacqueline Lecocq-Leiner, of Paris; Mr. Ronald C. Cooke, of Toronto, Ontario; and Mr. Ian Peyman of Vancouver, B.C., for their kind help extended to me at various stages of the preparation of this manuscript.

I am also greatly indebted to the Canada Council, whose generous grant has effectively assisted me in the publication of this study, and to Dean V. W. Bladen and the Social Science Research Council of Canada for their encouragement.

Parts of this book appeared in the *Proceedings of the Huguenot Society of London* (Vol. XIX, No. 1, 1953; No. 3, 1955), *Proceedings of the American Philosophical Society* (Vol. XCIX, No. 3, 1955), and in *Der Deutsche Hugenott* (Vol. XXI, No. 2, 1957; Vol. XXII, No. 2, 1958; Vol. XXIII, No. 1, 1959), and are published here by the kind permission of the editors.

The engraving of the anvil reproduced on the title page of this book can be found, among other places, on the title page of the *Histoire Ecclésiastique des Eglises Réformées au Royaume de France* (1580), attributed to Théodore de Bèze. The allusion is to the answer given by T. de Bèze to the royal envoy after the Vassy Massacre (1562) that persecutions are futile and that the Reformed church is like an anvil on which many hammers have been broken.

W. J. STANKIEWICZ

University of British Columbia
June, 1959

CONTENTS

Non. Il fut gallican, ce siècle, et janséniste! ...

Non. Il fut gallican, ce siècle, et janséniste!
C'est vers le moyen âge, énorme et délicat,
Qu'il faudrait que mon coeur en panne naviguât,
Loin de nos jours d'esprit charnel et de chair triste.

Roi, politicien, moine, artisan, chimiste,
Architecte, soldat, médecin, avocat,
Quel temps! Oui, que mon coeur naufragé rembarquât
Pour toute cette force ardente, souple, artiste!

Et là que j'eusse part—quelconque, chez les rois
Ou bien ailleurs, n'importe—à la chose vitale,
Et que je fusse un saint, actes bons, pensers droits,

Haute théologie et solide morale,
Guidé par la folie unique de la Croix,
Sur tes ailes de pierre, ô folle Cathédrale!

PAUL VERLAINE

INTRODUCTION

An inquiry into the problem of toleration provides interesting material for the semanticist, for the term has more than one meaning. In the period of French history examined by this study, "toleration" was used in at least three distinct ways: (1) to embody the philosophical principle of true tolerance, defended by Castellion and to a lesser degree by L'Hôpital, which was only vaguely related to any practical attitude and seldom explicitly and clearly expressed—certainly not yet an "homage to the rights of conscience";[1] (2) to designate a legal device desired by the Politiques and used by Henry IV; and (3) to describe a measure of expediency suggested by Omer Talon and "practiced" by Richelieu in the form of *tolerationism*—an attitude which attributed purely political meaning to the notion of religious toleration. But these distinctions, fascinating as they are, do not end the semantic problem, for the philosophical implications of the term were left vague at this period.

In the contemporary vocabulary of Catholic spokesmen, "toleration" was a term of contempt. The Catholics had no interest in promoting it; occasionally they practiced a quasi-toleration—a false attitude concealing some ulterior motive, a utilitarian attitude taking for granted that at some point toleration would be rejected, an expedient usually referred to with derision. Both Talon, in a famous speech,[2] and Meynier, in his treatise,[3] used "toleration" in this derogatory sense, although they recognized the necessity of putting up with this altogether undesirable phenomenon.

The Protestants as a rule, but with some notable exceptions, did not speak of tolerance in a disparaging way; for them, the concept was a valuable weapon in their struggle for political survival. Their attitude was hypocritical, for at their stage of religious development they could not sincerely believe in true tolerance. No doctrine can afford to find a place for tolerance while it is still asserting its own validity. Tolerance is the mark of achievement. It is the skepticism which crowns the struggle, but which is absent during revolu-

---

[1] J. E. Neale, *The Age of Catherine de Medici*, p. 53.
[2] Cf. below, chap. iii.
[3] Cf. below, chap. v.

tion and expansion. To recognize the plausibility and justification of another point of view is to admit limitation in one's own theory— an inadmissible act by a follower of any young ideology. A new doctrine, attempting to find a basis for its own existence and to promote enthusiasm, must claim to be the only purveyor of truth and must condemn all other theories as aberrations. Salvation comes only with unquestioning faith, and any laxity delays the march to the goal— the triumph of the new dogma. To promote such dogmas, it may be necessary to find room for the idea of toleration, but it will be for external use, as a weapon to be used in relations with opponents.

Toleration as a medium to achieve power was not accepted by Calvin and other sixteenth-century theologians, but it was practiced by some later Huguenots, who were less rigidly Calvinist and more politically minded. Both the earlier and, for the most part, the later Huguenots were intolerant, the only difference being that in the beginning the position was frankly stated, whereas later the meaning given to the principle of toleration was deliberately obscured. Toleration mattered only as long as it gave a hope of finding the right way to establish the predominant influence of the Reformed religion.

The weapon which the Huguenots made of the term "toleration" was wrenched from them by Richelieu, who replaced it with his peace formula. In his use of the term "peace," he simply gave a new name to the accepted meaning. Yet the scope of his term was more extensive; it concerned the state as a whole and not merely the oppressed minority; it was used in a far more subtle way and was far more successful. By "peace," he meant a period of quiet, of temporary toleration, which was to be extinguished later. By demanding toleration, the Huguenots expressed their desire for the political and religious equality which they would never have dreamed of preserving had the state been under their control.

❖   ❖   ❖

This investigation cannot survey the different meanings of the term "toleration" and their relation to contemporary ideas without showing the degree of religious and political freedom to which the party struggle led the Huguenots.

The over-all survey presents a somewhat gloomy picture of the fairly general contemporary attitude, in which it was not the principle of tolerance that counted, but the methods of achieving intolerance while preserving religious unity.

If at one time a certain degree of toleration was attained, this was due either to a concession to the strength of the other party or to submission to the exigencies of statecraft. While toleration was then "a plea without either moral or intellectual validity," [4] it was not merely a bogus issue in the dispute between parties or in the conflict between a party and the state. A policy of toleration would have meant the introduction of freedom of conscience not only within the Church but also within the state. The civil government could not remain undisturbed by the external manifestations of the same freedom of religious belief which demanded the right to examine the Scriptures.

No presentation of the political theory of the period would of course be adequate without due consideration of the problem of religious tolerance, which indeed formed one of the two main topics of contemporary political writings. When dealing with toleration, one cannot exclude the concept of sovereignty, the other problem of importance, by which toleration was affected both in its theoretical and in its practical aspect. Again, when speaking of the idea of toleration and presenting it against the wider background of political theory in general, one must try to relate contemporary doctrines to events, mainly those occasioned by, and developing alongside, the party struggle; one must interpret doctrines in the light of events, and events in the light of doctrines.

[4] H. J. Laski, *Communism* (London, 1927), p. 62.

I

THE BACKGROUND

"Libertatem conscientiis diabolicum dogma."—T. Beza.

He that is not with me is against me.—Sixteenth-century theology.

"Le but de la guerre c'est la paix."—Michel de l'Hôpital, Oeuvres complètes, II (Mémoire adressé à Charles IX, 1570), 175.

An adequate account of the political thought of the second half of the sixteenth century must take into consideration not only the events which occurred but also the economic developments which took place and the religious convictions which were held, since all these served either to foster or to hinder the emergence and evolution of the political ideas of the time.

The period between 1546, the date at which evidence of the existence of underground religious organizations is first found, and 1598, when the Edict of Nantes, a concrete measure of toleration, gave the Huguenots legal status, is one of great confusion—full of the clash of ideas, policies, and arms. The Reformation caused violent spiritual and mental upheavals, and though it preached nonresistance, civil wars were waged in its name. Violence bred violence. Soon the spirit of oppression was rampant, and mass murder became a common, if not an openly recognized, political weapon. The body of popular doctrine which emerged as a sequel, and at times as a justification, of events served two immediate purposes: to provide a program for vigorous party activities; and, in the sphere of ideas, to oppose the theory of the divine right of kings.

In such a setting the idea of religious toleration was a contradiction. Yet at the close of the century the Edict of Nantes brought a working compromise, which, if precarious, was at least partly effective.

The Huguenots were allowed to remain comparatively undisturbed for about two decades. The subsequent decline in toleration, which extended over a much longer period, culminated in the Revocation of the Edict of Nantes in 1685. The effective operation of the Edict of Nantes ended with Richelieu, who, in 1629, at Alais, made a new peace treaty on which Huguenot status was to be based. The Peace of Alais was the outcome of the war which closed a long list of civil wars that begins with the wars of religion of the sixteenth century. Though toward the end these wars ceased to have much in common with their predecessors, they sprang from the same root, and a key to many of the problems of the following century can be found in the sixteenth-century wars of religion and in the doctrinal conflict which enveloped them. The seventeenth century can perhaps be more easily understood because it provided clear, if disappointing, solutions to the problem raised by Protestantism. Furthermore, it is less confusing, because the previous century with its doctrines, which are brought to life in the pamphleteers of the Fronde and in Jurieu, had covered all the theoretical ground.

For these reasons a summary of certain events in the sixteenth century will be given in this prefatory chapter. The chapter will also set down certain guiding principles without which the complexities of the wars of religion are difficult to understand.

The first part of the chapter discusses the intolerance of an age when the idea of tolerance, although not unknown, had not as yet found acceptance. It tries to explain why this idea of tolerance was never considered seriously.

The second summarizes the causes of the wars of religion, with their long chain of alternating treaties of peace and fresh hostile outbreaks.

The third introduces the problem of political doctrines, and groups them into separate schools of thought. These doctrines were used by various political parties when they found themselves engaged in conflict, and therefore desperately in need of a theory which would strengthen the right of active disobedience, newly approved by Protestant opinion.

The fourth section deals with the prospects for toleration: grim, both in the sphere of theory and in that of practice, and on both the national and the international level; impracticable, because of a lack of liberal ideas and of broad conceptions of the various forms of coöperation.

The hope of a common understanding in the days of the Counter Reformation was dimmed by those characteristics of human behavior, based on unreason and passion, which the Reformation aroused in spite of its avowed belief in reasoned Biblical investigation and reasoned religious speculation.

THE INTOLERANCE OF THE SIXTEENTH CENTURY

The Edict of Nantes was a concrete measure of toleration, but it did not come into existence because the ruling ideas of the age demanded such a measure. They were too much directed toward certain limited and often conflicting objectives to permit of the wider perspective which genuine religious tolerance requires. The idea of tolerance was rejected both by the rank and file and by the leaders of Catholics and Protestants alike. It was alien to the theologians of both religions. Most people, irrespective of their religious opinions, regarded the principle as a foible of the Humanists, in particular of a few lofty spirits whose outlook was independent, and scarcely religious. These advocates of religious tolerance were not so uncommon as the negligible role they played would suggest.

The outstanding name is that of Castellion (1515–1563), who was influenced by Erasmus and Sebastian Franck. Like Erasmus (1467–1536), he believed in simple and undogmatic faith; like Franck (1499–1542), he regarded religion as a purely spiritual matter, outside the authority of the magistrates. He pointed out, first, the senselessness of killing people on account of ideas the truth of which cannot be defined with certainty;[1] and, second, the wickedness of doing so as being an unwarrantable interference with the individual's right to follow his own religious development. He pleaded that men know too little to be able to judge of what is and what is not heresy. He defined what is meant by a heretic: "Equidem cum quid sit hereticus, saepe quae siverim, nihil aliud deprehendi, nisi haereticum haberi, quisquis a nobis dissentit."[2]

---

[1] The case was made in Castellion's preface to the Latin version of the Bible addressed to Edward VI (1551). Cf. J. W. Allen, *A History of Political Thought in the Sixteenth Century*, p. 84. Hereafter cited as Allen, *A History of Political Thought*.

[2] Martinus Bellius [Sébastien Castellion], *De Haereticis; an sint persequendi*, p. 19.

The problem was not quite so clear to his follower Acontius, who in 1565 wrote *Strategematum Satanae,* in support of Castellion, opposing persecution on the ground that the meaning of heresy could hardly be clear to anyone. He had a low opinion of men's reason and of their conclusions and judgments, which were reached, in his opinion, mechanically, without conscious effort or honest application. He claimed that the bulk of theological argument was vain, vague,[3] and unrelated to human life, and that it reflected man's incapacity to suppose his own opinions to be wrong or to appreciate a spirit of doubt in others. Magistrates, in his view, were not justified in using force either to destroy heresy or to propagate true religion—a view which goes further than the opinions of typical Erasmian Protestant liberals such as Conrad Pellican, Otto Brunsfeld, Gaspar Hedion, and Coelius Curione. Arguing against those who wanted heretics to be killed, Brunsfeld struck an unexpected note: "Nevertheless I do not object if anyone feels that the magistrates, who have the sword as ministers of justice, should punish manifest blasphemers."[4] Hedion, in spite of his reputed moderation, toyed with the idea of suppressing the Anabaptists.[5] But Castellion, as well as Franck and Hesse, can be labeled "independent Protestant liberal,"[6] as they professed a more genuine kind of toleration.

Franck, whose ideas Castellion borrowed heavily, used in support of toleration the most varied methods of approach: dialectics, determinism, indeterminism, pessimism, and optimism. He preached a religion of the spirit—a belief in *das innere Licht* and in a God who did not demand worship in accordance with a particular form or creed. He believed that the division of Christianity into separate sects was obsolete, and on this principle he tried to build his theory of tolerance. Full of paradoxes and unexpected twists of thought, he considered that this religion of the spirit would suppress heresy and be hostile to the Church if it possessed institutional forms within

---

[3] This was a truly Castellionian touch; it reflected his dissatisfaction with the existing body of theological doctrines, his almost Cartesian spirit of doubt, and an attitude tinged with mild skepticism, which is a breeding ground for toleration.

[4] Otto Brunsfeld, *Annotation on the Gospels and Acts.* Cf. R. H. Bainton, ed., *Concerning heretics . . . an anonymous work attributed to Sebastian Castellio, now first done into English,* p. 90. Hereafter cited as Bainton, ed., *Concerning heretics.*

[5] See Bainton, ed., *Concerning heretics,* p. 80.

[6] *Ibid.,* p. 91.

the state, but that it would be quite suitable for a "community of the saints," although such a community might be intolerant.[7] That Franck had no objections to the creation of a group of this kind is shown by his attitude to the Anabaptists, whose views on religion were similar and who were far from tolerant.[8]

In 1569, Hesse opposed the idea of baptizing Anabaptist children by force, in order "to avoid a worse evil, and for the sake of Christian love." [9] The attitude of liberal Protestants to Anabaptism is doubly important, because the Anabaptists, although intolerant themselves, had a concept of the church as a voluntary organization,[10] which, if only indirectly and in a limited sense, helped to develop the notion of toleration.

Castellion met with little success in France, though he had a number of followers abroad. There were local manifestations of revolutionary "bellianism" in the year or two after the publication of his *De Haereticis* (1554). His ideas were exploited by Katherine Zell, in her remonstrance against persecution; by Bartolomeo Silvio, who in 1573 denied magistrates the right to act in religious matters; and by Minus Celsus.[11] The activities of Dirck Volckertszoon Coornhert after 1578 and of Arminius at the beginning of the seventeenth century showed that Castellion's influence had spread to Holland. Arminius founded a sect, known as the Arminians, which at length secured toleration in 1630 and thus reached the goal their spiritual father had not lived to see. At home, in the sixteenth century, Castellion was opposed by Protestants and non-Protestants alike. Sincere Reformers fought him in the name of the Christian unity which they thought was threatened by the growing number of sects. In their opinion, the multiplication of sects which would follow upon a peace embracing all dissenters would bring about the downfall of Christianity. After the publication of Castellion's book, Beza commented on the danger of its doctrine for Christianity: "Cela, di-ie, franchement ie declare, & a haute voix en advertis toutes Eglises Chrestiennes, que si de bonne heure on ne s'oppose a votre impudence, on verra que vous ruinerez toute la religion sans rien

---

[7] Cf. *ibid.*, p. 102.

[8] Cf. G. d'Aubarède, *La Révolution des Saints, passim.*

[9] Bainton, ed., *Concerning heretics,* p. 93.

[10] Cf. Allen, *A History of Political Thought,* p. 48.

[11] In his book *In Haereticis coercendis quatenus progredi liceat Mini Celsi Senensis disputatio* (1577).

laisser." [12] Beza's argument for persecution rested on expediency:
"Quand donc nous traittons en ce livret, a scavoir non si le Magistrat
doit pas punir & reprimer les heretiques ce n'est pas disputer d'une
chose de neant, ce n'est point aussi debatre d'un poinct duquel la
cognoissance ne soit gueres necessaire: mais nous parlons du salut
& de la conservation de l'estat de l'Eglise." [13]

Others opposed the practice of toleration for various reasons
of pure expediency, such as fear that it would interfere with sovereign rights, personal gains, or family interests. The situation
was eased by the "intellectual assumptions" [14] of the age, which
offered some protection against the shocks that the idea of persecution inflicted later. Until Arminianism proved successful, the pre-
cepts of Castellion were without force. The spirit of his ideas was
not even accepted by the Politiques, who merely believed in the
necessity for legal toleration [15] as the remedy for ills resulting from
the wars of religion.

The religious prophets left no room for such an idea in their respective systems. Luther (1483–1546) was not tolerant, though
his intolerance was deprived of its sharpness by the mysticism which
enveloped his thinking. The intolerance of Calvin (1509–1564)
was more pronounced,[16] and was only in part due to the practical
outlook of a great organizer who believed that only a strict and
all-embracing discipline could create the world-wide theocracy which
he hoped to see emerge from the pattern provided by the Genevan
religious state. Although Calvin's new ecclesiastical organism was,
as such, an original creation, his teachings were less so. He borrowed a great deal from his predecessors, notably Luther, expressing the old ideas in a brilliant new way. But his authoritarian outlook was not so original as his style. Like other Reformers, he
disparaged man's earthly existence in order to glorify God.

A connection can be found between his saying "L'homme n'est
rien" and the idea of freedom. A true authoritarian, Calvin did
not originally profess the principles of freedom of thought and

---

[12] Théodore de Bèze, *Traité de l'authorité du Magistrat en la punition des hérétiques,*
p. 58. Hereafter cited as Bèze, *Traité de l'authorité du Magistrat.* (Original Latin
version: *De Haereticis a civili magistratu puniendis libellus.*)

[13] Cf. *ibid.,* p. 426; cf. also p. 327.

[14] Cf. Allen, *A History of Political Thought,* p. 76.

[15] Cf. P. Doyle, *A History of Political Thought* (London, 1949), p. 165.

[16] Cf. R. Stéphan, *L'Epopée huguenote,* p. 60.

speech.[17] His plea for liberty was stated feebly: "Vray est que ... la préeminence de ceux qui gouverneront tenans le peuple en liberté, sera plus à priser." Further qualifications reduced the scope of this liberty, though not its importance:

> Et de fait, comme le meilleur estat de gouvernement est celuy-la, où il y a une liberté bien temporée & pour durer longuement: aussi ie confesse que ceux qui peuvent estre en telle condition sont bien-heureux, & dy qu'ils ne font que leur devoir, s'ils s'employent constamment à s'y maintenir. Mesmes les gouverneurs d'un peuple libre doyvent appliquer toute leur estude à cela, que la franchise du peuple, de laquelle ils sont protecteurs, ne s'amoindrisse aucunement entre leurs mains.[18]

These principles, primarily engendered in the Renaissance, were reversed by the Reformers, as the latter cared not for "freedom" but for "truth" as they saw it. Putting a premium on "truth," they gave a new interpretation to the concept of freedom. The new Huguenot adherents were, of course, "free" to join the system and were not yet "compelled to come in." Once reformed, however, they had to relinquish a considerable degree of the liberty previously enjoyed, and they could not go beyond certain rigidly imposed limits. Strict obedience to magistrates in a grimly austere daily life and far-reaching submission even to tyrant-rulers were Calvin's favorite commandments. He laid stress on the wretchedness of human life and advocated abasement as a necessary preliminary to virtuous existence. The latter, he held, is only to be attained by relentless human effort. Without discipline, Calvin preached, there is no moral life. Without moral life, one may add, there is no true freedom.

The outlook of the Reformers on these matters, however, could scarcely have had any influence on the passing of the Edict of Nantes, for this had no direct connection with religious activities. Although Calvin fought for toleration, he also preached intolerance. Nor could he be said to have been truly democratic in attitude.

---

[17] Even according to Viénot, Calvin had spread only the seeds of liberty. "Calvin avait malgré tout déjà jeté dans le monde des semences de liberté." J. Viénot, *Histoire de la Réforme française,* I, 272. Calvin's preference for governments that maintain liberty is not obvious. In any case he never did realize it in his "parochial state." In the long run, however, certain phenomena were observed. To quote Mesnard, "c'est du courant calviniste, débarrassé dans de terres nouvelles des étroitesses de la Ville-Eglise, que surgira, le temps venu, cette notion de liberté civique et personnelle." P. Mesnard, *L'Essor de la philosophie politique au XVI* siècle,* p. 671. Hereafter cited as Mesnard, *L'Essor de la philosophie politique.*

[18] Jean Calvin, *Institution de la Religion Chrestienne,* p. 672.

The organization of the Calvinist church and especially of the Genevan state had an outwardly democratic appearance, but there was, it would seem, little reality in its democracy. True, the principle of representation was enforced in the body ecclesiastic of the Reformed religion; and the Consistory, or lowest Protestant assembly, comprised a fairly representative cross section of the lower clergy. Ministers, elders, and deacons were made "equal." Another move of a democratic nature was to dispense with that practice of the Catholic Church whereby a priest could be imposed on a community against its will. The Huguenots had quickly discarded that practice and in addition lent their higher assemblies—the Colloquy, the Provincial Synod, and the National Synod—a parliamentary character by electing these bodies and by holding regular meetings. Generally speaking, then, the new organization was democratic in appearance.[19]

Yet it would be a mistake to take this democracy at its face value. In politics, what matters is not the formal perfection of a constitutional scheme, nor the precision of the theoretical structure, but the spirit that animates the whole. Democracy is not to be confused with liberalism. The Calvinist church may have been democratic in organization, but it lacked a liberal spirit. The political doctrine of Beza, the successor of Calvin, was in a certain sense democratic, since the people were regarded as the source of power. But that democracy had in it no trace of liberalism.[20] It gave to the individual no safeguard against a tyrannical ruler. And it should be remembered that Beza was something of a "corrective to the uncompromising spirit of Calvin." [21] Taking the Protestant church as a whole, one is entitled to ask whether liberalism could expand where intolerance was rampant, where religious toleration was regarded as impious and destructive of religion—if not a mortal sin—and where humiliating subservience to a tyrant was the rule.

It should be noted that a grave danger arises from the anach-

---

[19] Even such a cautious view is held in doubt by Professor Neale, who questions the democratic basis of the Calvinist church, describing it as oligarchic and conservative. The actual choice of a candidate for a spiritual post, he asserts, lay ultmately, not with the congregation in which the candidate was to preach, but with the body of ministers, who invariably tested the candidate's doctrinal and other qualifications. Cf. J. N. Neale, *The Age of Catherine de Medici*, p. 17.

[20] Cf. Mesnard, *L'Essor de la philosophie politique*, p. 325.

[21] R. H. Murray, *The Political Consequences of the Reformation*, p. 173.

ronistic use of political terminology. Apparently unequivocal terms take on completely different meanings when they are applied to different epochs. The task of the historian lies in finding a yardstick by which relatively similar events of different epochs can be measured. His aim is to show the relationship between past and present, and to explain the changes that have occurred. He would, of course, be unintelligible to his contemporaries if he did not use current terms. Such terms, however, must be applied with extreme care. The distance between present and past must be acutely felt. The reinterpretation of the past to suit modern requirements should not go too far. An author who is anxious to suit contemporary tastes or to illustrate his own theory with certain past events which he considers landmarks, in spite of minor facts which do not fit into the pattern, is treading on shifting sands. Only with precise definition should concepts with an obviously modern meaning be used with reference to the past.

Thus, if it is thought useful to discuss the sixteenth century in terms of "democracy," it is important that the reader remember the peculiar political and social climate of the time in which only those who were capable of holding public office were regarded as full citizens. Such were the views that Goslicius, a Polish political philosopher, advanced in his *De Optimo Senatore*.[22] By "the people," Hotman (1524–1590) meant only the possessors of wealth and rank, who could keep the royal power within its limits: "Il est plus que necessaire, qu'un Roy soit retenu en son devoir par la reverance & l'authorité des gens de bien & d'honneur, comme representans la personne du Peuple."[23] Similarly Beza, when defining the rights of subjects against tyrant-sovereigns, bluntly asserted that the "ordinary" subject, who has no state responsibilities, duties, and charges, has no right to resist tyrannic ordinances. No one below the rank of a minor state official can oppose a manifest tyranny.[24] A similar attitude was taken by the author of the *Vindiciae contra tyrannos*.

It is important to consider how far Calvin actually influenced

---

[22] Laurentius Grimalius Goslicius, *De Optimo Senatore* (Venetiis, 1568). Cf. my *The Accomplished Senator of Laurentius Goslicius* (Munich, 1946).

[23] F. Hotman, *La Gaule Françoise*, p. 12.

[24] T. de Bèze, *Du droit des magistrats sur leur sujets*, in Simon Goulart, ed., *Mémoires de l'Estat de France sous Charles IX*, II, 491, 492. Hereafter cited as Goulart, ed., *Mémoires de l'Estat de France*.

events. There can be no doubt that he had a tremendous hold over
people's minds—a hold that was strengthened by his essentially
practical approach to life. He felt the needs of a society tired of
an immoral and dissipated existence and unconsciously yearning for
a regulated and disciplined regime. In the words Taine used in
speaking of the German Reformers, he "put his finger on the secret
wound" of society.[25] Diagnosing a disease is the first step toward
curing it, and that step was taken early by Calvin, about the time
when he first wrote his *Institutio religionis christianae* (1536).[26]
The important point is that he also took the second step, in that
he devised ways and means to achieve the cure. That is the solution to the mystery of the limited success which he achieved. His
Genevan state in some way suggested a new Rome. It was the
working pattern of a political community in which the secular and ecclesiastical elements were ingeniously blended into a single structure, which nevertheless left to the church a wide margin of freedom.[27] Outwardly, Geneva had a democratic appearance. But it
had that before Calvin built his parochial state on its foundations.
Nevertheless, the Huguenot ideal was more adaptable and had more
appeal to the French than Luther's ideal. Whether it was "popular"
in the wider sense is quite another question. We have evidence to
show that in sixteenth-century France the Reformation was able
to achieve only local successes.[28] The causes of the failure of any
nationwide spread of Calvinism are to be sought outside the deficiencies of Calvin and of his Genevan state. The inherent, almost
atavistic conservatism, pride, and sense of duty to their ancestors
felt by most people make them reluctant to discard an inherited religion, although, of course, the problem cannot be reduced to one
generalization. To a certain extent, human sloth and dislike for

[25] "Les Allemands du seizième [siècle] ont mis le doigt sur la plaie secrète. On ne
fonde pas une société sur le culte du plaisir et de la force; on ne fonde une société
que sur le respect de la liberté et de la justice." H. Taine, *Histoire de la littérature
anglaise,* II (Paris, 1899), 288.

[26] "Calvin est l'homme d'une seule idée et d'un seul livre. Le livre, c'est la Bible;
l'idée, c'est la gloire de Dieu. Dieu est glorifié dans la création, dans le gouvernement
du monde physique et moral, enfin dans l'oeuvre de la Rédemption et dans l'économie
du salut: tel est le plan général de *l'Institution chrétienne.*" A. Bossert, *Calvin,* p. 53.

[27] Cf. E. Choisy, *La Théocratie à Genève au temps de Calvin,* pp. 51–54.

[28] About 1573 the numerous Huguenot communities were those of Languedoc, Gas-
cony, Dauphiné, the Vivarais, the Quercy. Viénot, *Histoire de la Réforme française,*
I, 433.

hard thinking are also present, as is a skepticism about which religious camp has the right to save souls. This skepticism, however, without which there can be no true tolerance, did not appear until much later.

Although the number of followers is no measure of the part played by a religious reformer, it is perhaps some indication of the spread of Calvin's influence that during the last years of his life the number of his followers was increasing.[29] In spite of this, however, there were factors at work beyond his control which were to put an end to the glorious revolution. He failed to anticipate the Machiavellian capacities of the Court.[30] The fact that the Calvinist church failed to become an organization with nationwide status and that its development was brought to a standstill did not prevent the spiritual process. Calvin had taught people to read the Bible and to accept his interpretation of it. His approach was not so much conscious and critical (since limits were defined) as it was startling. It simply meant that the Bible was to be regarded as a revolutionary manifesto. This new interpretation of the Bible, a new outlook on the ritualistic side of religious activity, and a new approach to men as mature, conscious, thinking individuals were the signs of the spiritual revival of the age. A feature of this spiritual revival was that it seemed to touch mainly on problems of a spiritual, rather than political, nature. In the long run, Calvin's party stopped short of political revolution. The reason for this development lay in the contemporary trend toward separating the sphere of politics from that of religion.

Politics and religion had begun to follow divergent paths, and were no longer united, as they had been throughout the Middle Ages; their medieval "marriage" was in a state of dissolution and there was a growing feeling that the balance between them was changing. The primacy which had been assigned to religious issues was gradually being accorded to political and social matters, and the change heralded a new epoch in which they were to be unquestionably the center of interest.

The issue had always been complicated, and it now appeared even more so. The Reformation, which preceded the final divorce

---

[29] Four hundred thousand in 1558; cf. *ibid.,* p. 270. Substantial progress was made at the time of the *colloque* at Poissy in 1561.

[30] "Ce qui ... fit échouer [la Réforme] ce fut le machiavélisme des maîtres du jour." *Ibid.,* p. 280.

between the religious and the secular, attempted to find new links
between them to take the place of the old ones, which were losing
their effectiveness. But the Reformers were not to achieve their
aims, for their own critical spirit widened the split which had been
made by the Humanists. To be sure, in the Middle Ages a distinction was made between secular and religious life, between natural
ethics and Christian ethics, between political and moral obligation;
yet a spirit of universalism prevailed. The medieval way of life expressed a unity in which religion predominated. The Reformers
failed to realize that, in defending the primacy of religion, they
were defending a lost cause; they failed to see that this was a feature which had survived from the Middle Ages but which Humanism had shaken to its very foundations. They condemned the supremacy of law over religion, regarding it as a remnant of the
Middle Ages. Their attitude was no doubt inspired by a desire
to gain control over the entire spiritual life of the age; but, as the
split between spiritual and temporal matters widened, the claim
put forward by the Reformation that political obligation should
be one with moral obligation had little effect.

Another cause of Calvin's failure to achieve complete success
lay in the customary inability of a theorist to reach the desired practical objectives. Here we are faced with an instance of the broader
problem of the influence of prophets and revolutions upon each
other. The activity of thinkers runs parallel to historical trends.
The task of ideological leaders is to formulate ideas which already
exist and of which society is already aware. Political writings are
a result of existing situations. An entirely new program cannot be
accepted immediately and therefore has no chance of influencing
contemporary history. Leaders and men of thought are in a position to formulate doctrines and precipitate events, but they are
neither able to control the latter according to their will nor capable
of clearly foreseeing the results. Events create men to no less a degree than men create events. Without Hotman and Beza, religious
wars would in all probability have been fought. Calvin did little
to prevent them, although he repeatedly maintained that kings
should be obeyed by their subjects. Without his elaborate doctrine,
the tension between the Catholics and those who had absorbed new
ideas and were attracted by the new style of life would have taken
a more or less violent form. Calvin disapproved of his followers
bearing arms against the monarch, but he was helpless to prevent it.

He had engendered in people's minds certain ideas which produced unpredictable effects. His ardent plea for religious autonomy carried the seeds of revolt into social and political matters, revolutionizing the whole of contemporary life.

Once the spirit of unrest was abroad in society, the revolutionary forces were beyond the control of the spiritual leaders who had started the movement. Moreover, the rigid intolerance of the Reformist leaders helped to create a desire for revenge on the part of their Catholic opponents. Calvin's intolerance, in particular, had serious consequences. It was, in part, responsible for his inability to obtain recognition for his church. He furnished a perfect pretext for his opponents by establishing a pattern of behavior which served their purposes; he supplied a formula by means of which governments could later justify persecution but hide the real reasons for it. Furthermore, he invited a refusal when demanding rights for his followers, because he denied these rights to other religious groups, particularly the Catholics and the Anabaptists.

The idea of toleration failed to gain ground not only because it was denied by religious leaders and only feebly advocated by lesser men, but also for many other multiform and intricate reasons. Arguments in political philosophy were about to be freed from religious trimmings. The struggle for redistributing material wealth, for acquiring vested interests, and for promoting family aggrandizement—a struggle which was visible through the party strife on a background of newly formed national concepts—overshadowed the purely religious struggle, which, indeed, was used merely as a cloak to hide the real interests at stake.

International religious organizations were still strong, but a man who owed allegiance primarily to an international body, and only secondarily to his king and country, was soon to be regarded with suspicion. The world of ideas and of action, instead of opening out and being made more free of access, was becoming more constricted. The existence of boundaries and limitations, which in later centuries became more and more rigid, was destroying the medieval sense of belonging to one community. The retrograde tendencies of the times could not have been avoided even if there had been general acceptance of the idea of tolerance. Theodore Beza, Calvin's principal disciple and successor at Geneva, for long saw the problem as Calvin did. He considered liberty of conscience a diabolical dogma recognized only in two countries: "Et illa est diabolica libertas quae Poloniam & Transylvaniam hodie tot pestibus implevit, quas nullae alioqui sub sole regiones tolerarent." [31] He sided with his teacher in trying to justify the execution, at his instigation, of the unfortunate Spaniard Servetus. In his *De Haereticis* he maintained the view that all Christian heretics should be punished by death: "Qu'il eschat bien, et est expedient quelques fois de punir mesmes de mort les heretiques." [32]

In 1576, as Professor Tawney puts it, "no one yet dreamed that tolerance was possible." [33] But by 1580, Geneva began to believe less in persecution, which had formerly been a component part of the orthodox doctrine. In that year Beza, whose views, though firm, were not so uncompromising as Calvin's, published his *Icones,* a book of "portraits" of those Protestants "famous for their piety and doctrine." [34] Among many other portraits of orthodox Protestants, selected for obvious reasons, the *Icones* included panegyrics of two liberal Erasmians, Conrad Pellican and Gaspar Hedion, and of Michel de l'Hôpital, a liberal who was regarded as neither a good Catholic nor a true Protestant, because he believed in a policy of compromise and advocated tolerance. It looked for a while as if the dawn were imminent; for, without a gesture from the Protestants, the other camp would hardly have been expected to offer in the future edict what it had been denied by its opponents. But the offer was not yet forthcoming, and intolerance continued to inspire both parties with the idea that war was the only solution.

THE WARS OF RELIGION AND THEIR IMPACT

The wars of religion are of central interest for the study of religious developments in the second half of the sixteenth century, not merely because they force our attention by extending over so long a period, but also because they focus it on the political as well as the doctrinal importance of theology at that time. It was perhaps the last time that theology was to be used as a political weapon,

---

[31] T. Beza, *Epistolarum theologicarum,* I, 21.
[32] Bèze, *Traité de l'authorité du Magistrat,* p. 327.
[33] R. H. Tawney, *Religion and the Rise of Capitalism,* p. 118.
[34] Beza, *Icones, id est verae imagines virorum doctrina simul et pietate illustrium.*

although, of course, the wars were by no means fought for purely religious reasons. Strong political motives, such as the struggle for supremacy of the three most powerful families in France, also played a part. The wars, however, were all begun and all waged in a spirit of intense hatred, matched by a deep-rooted intolerance which the theologians sanctioned. The one constant factor in the long series of wars, which more than anything else shows that it was in fact a single prolonged conflict, was the reciprocal hatred between the believers in the old and the supporters of the Reformed religion. Hatred and intolerance alike found expression in philosophical and theological terms, but it was the profound underlying feeling of antipathy [35] between the contestants that sharpened the conflict far more than any differences of opinion could have done. It seems that the principle put by Michel de l'Hôpital to Charles IX in 1570, that the end of war is peace, has seldom been so entirely forgotten.

Tempers rose as war succeeded war; the blinding spirit of intolerance intensified the worst emotions and transformed the best: "We fought the first war like angels, the second like men and the third like devils." [36] The spirit of intolerance which had evoked these wars was in turn heightened by them, in this way prolonging the struggle.

It is not, however, only because of the light they throw on the spirit of intolerance and on the theological sanction which it enjoyed that the wars of religion deserve analysis. Another reason lies in the clues afforded by such an analysis which help to disclose the formative influences accounting for the growth of the Huguenot party. While the wars continued, the Huguenot party was becoming politically stronger and militarily weaker, though on the whole there was a steady upward trend in its prestige. By the time the Edict of Nantes was passed, the party was a mature military and political organization. The insecurity and uncertainty of the ensuing peace compelled the Huguenots, after 1612, to consolidate the position they had gained under the impetus of war. But, owing to the intricate situation developing from the lack of adequate leaders, that party organization was later engulfed in further chaotic wars. Adequate military leaders of the earlier wars were no longer

---

[35] Cf. L. R. Lefèvre, Le Tumulte d'Amboise, p. 28.
[36] A contemporary opinion quoted in Neale, The Age of Catherine de Medici, p. 71.

available, because after 1610 the nobles drifted away from the Huguenot party. The subsequent wars were more like squabbles than bitter conflicts. The constant factor of that earlier conflict was now missing.

At the outset of the wars of religion, toward 1560, two Huguenot groups had been thrown together by the state of emergency: the "Huguenots of religion" and the "Huguenots of State," [37] the "religious" and the "political" Huguenots. The activities of these two groups merged because of the nature of the Reformed church, whose authority extended over matters political and social as well as purely religious. Before the outbreak of the wars, the religious Huguenots had revolted against the Church and the political Huguenots against the monarchy, but the civil war united them all against the state. The reason was simple. When the "papists" allowed their holy hatred of the Huguenots to lead them into an alliance with the state, the one alliance determined the other: on the one side were Catholics and the state; on the other, both wings of the Huguenot group.

The composite character of the Huguenot group was in line with the character of the wars of religion. Although the wars produced a unifying effect, merging the religious Huguenots with the secular, all the natural revolutionary propensities of the Huguenots were increased. The process was started in 1559 with the terrorist persecutions carried out by the Guises. "Six score commissions are sent forth for the persecution for religion and that they may be more speedily executed, all appellations usually made at Paris, are restrained for a year" read the report to Queen Elizabeth I.[38] But terrorism failed; it only provoked revolt and contributed to Protestant unity.

It was generally felt that unorthodoxy necessarily led to rebellion against the state's authority. Here the Huguenot point of view was not different. Ramus argued that "the first Bond . . . which confirmeth, knitteth, and retaineth the obedience of Kings, is Religion." [39]

---

[37] The terms used in J. W. Thompson, *The Wars of Religion in France,* p. 17.

[38] Killigrew and Jones to the Queen, Blois, December 18, 1559. *Calendar of State Papers,* Foreign Series (1559–1560), No. 451.

[39] Petrus Ramus, *The Three Partes of Commentaries, containing the whole and perfect discourse of the civill warres of Fraunce,* Part I, p. 89. Hereafter cited as Ramus, *Commentaries.*

For a brief period, Catherine's policy of building up the Huguenot party successfully delayed hostilities. Such a policy was expedient but shortsighted. It did not mean that Catherine was not afraid of the Huguenots, should they rise against the monarchy, or that she underestimated their potential strength. But it did mean that she planned to use them against the powerful triumvirate, and that ultimately led to war. In 1562, as soon as she discovered their weakness, especially in the military field, and their disunity, she dismissed the idea of conciliation and discarded her previous plans.

She was able to grant the Protestants the right of religious freedom without undue fear of an antimonarchist rebellion, but she was not religious and, although in a limited sense a Politique, she was a practical woman concerned with immediate aims. Not being a theoretician, she misunderstood the implications involved in the composite structure of the Protestant group. She managed to achieve a short delay, but otherwise did little to prevent war. She did more harm than good in creating a great deal of the chaos which characterized the wars from the start. Catherine had thus committed the unpardonable error admirably described by Professor Neale: "She contemplated a temporary policy leading to a permanent solution." [40] The incoherence of her later policy can be traced to this source.

She envisaged the building up of the Protestant military party as a means to end the war and to solve the Protestant problem. All that she achieved was the strengthening of the opposition against the triumvirate, to which a counterbalance was much needed. But "the Triumviri [remained] . . . the authors and causes of the war and these troubles." [41]

Taking energetic action in 1561 to assist the Calvinist military plans, Catherine asked 2,500 churches to prepare to repel an "attack by foreigners." She authorized Beza to hold the first public meeting, which took place on November 1, 1561, and which was attended by 15,000 Huguenots. She promulgated the Edict of January, 1562, granting the Huguenots full civic status. The fears that had haunted the Huguenots since the Edict of Compiègne, 1557 (which introduced the death penalty for dissenters), and which had been only diminished by the Edict of July, 1561, were now dispelled.

[40] Neale, *The Age of Catherine de Medici*, p. 53.
[41] Ramus, *Commentaries*, Part I, p. 126.

But even before the military strength of the Huguenot party could mature (the process, it is true, was delayed by Protestant disunity), she abandoned her project. When the Peace of Amboise was signed in March, 1563, the Protestant cause was doomed. A "little" League, an anti-Protestant organization, was formed in anticipation of the "great" Catholic League. The spirit of the latter was already present. Liberty of conscience was nominally preserved, but liberty of worship was restricted.

Even then, Catherine's policy was not brought to its logical conclusion: it appears to have vacillated; it was in fact incoherent; it was ruled by external forces and led her from one crisis to another.

It appears likely that the plans to destroy the Huguenots were hatched in 1565 at Bayonne, during the meeting of Catherine, Charles IX, the Queen of Spain, and the Duke of Alva, acting for Philip II. It seems probable, too, that in their minds an idea of some radical measure to dispose of the Huguenots once and for all, though not necessarily a St. Bartholomew's Eve, was then born. It is also possible that Catherine made certain promises. A few days before the St. Bartholomew Massacre, Admiral Coligny received many letters from the distressed inhabitants of La Rochelle and other Huguenot communities, warning him of the danger. One of the letters said: "Ne doutez pas aussi que la Reine mère n'accomplisse ce qu'elle a promis au Duc d'Albe pour le Roi d'Espagne à Bayonne: de rompre les édits de paix et ruinner les Huguenots de la France avec la peau du lion ou avec la peau du renard." [42]

Again, no oppressive measures immediately followed the Bayonne meeting, but Chancellor L'Hôpital, a defender of toleration, whose policy Catherine had sponsored since 1560, was no longer trusted.[43] He was dismissed in 1567, and the road lay open to intolerance. But, in March, 1568, the Edict of January, 1562, found confirmation in the Peace of Longjumeau, although the peace treaty omitted the concessions of the guaranteed strongholds. It was only in September of the same year (1568) that the Edict of Saint Maur-des-Fossés abolished the Edict of January, 1562, and forbade the exercise of the reformed religion altogether.[44]

---

[42] Goulart, ed., *Mémoires de l'Estat de France,* I, 254.

[43] Cf. T. Seitte, *Un Apôtre de la Tolérance au XVI⁰ siècle: Michel de l'Hospital, Chancelier de France, 1506–1573,* p. 58.

[44] "The very cause of the Civill warres was the breaking of the Edict of January." Ramus, *Commentaries,* Part II, p. 2.

The Edict of September, 1568, meant a complete departure from the policy of compromise and toleration that had been enunciated by L'Hôpital, who was said to have been the "mouthpiece" [45] of Catherine de Médicis. What it meant in fact was that, during his chancellorship, he was given the power to put in practice his own declared ideas on tolerance. His term of office coincided with a period of respite for the Huguenots. As for Catherine, her enthusiasm for the Protestants very soon wore thin, and thereafter she barely tolerated them. The responsibility for the policy was the Chancellor's. He saw to it that the opportunity to practice toleration was not wasted. As Chancellor, he behaved as a true Politique. Catherine was neither a mature nor a sincere Politique; she had merely followed for a time a milder, if expedient, policy, hoping to reap permanent benefits from a series of desultory and halfhearted acts. L'Hôpital went to the heart of the matter. He analyzed the disturbances of his time, trying to ascertain the main cause of the troubles. It was on theoretical foundations, clearly laid down in 1560, that he built his policy. "C'est follie," he said to the States-General at Orléans, on December 13, 1560, "d'espérer paix, repos et amytié entre les personnes qui sont de diverses religions." [46] He started immediately to cope with the problem. "The Chancellor," wrote Peter Ramus, "therefore began to shew that . . . disordered matters in Religion which concerned both doctrines and money might be reformed: he understanding that this was the onelye cause of all troubles, woulde diligentlye provide for them as his office required." [47]

Ramus himself indicated the connection between religion and the problem of obedience to monarchy:

> . . . if the King will be loved, and obey the commandments of God and retaine the obedience and love of his subjects, he must of necessitie establishe Religion . . . [And further] Where upon it cometh to passe, that Religion which is a most assured bonde of humane actions and of the true obedience of subjects towards their Kings, ought to be reformed, preserved and maintained. [48]

---

[45] A. J. Grant, "The Problem of Religious Toleration in XVIth Century France," *Proceedings of the Huguenot Society of London*, XIII, 159.

[46] Michel de l'Hôpital, *Oeuvres complètes*, ed. by P. J. S. Dufey, I, 396. Hereafter cited as L'Hôpital, *Oeuvres*.

[47] Ramus, *Commentaries*, Part I, p. 187.

[48] *Ibid.*, p. 89.

Ramus prophesied that if this was not done the future was uncertain:

> These two things [religion and good will] therefore must be established and confirmed to prevent that ruine which is like to come: and to this ende (as both common profite and necessitie requireth) all our Counsels, reasons, devises and deliberations ought to tende: seeing hereupon both the due obedience to the King, and the conservation of the people dependeth.[49]

Clearly Ramus shared the utilitarian attitude stressed by L'Hôpital. But there was one minor difference between the Huguenot point of view, as represented by Ramus, and that of L'Hôpital. Ramus believed in the need to preserve "the integrity of religion."[50] L'Hôpital was also concerned with the unity of religion, but was equally determined on peace and order. What he wanted to avoid at all costs was civil war: "Reste à délibérer par quelz moyens nous pourrons apaiser ces séditions, et pourvoir qu'elles cessent à l'advenir."[51] There the ground was laid for legal toleration. For the sake of peace he opposed the contention that it is the duty of a government to safeguard true religion, though he believed in conversion by gentle means.[52] He was equally careful to exclude the element of constraint and force in the dealings of the state with religious problems. "Le roy, s'estant déclaré d'ung costé, debvroit assembler une armée pour ruyner l'aultre: chose qui est non seulement répugnante au nom de chrestien que nous portons, mais à toute humanité."[53] His system assured freedom to dissenters and excluded any attempt at their punishment by the state.

L'Hôpital's utilitarian approach produced a curiously ambivalent effect. Though tolerant (even in a legal sense), he objected to the idea of two religions in one state,[54] particularly in the troubled time in which he lived. Fearing that disunity would bring disaster, he advocated the absolute rule, "Une foi, une loi, un roi"—a Huguenot ideal. "La division des langues ne foict la séparation des

---

[49] *Ibid.,* p. 88.

[50] *Ibid.*

[51] L'Hôpital, *Oeuvres, I (Harangue à l'Assemblée des Etats Généraux à Orléans,* 13 Déc. 1560), 387.

[52] *Ibid.,* p. 402.

[53] *Ibid. (Harangue à l'Assemblée des Etats Généraux à Saint-Germain-en-Laye,* 26 Août 1561), p. 448.

[54] "Et portant, les Romains, qui ont esté les plus sages policiers du monde, ont défendue et prohibé, nova sacra, novos vitus inducere in rem publicam. N'ont voulou qu'il y eust diverses religions en une maison." *Ibid. (Harangue à l'Assemblée des Etats Généraux à Orléans,* 13 Déc. 1560), p. 398.

royaumes, mais celle de la religion et des loyx, qui d'ung royaume en faict deux. De là sort le vieil proverbe, Une foy, une loy, un roy." [55] Had he been in office longer, he would, as he had stated earlier at Poissy,[56] have had the Huguenots tolerated but subjected to gentle persuasion in order that the two religions might merge in peace and obedience to the King. Hence the ambiguity ascribed to his policy, the mistrust which he met with in both Catholic and Huguenot circles, and the impossibility of realizing his hopes of introducing peace and order where confusion reigned.

His was a system of constitutional monarchy. Yet the authority of the monarch was to be recognized, and obedience required of his subjects: "Gardons et conservons l'obéyssance à notre jeune roy." [57] The argument that arms could be taken up against the King in self-defense was condemned.[58] But the case for liberty of conscience persistently put forward by L'Hôpital was very strong. In 1570, when urging the King to give peace to the Huguenots, he argued that concessions of that kind are not a proof of weakness:

> Or, veoyons ce que le roy leur donne par les traictés. ... Il leur donne une liberté de conscience, ou plus tot il leur laisse leur conscience en liberté. Appelez-vous cela capituler? Est-ce capituler quand ung subject promet pour toute convention, qu'il recognoistra son prince et demeurera son subject? ... en leur accordant ceste liberté, il se constitue vrayement leur prince et protecteur, et eulx se déclarent ses subjects, obligez à maintenir son estat.[59]

Hence the atmosphere which made it impossible for him to play the role to which he was suited by his statesmanship, broad views, and scholarly wisdom. His failure was avenged only by the passing of the Edict of Nantes: a triumph of the *politique* way of thinking which he had promoted. His example had shown the dangers involved in the spirit of compromise which was his political legacy to the Politiques.

After the dismissal of L'Hôpital, departure from legal toleration was given formal expression in the Edict of Saint Maur-des-Fossés. Apart from this single act, there was little which could

---

[55] *Ibid.*

[56] Cf. *ibid.* (*Harangue à l'Assemblée des Etats Généraux à Poissy*), pp. 478–479.

[57] *Ibid.* (*Harangue à l'Assemblée des Etats Généraux à Orléans*, 13 Déc. 1560), p. 399.

[58] *Ibid.*, p. 395.

[59] *Ibid.*, II (*Mémoire adressé à Charles IX*, 1570), 199.

justify the opinion that there was some method in Catherine's folly. But, obstinate and energetic, she knew how to put into operation short-term plans. Her role in preparing St. Bartholomew's Eve was important, even if one accepts the view that the measure was not premeditated, but decided on on the spur of the moment.[60] She thus influenced the wars of religion, for the massacre prompted an outburst of new troubles.

The slaughter was prepared and executed as she had planned.[61] It was in accordance with her plan that Admiral Coligny, the Huguenot leader, was shot from the window of the house belonging to a dependent of the Guise family.[62] She did not, however, succeed in promoting the conflict between the family of Châtillon and Guise, which was one of her cherished hopes. Yet a situation was created in which mass murder appeared as a reasonable defensive measure against the Huguenots' probable vengeance. Although seemingly successful, the move was a great blunder. General indignation was aroused abroad. Only the Pope and the King of Spain celebrated the news; the Protestant states were greatly alarmed and demanded an explanation. Here Catherine's invention utterly failed her. Explaining and apologizing with elaborate lies, she became deeply involved and was unable to avoid contradicting herself. Indeed, she never provided a plausible excuse.

Her subsequent attitude to the Protestants, especially after the Peace of Bergerac (1577), is an indication of her cynicism and her utter lack of moral principle. Once again she tried to win back her influence over the Huguenots by providing Protestant nobles

---

[60] Divorce was discussed with Marguerite de Valois immediately after her wedding to Henry of Navarre. Cf. *Mémoires de Marguerite de Valois,* pp. 35–36. Pierre Bayle, in "Navarre," *Dictionnaire historique et critique,* testified that Catherine was resolved to break the marriage of her daughter. Yet in view of Catherine's cunning, the wedding festivities held in Paris could have been planned as a trap for the Huguenots. She would certainly not have hesitated to involve her daughter in a scheme of this kind.

[61] Goulart quotes from a letter of Catherine written a few days before August 24, 1572, with an instruction to open it on the fateful day: "Strozzi, je vous avertie que c'est aujourd'hui le 24 août. L'Admiral et tous les Huguenots qui étaient ici avec lui ont été tués. Partant avisez diligamment à vous rendre maître de la Rochelle et faitez aux Huguenots qui vous tomberont entre les mains que nous avons fait à ceux-ci." Goulart, ed., *Mémoires de l'Estat de France,* I, 220.

[62] Other plans were that of the King, who planned to kill Coligny and thus cause a Huguenot uprising, after which he would massacre the Hugenots; and that of Guise, who wanted the King to kill Coligny personally. Cf. *ibid.,* p. 265.

with titles and sinecures. She resorted again to the expedient of
legal toleration, which this time lasted for just over three years.
This measure was apparently caused by her fear of public opinion.
Her expedient was not effectual. The situation was deteriorating.
France had suffered a considerable loss of manpower directly,
through the slaughter [63] carried on throughout the country, and
indirectly, through the emigration which followed the massacre.
New civil wars, whose outbreak was beyond the control of both
Catherine and Charles IX, were imminent. Also beyond their control was the furious battle of ideas. Hotman's *De Furoribus Gal-*
licis (1573) and his *Franco-Gallia* (1573), Beza's *Du droit des*
magistrats (1575), Le Roy's *De l'excellence du gouvernement*
royal (1575), La Boetie's *Le Contr'-Un* (1576), Bodin's *La*
République (1576), and the *Vindiciae contra tyrannos* (1579)
were all published during the next few years. This flood of writings deflected political thought into new channels [64] which provided
a challenge to the blind spirit of intolerance.

Yet, for a long period, no ray of hope was visible. Conditions
were inadequate even for a state of legal toleration. The work of
L'Hôpital was undone by Catherine and her successors. The numerous edicts passed before the Edict of Nantes were of little use.
"On a fait infinité d'Edits," wrote Coquille in 1590, "ausquels on
fait parler le Roy ... avec des propos specieux, beaucoup de langage
et rien de vérité." [65] At best, they meant only limited toleration.
They were neither adhered to nor accepted by all parties, and they
were soon repealed. The edicts could ensure only a period of truce,
which, as a rule, meant preparations for further hostilities. New
treaties were signed because both parties felt too weak and had no
other alternative, since further war meant utter exhaustion.

In these circumstances, measures introducing peace and toleration alternated with revocatory enactments. The Edicts of Ro-
morantin and of April, 1561, were revoked in July of the same

---

[63] The number of victims in Paris alone amounted to 8,000. Cf. N. Weiss, *Bulletin de*
la Société de l'histoire du Protestantisme Français, XLVI, 481. Professor Savory, however, accepts the number mentioned in the *Martyrologie* of Crespin (10,468). Cf. D. L.
Savory, "Pope Gregory XIII and the Massacre of St. Bartholomew," *Proceedings of*
the Huguenot Society of London, Vol. XVII, No. 2, p. 96. The total number of Huguenots murdered in France in the few months after St. Bartholomew's Eve is quoted as
100,000.

[64] See below.

[65] Guy Coquille, *Oeuvres*, I (*Dialogue sur les causes des misères de la France*), 219.

year. The Peace of Longjumeau (March, 1568) was annulled by
the Edict of Saint Maur-des-Fossés (September, 1568). The
Treaties of Nérac (1579) and of Fleix (1580) were followed by
the ineffective Treaty of Nemours and Paris (July, 1585) and the
Edict of Union (1588).

The lack of a spirit of conciliation not only shortened the life
of the edicts but also accounted for their character—their incom-
pleteness and their want of general principles. The only measure
of note (enforced before the Edict of Nantes) was the Edict of
Beaulieu, or of "Monsieur" (1576), which was resuscitated the
following year, after the Peace of Bergerac, as the Edict of Poitiers.
Its authors had the courage and vision to make it a matter of broad
principle:

> And to remove all occasion of Contentions and Differences among our
> Subjects, We have allow'd and do permit those of the said pretended
> Reform'd Religion, to live and inhabit in all the Cities and Places of
> this our Kingdom and Territories under our Obedience, without being
> troubl'd, vex'd, molested, or constrain'd to do any thing against their
> Conscience, or disturb'd in the Houses and Places where they shall think
> fit to inhabit . . .[66]

Notable as it was, the Edict remained an exception and brought
no essential change. The uneasiness of the period persisted, and
was reflected in chaotic conflicts. The importance of the Edict of
Beaulieu is measured only by comparison with the Edict of Nantes.
The latter was a compendium of edicts previously passed, yet contained no statement giving broad religious liberty.

The halfheartedness with which edicts were passed was in part
responsible for the prolonged conflicts. Even the Edict of Beaulieu
did more harm than good. The Protestants did not believe in the
sincerity of the intentions of Henry III, who so readily disavowed
the policy of St. Bartholomew, which he himself had helped to
frame. The Catholics were even more discontented. The fact that
their tempers were aroused helped in the formation of the League
(1576–1595). The League was, indeed, the outcome of the need
to form an alliance outside the monarchy, which was unable to deal
with the Protestants.[67] It was the outward sign of a complex variety
of causes accounting for the wars of religion.

To some individuals, particularly the military, wars were highly

---

[66] Edict of Poitiers (October, 1577), par. IV, as quoted in Elie Benoit, *The History
of the Famous Edict of Nantes*, I, 478.

[67] Cf. M. Wilkinson, *A History of the League or Sainte-Union: 1576–1595*, pp. 1 ff.

advantageous, because they offered tremendous opportunities for the rapid acquisition of wealth. Corruption in the armies of both sides was cogently described by Saint Romain: officers and soldiers of both religions trade with members of the opposite camp whom they "... trahissent, vendent ou eschangent les ungs aux aultres, pour les rançonner et se départir puis après le butin, sans metre en compte les blasphèmes exécrables qu'ilz vomissent ordinairement de leurs bouches." [68]

On the other hand, wars were injurious to the state, which found their cost a heavy burden. When the States-General met at Orléans in December, 1560, it was apparent that Diane de Poitiers, Marshal de St. André, and the Guises [69] had for years been squandering the financial resources of France, and that the state was running heavily into debt. The deficit estimated by L'Hôpital in January, 1561, was forty-three million livres, or four times the amount of the annual revenue of the state. [70]

The general unrest in France was also in part a product of defects in the social system. The lower classes, kept in servitude in the preceding centuries, had been partly released from their bonds by the advent of Humanism, and they now tried vigorously to assert themselves. The feudal underdog, fighting for a new place in society, naturally favored violence as a method, since it gave hope of more rapid improvement in living conditions. The military class, also, swollen in number and ambition and largely unemployed since the cessation of the Italian wars, constituted a factor making for disturbance and warmongering.

Political factors exerting a constant pressure on the genesis and continuance of the religious wars were both international and purely native in origin. Externally the flame of war was being constantly fed by the Pope, the Spanish Monarch, the Italian princes, and the Swiss, who supported the Catholic League; and by the Protestant German princes and the English, who supported the Calvinists. [71]

[68] Quoted in Oudot de Dainville, "Contribution à la biographie de Jean de Saint Chamond," *Annales de l'Université de Montpellier,* Vol. III, No. 1, p. 21.

[69] "Among these latter sort [being called to give up their accounts] the chiefe were the Guises, the fatall destruction of the Kingdom of France: who also as yet were to make their account for great sommes of money taken out of the King's Treasury . . . in the time of King Fraunces the second." Ramus, *Commentaries,* Part II, p. 2.

[70] Cf. Viénot, *Histoire de la Réforme française,* I, 325.

[71] Foreign intervention coincided with a certain Calvinist internationalism, apparent in Beza's official permission, given to the magistrates who were unable to deal with the tyrant-ruler, to seek help abroad.

"D'ailleurs," wrote L'Hôpital, "il y a de puissans princes et peuples estrangers qui estiment ceste cause leur appartenir, et ne leur ont y-devent failly, moins à ceste heure qu'ilz sont liguez, et participent ouvertement à leurs entreprinses." [72]

Coquille, in his *Dialogue sur les causes des misères de la France entre un Catholique ancien, un Catholique zelé & un Palatin* (1590), made the same point: "... peut être aussi qu'il y a quelque chose de mêlé des Princes Etrangers, parce que si cette Monarchie se défait d'elle-même avec ses propres forces, les Seigneurs voisins tous frais & reposez auront meilleur moyen de l'envahir." [73]

Internally the political roots of the trouble lay with the three most powerful families, the Bourbons, the Guises, and the Montmorencys, who combined the pursuit of private feuds with the encouragement of different causes, and added their own unquenchable zeal for profitable war to the motives inspiring the religious camps. The plans of the Guises were most ambitious: as the house of Lorraine, they put forward a claim to the throne. They hoped to dethrone the King by stamping out both heresy and its supporters at the same time. They barred the way to the Protestant pretender to the throne (Navarre). They posed as defenders of orthodox Catholicism and rejected the Gallican doctrines. "Plusieurs ont en opinion que le secret du Conseil étoit d'entretenir la guerre civile, sans que l'un ou l'autre fut ruiné, pour par cette occasion faire mourir les Chefs & principaux aides des deux partis, comme c'est l'ordinaire en telles guerres." [74]

Members of these families had key positions in the three main forces, the monarchy, the Catholic League, and the Protestants. It was as a struggle between these forces that Richelieu epitomized the wars of religion:

> Le regne de Henry 3me n'a esté non plus que celuy de Charles 9me sinon une continuelle guerre contre l'hérésie; ce prince ayant été contraint d'avoir tousjours autant d'armées sur pied, qu'il y avait de provinces en son Royaume, où elle estoit cantonnée contre son service, jusques à ce que la Ligue s'estant eslevée contre sa personne et son Estat, alors comme un cloud respouse l'autre, il se sentit forcé de quiter celle là pour s'opposer

---

[72] L'Hôpital, *Oeuvres*, II (*Mémoire adressé à Charles IX, 1570*), 177. "C'est à cette double intervention des étrangers qu'il faut attribuer la durée de nos guerres de religion, qui se sont perpétuées pendant quatre règnes." (Editor's note.)

[73] Coquille, *Oeuvres*, I (*Dialogue sur les causes des misères de la France*), 218.

[74] *Ibid.*

à celle-cy, appellant pour cest effect à son secours Henry 4me à qui pour lever tout ombrage de n'estre pas avec les siens en assurance auprès de sa personne, il consigna entre se main des villes d'ostage.[75]

Finally, the causes of war were doctrinal. The wars were not of course purely religious. They were waged, according to Coquille, "pour le fait ou sous le pretexte de la Religion." [76] But even though religion was not their real cause, there were some doctrinal aspects. Taking upon itself the defense of the purity of the Christian doctrine, the League professed that no peace with the heretics was possible.[77] In its vigorous program for action, as set forth in *Les Articles de la Saincte Union des catholiques françois* (1588),[78] the League included war as a means of achieving its aim of perfect religious unity. It regarded religion and the state as so closely linked that relinquishing the former would lead to the betrayal of the latter. To make its appeal popular, the League sought to relieve the populace of the burden of war expenditure by financing the campaigns through voluntary donations. It also attempted to bring about Christian unity and to widen the scope of popular rule by closer and more frequent intervention of the States-General in the burning issues of the day, particularly in the struggle against all dissenters.

The Calvinists were weary of docile martyrdom, having had too long an experience of the Paris prisons, the Châtelet and the Conciergerie, ironically called "la fin d'aise" or "la poche ou la chausse à l'hypocras." They refused any longer to submit unresistingly to slaughter, though Calvin had taught that martyrdom must be endured "as the will of God." Theoretical justifications of the new attitude duly followed. In his *De Jure magistratuum* (*Du droit des magistrats*), Beza upheld the view that armed resistance is acceptable, and a call for foreign aid entirely justifiable in case of need, provided this is done in a "legitimate" way.[79] The danger inherent in the new attitude of the Huguenots was not ignored by their

---

[75] G. Hanotaux, ed., *Maximes d'Etat et fragments politiques du cardinal de Richelieu*, No. XIX, p. 10.

[76] Coquille, *Oeuvres*, I (*Dialogue sur les causes des misères de la France*), 217.

[77] Cf. *ibid.* (*Discours sur les maux presens du Royaume pendant la Ligue* [unfinished work]), p. 241.

[78] Bibl. Mazarine, recueil 33238, pièce 5; quoted in Mesnard, *L'Essor de la philosophie politique*, p. 379.

[79] Pp. 280 ff. Cf. E. Troeltsch, *The Social Teaching of the Christian Churches*, II, 651.

enemies. "Depuis ces guerre civiles," wrote Coquille, "les gens d'Eglise sont devenus beaucoup plus déreglez, & se sont contentez de prêcher & crier contre les Heretiques, refuser leurs opinions, les mettre en detestation envers le peuple, exhorter tout le monde à leur faire la guerre." [80]

Toward the end of the century, when the fighting was interrupted out of sheer exhaustion, the passions of intolerance were also partly spent. The peace that resulted was precarious from the start because it did not signify any changed attitude, but merely the human inability to wage war indefinitely. The years of peace after 1598 were not, of course, without influence on subsequent ideas; the tranquillity of men's minds was conducive to a certain liberal movement which won the right to existence, however precarious. But the liberalism of the early seventeenth century was as much a reaction as a defense against any recurrence of the wars of religion.

THE VARIOUS FRENCH SCHOOLS OF THOUGHT

In order that their behavior should appear legal in the eyes of the Court and the Catholic party, the Protestants made some strange moves. After the Vassy Massacre (1562), they claimed that Catherine and Charles were prisoners of the Duke of Guise. Declaring that the aim of Condé was to liberate the King, they objected to being called rebels, since, as they claimed, they had no cause for rebellion. These were clever moves. Rebellion either for a "cause" or for self-defense had been criticized by L'Hôpital in 1560:

> Ne veult l'argument dont ils s'aydent, qu'ilz prennent les armes pour la cause de Dieu .... Nostre religion n'a prins son commencement par armes n'est reteneue et conservée par armes. Si l'on disoit que les armes qu'ilz prennent ne sont pas pour offenser aulcung, mais pour se défendre seulement, ceste excuse vauldroit peut-estre contre l'estranger, non contre le roy leur souverain seigneur: car il n'est loisible au subject de se défendre contre le prince, contre ses magistrats.[81]

---

[80] Coquille, *Oeuvres,* I (*Discours sur les maux presens du Royaume pendant la Ligue* [unfinished work]), 241.

[81] L'Hôpital, *Oeuvres,* I (*Harangue à l'Assemblée des Etats Généraux à Orléans,* 13 Déc. 1560), 395.

After 1567, when it was no longer possible to maintain the same excuse, as it was obvious that the royal party had not been deprived of liberty, a new claim was put forward—that the law had been violated and Protestants were fighting to reëstablish it. This constitutional argument had been an official party line from the beginning of the religious wars until approximately St. Bartholomew's Eve, a period during which, especially in its early years, tempers were not so fiery as they later became. The character of these campaigns was milder, and the wars were fought more for self-assertion on the part of the Huguenots than for sheer self-preservation, as was the case in the next decade. The doctrine of nonresistance was officially accepted by the Huguenot leaders until 1572, although for the last few years many Huguenots had felt critical, and, as it were, Knoxian, regarding the question of obedience.

The constitutional argument and the Huguenot claim to limit the royal power found their advocate in Hotman. In his *Franco-Gallia*, a comprehensive, but rather confusing, treatise, he set himself the task of proving that in the past the power of the French kings had been neither absolute nor unlimited,[82] and that it had been limited by the authority of the people: "... ces Roys ... n'avoyent point une puissance absolute & infinie, ny ne pouvoyent faire tout ce qu'ils vouloyent: ... ils estoyent autant sous la puissance & authorité du peuple, comme le peuple sous la leur: au moyen dequoy ces regnes, à dire vray, n'estoyent autre chose que magistrats perpetuels."[83] Hotman praised this system of limited popular monarchy:

> ... c'estoit la plus parfaite, & la plus seure forme de Police que celle-la: pourautant que la puissance Royale, si on ne luy donne quelque mors, comme dit Platon, que ca tienne un petit en bride: & qu'on luy souffre de s'elever iusques en un degré supreme de souveraineté & de puissance absolue en toutes choses adonc il y a grand danger qu'estant là, ne plus ne moins que sur un precipice glissant, elle ne se laisse choir en tyrannie.[84]

---

[82] This is not a new view. It goes back to the lawyers of Louis XI at least. What was newer here was the emphasis on the "authority" of the people—but the idea of the king as the "representative" of the people was much older and in some ways similar. In France the concept of royal power was flexible. "La royauté entre en scène à la fin Xᵉ siècle" [*sic*], writes Viollet, "faible, chétive, étouffée par une féodalité puissante. Elle s'élève de degré en degré. ... Dans son origine et dans sa nature, elle est essentiellement indéfinie, flexible, capable de se resserrer et de s'étendre, de s'adapter aux circonstances les plus diverses, de jouir les rôles les plus différents." Paul Viollet, *Histoire des institutions politiques et administratives de la France,* II, 185.

[83] Hotman, *La Gaule Françoise,* p. 11.

[84] *Ibid.,* p. 12.

He maintained that the sovereignty of the people was vested in
a representative body—"the sacred authority of the States-General." He argued that political administration of the kingdom had
been the prerogative of the States-General: "... toute l'administration politique du Royaume estoit entierement en la disposition de
l'assemblée des Estats." [85] Obviously, *Franco-Gallia,* published in
1573, produced little if any effect; since, in the years to come, no
indication can be found of sovereignty residing in the States-General.
Moreover, if the constitutional argument had any appeal before St.
Bartholomew, it ceased to have it altogether after that event. Huguenot political thought began to follow a different path. A new
program had to be worked out; otherwise, the party would have
lost its grip over the rank and file of its members, who wanted an
ideology suitable to the changed conditions. The earlier struggles
for mere self-assertion became wars for self-preservation.[86] For the
Huguenots, Hotman's work was out of date even on the day of
publication, because it could teach them no lesson in practical politics.[87] Soon indeed he might well have been understood by the Catholics, who, after 1576, were to become convinced constitutionalists.

After St. Bartholomew, when the Huguenot party turned to the
doctrine of resistance as its new creed, Huguenot political theory,
contained in the massive *Mémoires de l'Estat de France* edited by
Simon Goulart (1576) and in the *Vindiciae contra tyrannos*
(1579), followed its own path away from what was understood as
the Calvinistic approach and closer to the political philosophers of

---

[85] *Ibid.,* p. 121.

[86] The testimony of Charles IX given at the end of 1568 is striking, not only because
it can serve as a proof of his good feelings toward the Calvinists at that period, but
also because he bluntly stated that the Huguenots had begun to fight for their existence.
Goulart described this as follows: "... aux premiers troubles ceux de la religion s'étaient
armés pour son [Charles IX's] commandement et pour son service: aux seconds qu'il
n'avait pas bien entendu leurs intentions. Mais qu'aux troisième ils avaient bien fait
de prendre les armes: autrement, disait-il, ils eussent été mal à cheval, c'est-à-dire ils
étaient ruinés." Goulart, ed., *Mémoires de l'Estat de France,* I, 5.

[87] According to Figgis, there is an affinity between Hotman and the author of the
Vindiciae; for, if one disregards Hotman's constitutional argument, one realizes his
anxiety to trace back in history the spirit of freedom. "He seeks to show that the nation
of France is really one of free men." J. N. Figgis, *Studies of Political Thought from
Gerson to Grotius: 1414–1625,* p. 179. Hereafter cited as Figgis, *Studies of Political
Thought.* From such a point of view he may be placed as a link between the two epochs
of Huguenot thought, the constitutional and the revolutionary. He was rooted in the
first but anticipated the second.

the late Middle Ages, such as Nicholas of Cusa, William of Occam, and Aquinas.[88] All these writings are typical in that they deal with the problem of obedience, but they also have peculiarities of their own.

The *Vindiciae*, for instance, clearly and boldly asserts that all rights, even the right to resistance, are divine, since all political obligation is an obligation due to God. The right of resistance is also divine, because all authority is given conditionally. The only absolute sovereignty is that of God, and the power of all magistrates must therefore be limited. Magistrates are created by God, but with the consent of the people. The king is God's creation and representative; and, as he must serve the people's good, his status can never be unconditional. His duties are to serve God and to be just. The sovereignty of the people, second to the sovereignty of God, lies within the class of people who are capable of holding public offices and have a recognized superiority over the masses—a view commonly shared all over Europe at that period.[89] "When we speak of all the people, we understand by that, only those who hold their authority from the people, to wit, the magistrates, who are inferior to the King, and whom the people have substituted, or established . . . to restrain the encroachments of sovereignty, and to represent the whole body of the people." [90]

The problem of resistance, however, found in the *Vindiciae* an original interpretation. Action against a tyrant, it was claimed, can be undertaken only by communities [91] and not by single individuals. "Particulars or private persons are not bound to take up arms against the prince who would compel them to become idolaters." [92] Thus, according to the *Vindiciae*, every community has the right to rebel against a common tyrant. This rule, however, was qualified by a provision that the representatives of the people can act as communities. "In like manner, that all, or at the least, the principals of provinces or towns, under the authority of the chief magistrates, established first by God, and secondly by the prince, may ac-

---

[88] Cf. Allen, *A History of Political Thought*, p. 313.

[89] Cf. above.

[90] Junius Brutus (pseud.), *A Defence of Liberty Against Tyrants*, p. 97.

[91] "All the people by the authority of those, into whose hands they have committed their power . . . may, and ought to reprove and repress a prince who commands things against God." *Ibid.*, p. 109.

[92] *Ibid.*

cording to law and reason, hinder the entrance of idolatry within the enclosure of their walls, and maintain their true religion." [93]

The principle of representation, which ignored the rule of the majority, was putting dangerous and powerful weapons into the hands of those few in whom the sovereignty of the people was invested. The unknown author of the *Dialogue d'Archon et de Politie* assumed that a minority is perfectly entitled to rebel if it does so for a just cause. This view, taken by a Huguenot writer, was neither unique nor original. Almost ten years earlier, numerical superiority had been rejected by Goslicius as of no deep significance. The decisions of the elite were regarded as the only ones of importance, and they were to enjoy the common obedience of the community. Obviously, oligarchic ideals had not yet lost their appeal.

The *Vindiciae* should be regarded as the main and classical work of the Huguenot Monarchomach theory. It was written in a pioneering and revolutionary period, which had come to a close by 1589 with the complete abandonment of the doctrine of resistance. As the feeling grew that Henry of Navarre would be King of France, Huguenot thought reversed its trend. Rebellion was rejected and regicide condemned. Speaking of the death of Henry III, Hurault brands the partisans of the League as guilty of the murder: "Ce meurtre cruel & horrible de leur Roy les rendant execrables à toutes personnes de courage, maintenant pour couvrir les artifices dont ils ont usé afin d'y parvenir : ils donnent cette impression au peuple par leur declaration, que la mort de nostre Roy est un coup du ciel. O impieté abominable." [94] The doctrine of obedience, which previously had been denied in all circumstances, was now more and more boldly asserted. The way was made clear for a general acceptance of the doctrine of the divine right of kings, and of an absolutist idea of the state.

The Catholic cycle of thought followed, on the whole, a similar pattern; climaxes and anticlimaxes had, of course, occurred at times different from the corresponding phases of the Huguenot cycle, and their duration and intensity correspondingly varied, since they were the result of changing circumstances. Similar conditions produced relatively similar effects. Thus in the period between 1576 and 1585, the situation of the League roughly resembled that of the Hugue-

---

[93] *Ibid.*

[94] Michel Hurault, *Quatre excellens discours sur l'estat present de la France*, p. 170.

nots in the period between 1562 and 1572, which was the period of self-assertion rather than self-preservation. The Huguenots fought violently for life between 1572 and the late 'eighties, until they realized that their battle was won. The Leaguers, feeling themselves to be on the losing side, started to go through the same process before the Huguenots ceased to profess the principles of resistance, disobedience, and violence.

So long as the Catholics wanted only to preserve their *status quo,* when their existence was not directly threatened, the detailed development of their theory was neither spontaneous nor particularly original. Especially in the late 'sixties and early 'seventies, before the formation of the League and the splitting up of the Catholic party into many factions (1572–1574), the theoretical part of the religious controversy was rather dull. Under the ascendency of the League (1576), in the decade that followed, the Catholics still created nothing important, not even a coherent theory. Their interest lay in constitutional tendencies, with a limited sovereignty and a limited right of resistance. The latter was not advocated for all circumstances, but became a duty if a king should tolerate heresy or act against the law of the land. Popular rights were warmly espoused, and the Leaguers put perhaps a greater stress than did the Huguenot writers on the monarch's being checked from below, that is, by the States-General.[95] The true claim of the Catholics to originality rests in their interpretation of religious unity, which they regarded as the most solid basis of the state. This view led them straight to intolerance; they maintained that, since a society cannot be integrated, according to "divine" law, without a single religion, the king should be a Catholic and should fight heresy. They also asserted that no heretic king could be recognized.

The radical spirit gained in intensity in the ensuing decade (1585–1594), when the League's official policy was reversed and constitutionalism gave way to a rather chaotic theory of popular rule. In the sphere of theory, violent disobedience was acclaimed as the guiding principle; in the sphere of practice, there followed a further disintegration of the Catholic bloc, which had never possessed the Huguenot unity. The confusion of ideas was a sequel to

---

[95] Such was the opinion of Jean Boucher and of several authors of writings collected in the *Recueil contenant les choses mémorables advenus sous la Ligue* (*Mémoires de la Ligue*).

that disintegration, and the writer who best exemplified such a state
of affairs was Boucher.[96] The Catholics were constantly in difficulties through their assumption that they alone possessed anything
which could be called "truth," and that therefore they were in-
fallible. The Calvinists also played with the notion that they alone
were on the right path, and that no one else had any chance of salvation. Consequently, no serious discussion was possible; the argument
either lapsed into monologue or moved in a vacuum. Such was the
attitude of the author of *Dialogue entre le Maheustre et le Manant,*
who staged a discussion between a Leaguer and a Politique. The
Leaguer, represented by Manant, insisted that a heretic king, if
he did not persecute Catholics, would debase himself and become an
atheist. Therefore, argued Manant, a heretic monarch has no alternative but to be intolerant toward the Catholics. But on the
whole it was the pamphleteers, whose numerous writings were included in the *Mémoires de la Ligue,* who produced the works which,
together with those of Rossaeus, give the best and most illuminating
contemporary expression of the ideas of the Catholic Monarchomachs.

The Catholic Monarchomachs continued what the Protestant
Monarchomachs had begun some fifteen years before, and the re-
statement of political theory was one of the sources of their real
strength. The power they possessed was exactly the same that the
Huguenots had had, before they knew that Henry of Navarre
would succeed to the throne—the power that is invigorated by
righteous indignation and by a sense of just revolt; the power that
makes certain minds intensely active in times when external events
are playing havoc with the lives of many, disrupting the existing social pattern, and destroying the structure of existing government.
On the Huguenot side, Duplessis-Mornay was a living example of
the theory that men can be highly creative in spite of an extremely
hostile environment.[97]

In the period of their Monarchomach leadership, the Catholic
writers were perhaps more aggressive, but not so original, as their
Huguenot counterparts had been. Louis Dorléans and Rossaeus
certainly wrote well, but their writings suggest that the subject mat-

---

[96] Boucher's works are *De Justa Henrici tertii abdicatione a Francorum regno*
(Parisiis, 1589) and *Sermons de la simulée conversion et nullité de l'absolution de
Henri de Bourbon* (1594).

[97] His *Mémoires* do him full justice.

ter had been recently fully discussed by their predecessors, and therefore in a sense exhausted, and that some time must elapse before
any fresh ideas would reach full maturity. Moreover, the position
of the Catholics had never been so desperate as that of the Huguenots after St. Bartholomew, and their intellectual revolt of the
'eighties, although violent, was never so sincere or profound. They
had now to experience the conditions for which they themselves
were partly responsible—conditions which could have been avoided
had their leaders possessed more foresight. Even then, however,
the typical Monarchomach leaders could not see very far. They
could not rid themselves of the obsession that the tyranny under
which they suffered would have dire consequences. They could not
free themselves from that obsession, as the party of Politiques had
done, or devise working methods by which the tyranny could be
put down.[98] The remedy lay partly in the growth of a spirit of toleration; but the Catholic Monarchomachs believed that toleration
destroys religious unity, without which, in the eyes of all Leaguers,
no state could have a secure basis.

Rossaeus,[99] who ranked among the more prominent writers of the
day, wrote his *De Justa reipublicae* (1590) embodying those principles. In his view, true religion should be protected by the government, and heresy suppressed. From this, the right to depose a king
naturally follows: "Regi haeretico obedientia non debitur." [100] A
heretic king or a king who tolerates heretics should be dethroned;
for, in dethroning him, the punitive hand of the subjects acts on the
authority of the law of God. "Lex Dei armat subditos contra regem
haereticum." [101] Numerous pamphleteers of the League advocated
a "sovereignty" of the people that empowered them to depose their
kings. On the whole, however, the sovereignty that the Catholic
Monarchomachs attributed to the people had a limited scope, since
it was ineffective against a Catholic monarch. Rossaeus was rather
more radical. He openly declared that a heretic king may rightly

---

[98] H. J. Laski, Introduction to *A Defence of Liberty Against Tyrants,* by Junius
Brutus (pseud.), Section iii.

[99] This was a pseudonym attributed to Bishop Guillaume Rose, to William Reynolds,
an English exile, and to Boucher. Cf. Allen, *A History of Political Thought,* p. 351.
Professor McIlwain collected evidence in favor of Reynolds. Cf. "Who was Rossaeus?"
reprinted in C. H. McIlwain, *Constitutionalism and the Changing World,* pp. 178 ff.

[100] G. G. Rossaeus, *De Justa reipublicae christianae in reges impios et haereticos
authoritate,* p. 609.

[101] *Ibid.,* p. 610.

be killed by any of his subjects. He questioned the validity of hereditary right, denying its absolute character. "Regis & populi obligatio," he stressed, "est reciproca." [102] A king must be approved by the people, whose consent is not irrevocable and can be withheld. "Et haec de regum origine & potestate dicta sint, e quibus circumscripta esse regum omnium Christianorum sceptra confirmatur, eosque ita singulis membris & universae quoque reipub. praesse, ut tamen eorum potentiam respublicam dilatare, restringere, commutare, adeoque & . . . penitus abrogare, aliam que substituere possit." [103] Heresy, according to Rossaeus, is not the only error for which kings should be condemned. It is for the Church to decide on what grounds the king is to be deposed and to sanction the deposition. Rossaeus believed that of necessity Christian kings must be under the control of the clergy.[104]

To sum up: the Catholic doctrines were not different in essence from those of the Huguenots; they were only belated. In spite of this, they did not lack a certain originality. In 1560, the Catholic cycle had started, just as had that of the Huguenots, with the doctrines of divine right and obedience; its further trend, however, was not the same, although the reactions of doctrines to changing conditions often resembled each other. Finally, what corresponded to the Huguenot anticlimax, expressed in the 'eighties by a return to the doctrine of obedience, was the Catholic climax of the theories justifying rebellion and resistance to unworthy rulers. The last manifestation was coupled with a phenomenon which confirmed what had already been in the air for some time. In the 'eighties, the trends of the two cycles met—the Protestant heading for full obedience, and the Catholic turning in the opposite direction—and people must have realized that there was no fundamental difference between the programs of the two parties.[105] Both the Catholics and the Huguenots had the same goal in view—liberty. In theory they wanted to attain this goal by working out the concept of the original contract, which was based on the assumption (opposed by the advocates of divine right) that the king derives his power from the

---

[102] *Ibid.,* p. 68.

[103] *Ibid.,* p. 104.

[104] Cf. *ibid.,* p. 615.

[105] It seems easy to multiply resemblances, which were considerable; e.g., between the author of the *Vindiciae* and Rossaeus, as discussed by Figgis, *Studies of Political Thought,* chap. v.

people. That liberty, however, was never understood by the Huguenots in the same broad sense as expressed in the *Vindiciae*. They were primarily, if not solely, concerned with the freedom to practice their own religion. The Catholic idea of liberty, on the other hand, never meant the liberty of any people other than themselves; they condemned the idea of suffering any dissenters within the country and could not bear the thought of having a heretic king on the throne.

In these circumstances, no prospect of freedom could be envisaged, and there was no hope of conciliation without a third party strong enough to take the lead. The third party was the Politiques, who knew how to restrain and master their desires in order to secure future gains and successes. Consequently, their policy of clemency and prudence was opposed to the uncompromising attitude of the Monarchomachs. This difference was reflected in William Barclay's *De Regno,* directed mainly against Buchanan, Junius Brutus, and Boucher. Barclay, arguing against the Monarchomachs, wrote: "Vos, quia existis de nobis, retrahi a nobis ut perditi & profugi libet . . . Nos contra, quoniam inter vos nullum unquam numerum tenuimus: nunquam coitionibus vestris interfuimus: nunquam religionis & rebellionis vestrae participes facti sumus, compelli ad nefarios caetus vestros non debemus." [106] The Politiques weighed the heavy price to be paid for the cause of dissent against the doubtful and insecure profits that an uncompromising minority was likely to achieve. They wanted unity in the state as much as the Catholics wanted religious unity, or the Huguenots the preponderance of their own church. Theirs was a utilitarian conception of the state as a self-sufficient entity taking precedence over religious, spiritual, and other matters. To achieve their goal of unity, they made room for compromise as a matter of expediency. They believed in a system of popular monarchy in which the two elements, the popular and the monarchical, could best coexist if they were blended together: "Et vero regnum," said Barclay, "nihil aliud est nisi Monarchico populi gubernatio." [107] Yet Barclay focused his attention on the unique authority of the prince as established by the will of God [108] and by the support of the people:

---

[106] William Barclay, *De Potestate papae . . . eiusdem de regno et regali potestate,* pp. 464–465.

[107] *Ibid.,* p. 643.

[108] *Ibid.,* p. 280.

"Populus lege regia omnem suam in Principem potestatem contulit." [109] Similarly, toleration was accepted simply for the sake of convenience. It was a typical reaction of the practical *politique* mentality, shocked by the futility of the violence and persecutions practiced by the Monarchomachs.

A wide range of writings forms a background and gives a solid frame to this utilitarian outlook of the Politiques. L'Hôpital's proposals to amend the system of justice came first, in the form of his *Traité de la reformation de la justice*. The other works were extremely varied in scope and form. They range from political treatises of first-rate importance such as Bodin's *La République* (1576) and Barclay's *De Regno et regali potestate* (1600), from legal arguments like Servin's *Vindiciae*, to the almost journalistic apologies contained in Hotman's *Brutum Fulmen* (1586) and in Belloy's *Apologie Catholique* (1585), which defended the cause of Henry of Navarre.[110] They also comprised the famous *Satire Ménipée* (1594), which parodied the States-General of the League. Unlike Bodin's *La République* and Barclay's *De Regno,* the books of Hotman and Belloy were primarily concerned with vital problems of the day. In his book dedicated to Henry of Bourbon, Belloy wrote:

> La maladie et vieille en nous, nostre Medecin qui est le Roy, avoit au paravant usé de quelque sorte de potions, par le moyen desquelles nous estions allegez. Maintenant sur cest recheute, le breuvage qu'on nous a fait humer, sans l'advis, ordonnence & authorité du Medecin, lequel nous avons contraint d'ordonner ce que nous voulions prendre à nostre fantasie, ne proffite point aux malades. Nous l'avons rejetté dont nous sentons plus de douleur qu'auparavant. Le Medecin avoit veritablement deliberé de changer d'ordonnance & de regime pour nostre guerison. Il nous voiloit traicter plus doucement.[111]

They defended the Bourbon heir to the throne against the Guises and the Pope,[112] and they fought the Monarchomachs and the

---

[109] *Ibid.,* pp. 335–336.

[110] "La maison de Bourbon, vraye & seule heritiere de la couronne." E. D. L. I. C. [Pierre du Belloy], *Apologie Catholique contre les libelles declarations, etc., publiée par les Liguez,* p. 12ʳ.

[111] Pierre du Belloy, *De l'authorité du Roy et crimes de leze majesté,* pp. 71–72. Hereafter cited as Belloy, *De l'authorité du Roy.*

[112] ". . . totamque illam furibundam execrationem nihil esse, nisi brutum Papatus R. fulmen, cuius inanes, vani ac ventosi sunt impetus: idque quattuor praecipue de caussis: nempe, propter temerarii iudicis incompetentiam, allegationis falsitatem, ordinis

Leaguers on the ground that they were heading for universal chaos.

> Que ces beaux ligueurs me disent, qu'est-ce qu'ils ont gagné depuis trois ans, qu'ils ont fait semblant de prendre les armes pour exterminer ceux qu'ils appellent heretiques. C'est qu'ils ont apporté la famine, & la peste à tous les coings de ce Royaume ... Comment voulez vous qu'ils nous guerissent de la maladie que les huguenots on apporté, puis qu'il nous font user de leur medicament.[113]

But they all regarded secular power as being, to put it mildly, outside the arbitrary control of the spiritual authority—"Papa non potest sine causa quenquam in dignitate constitutum deponere" [114]— and in their plea for divine right they stressed the importance of a rigidly observed hereditary principle and of a strict legalism. The latter was illustrated by their claim that the Salic Law, the only hope for Henry of Bourbon, was inviolable. "La loy Salique ... qui tombe si souvent en propos: laquelle mesmes du temps de nos ancestres ... pacifia un different de merveilleuse consequence, touchant la succession du Royaume." [115]

Clearly, the Politiques was not a religious party, although most of its members were Catholics. They attached no importance to religious questions, which they regarded as subsidiary to those of the state. What proved to be their chief legacy was the fact that their victory necessarily meant an interchange of roles between religion and politics. Religion was no longer to play a leading role in international politics, but to become a problem for each individual. Second, posterity inherited from them the spirit of an absolutist rule, upon which the Politiques were inclined to theorize. Third, in the sphere of everyday activity, they impregnated other people's minds with the incomplete Machiavellian notion of toleration, which they used as an *ad hoc* measure, always subservient to secular aims such as the good of the state.

Spiritually, they were a strange combination of the doctrines of L'Hôpital and Machiavelli. The career of Henry Montmorency-Damville is most illuminating in this respect. He was an independ-

---

indiciatis defectum, & conceptae formulae stultitiam." Hotman, *Brutum Fulmen Papae Sixtii V, adversus Henricum Serenissimum Regem Navarrae, & illustrissimum Henricum Borbonium, Principem Condaeum*, p. 8. Hereafter cited as Hotman, *Brutum Fulmen*.

[113] Belloy, *De l'authorité du Roy*, p. 70.
[114] Hotman, *Brutum Fulmen*, p. 177.
[115] Hotman, *La Gaule Françoise*, p. 80.

ent, Catholic, aristocratic despot who played a solitary game, winning over the Huguenots from the King and vice versa, but above all desiring to ruin the Guises, against whom he would have allied himself with anybody. The secret of his success was his practice of siding with the weaker partner in order to destroy the stronger: with Henry of Navarre, he conspired against the League, while at the same time stressing his loyalty to the Catholic world; his "loyalty" to Henry III was assumed in order to gain greater authority in Languedoc, where he was Governor, and in order to subjugate more easily the Huguenots whenever they rebelled. However, he never fought the Huguenots wholeheartedly, fearing to destroy them and thereby the balance of power. He also endeavored to gain and retain the friendship and support of the most powerful men on all sides: the Pope, Henry of Navarre, and the Duke of Savoy. Finally, he tried not to commit himself to any group or person, and thus to preserve an almost irresistible attraction for many and to be a center of general interest. Probably his spirit of toleration was of the same kind as his loyalty to the King: it was the only policy which in his opinion would bring him glory and establish his autocracy in southern France.

THE PROSPECTS FOR TOLERATION

Toward the close of the century, some practical expression of the idea of toleration was recognized as a politically necessary evil and was, moreover, demanded by the economic situation, even though the idea itself seemed to be disregarded by most people. Some stop had to be put to the wars; because France, already financially ruined in 1560, had been brought by the continuous hostilites, devastation, waste, and extravagance of some thirty years to a pitiful and, indeed, appalling plight.[116] The financial policy of the Court had always been inadequate. True, the kings refrained from coining bad money (their predecessors had learned the danger involved), but they did not hesitate to drain recklessly the financial resources of in-

---

[116] The writings of the epoch, collected by Goulart and others, do not show the inevitability of the Edict of Nantes but rather the impossibility of the situation created by endless civil wars.

dividuals, towns, and certain classes or professions. Individual persons were hit by direct taxation, for instance by *la taille,* which became exceedingly heavy by the end of the century.[117] From the towns the French rulers borrowed money on a grand scale, and from the organized social groups they exacted semivoluntary contributions, as they did from the clergy.

With the progress of the wars, the needs of the Court grew, and the burden of taxation therefore increased. This, together with the general feeling of insecurity inseparable from war and an unprecedented influx of precious metals, precipitated a rise in prices.[118] The first two dates connected with nationwide inflation were 1557 and 1558, after which a series of further crises followed. In the course of the century, the purchasing power of money had diminished by 75 per cent, and if it had not been for the Financial Act of September, 1577, the sequel might have been even worse. The act aimed at restoring equilibrium by forbidding the circulation of all foreign currencies in France and by stabilizing the value of the livre at three francs, fourteen centimes for some twenty-five years.[119] This measure had a direct influence on purchasing power and saved France from complete fiscal disaster. It was abandoned by Henry IV in 1602, and the consequences were felt immediately; in the period from 1590 to 1598, the purchasing power of the franc dropped to 25 per cent of its value in 1500. But in 1599, with the cessation of hostilities, prices began to fall, and the purchasing power rose by 6 per cent until 1603, when it dropped slightly, to remain practically stable until 1640.

There was not the least chance for stabilization in the course of the sixteenth century. Nominal wages were rising, but were swamped by the pressure of inflation; real wages had fallen. The social consequences were far-reaching: they brought ruin to the *rentier* class and to salaried employees, but windfall prosperity to agriculturists, merchants, speculators, and financiers. This last category enjoyed even greater prosperity than the merchants, for op-

---

[117] *La taille* amounted to 7,000,000 livres in 1576; 18,000,000 in 1588. See P. Raveau, *L'Agriculture et les classes paysannes: La Transformation de la propriété dans le Haut Poitou au XVIe s.,* chap. iii. Hereafter cited as Raveau, *L'Agriculture et les classes paysannes.*

[118] Jean Bodin's *Réponse aux Paradoxes de M. de Malestroit* (Paris, 1568), as quoted in H. Sée, A. Rébillon, and E. Préclin, *Le XVIe siècle* (Paris, 1942), p. 25, shows that its author was one of the few who understood the economic causes of the crisis.

[119] Raveau, *L'Agriculture et les classes paysannes,* pp. xxvi ff.

portunities for fiscal speculations were enormous. The roots of big financial capitalism can be traced to this period.

The economic policy of the Valois favored *étatisme* and mercantilism. The former system, establishing industrial state monopolies, mostly in luxury goods, foreshadowed the later policy of Colbert. The latter, on the other hand, was strongly supported by the States-General, especially in 1576 and 1588, and probably by the general public as well, as mercantile notions were rather popular. Protectionist legislation began as early as 1539. The mercantile way of trade was imposed in stages: in 1572, when restrictions were put upon the export of certain products, such as woolen, flax, and hemp merchandise, and on the import of textiles (velvet, cloth, tapestries); and in 1581, when excessively restrictive legislation was passed on imported, chiefly manufactured, goods.[120] Thus France on the verge of bankruptcy seemed to do everything possible to impoverish herself still more. But with that protectionist conception, mercantilism was evoking a new interest. An outlet had to be found for monopolistically produced goods; interest turned to colonial expansion, which meant profitable markets for the mother country. Trade, of course, could not be conducted in the state of constant tension resulting from the wars of religion. The feeling that religious toleration must follow trade expansion on a world scale had yet to find its way to recognition. "Tolerance came," wrote Laski, referring to the seventeenth century, "because intolerance interfered with the access to wealth."[121] Until then, trade suffered from the fact that countries were divided internally into many fragments and remained in a state of almost constant war with one another.

Nevertheless, the odds against the Huguenots were overpowering, and the future of toleration was precarious, in spite of the many good reasons in its favor. The struggle between the Huguenots and the Catholics, which, reaching its climax during the wars of religion, was not indeed to end with the close of the century, was in the strict sense a "party struggle." This term is by no means an historical anachronism, as is the conception of "democracy" in connection with the sixteenth century. The same machinery was developed and the same methods were used as in later times: peaceful propaganda, revolutionary practices, assassination, open warfare. The circumstances in which these methods were used show that

---

[120] Cf. Sée, Rébillon, and Préclin, *Le XVIᵉ siècle*, pp. 244–245.
[121] H. J. Laski, *The Rise of European Liberalism*, p. 131.

what was at stake was the welfare of the big families on the one hand—the Bourbons, Guises, and Montmorencys, who sponsored the Huguenots—and on the other, the Leaguer and the Politique parties. The religious cause was also, as a rule, espoused by the leaders, but there were few who took seriously the religious side of party activity. True, there seemed no end to doctrinal controversies backed by lengthy quotations from the Scriptures, but these habitual references to the Bible were made almost mechanically.[122]

The religious side of party strife, however, had an important international aspect: internationally minded Calvinism invited an international Catholic reaction, and this process went on without a hope of solution until the advent of Richelieu. In addition, Geneva, the center of Calvinist doctrine, was attracting, educating, and sending out all over Europe a host of teachers, who were infecting distant countries with the new concepts. Knox, the foremost personality of the Scottish Reformation, was to all intents and purposes a Geneva man.

The conflict was international in a variety of ways. The European countries ought to have realized that economically they were members of one body, susceptible to the same diseases. The catastrophic rise in prices in France and in the other European countries indicated unequivocally that no country could be completely cut off from the economy of Europe as a whole. In England the pressure of inflation was marked by the increase of seigneurial rents.

In politics there were numerous examples of this relationship. Monluc, bargaining for the Polish crown on behalf of the Duke of Anjou, promised to stop religious persecutions in France. "Le fondement de ses ruses," wrote Goulart, "estoit un langage, accompagné d'escrits, excusans le massacre, & de grandes promesses aux gentils hommes Polonais." [123] Under the pressure of the Polish electors, who looked with favor on the idea of having a Valois on the throne, but were unwilling to accept him at the height of civil war and religious persecutions, France restored internal peace by the Treaty of La Rochelle in 1573.[124]

Yet this was of small importance compared with the constant pres-

[122] Allen, *A History of Political Thought*, p. 302, asserts that very few people believed in their usefulness.

[123] Goulart, ed., *Mémoires de l'Estat de France*, I, 513.

[124] "Plusieurs ont disputé des raisons pour lesquelles le duc d'Anjou & les siens qui avoient tant fait les mauvais du commencement devindrent si souples sur la fin. Aucuns ont estimé que la venue des ambassadeurs de Pologne fut cause que leur Roy accorda aux Rochelois plus qu'il n'eust fait sans ceste venue." *Ibid.*, II, 293ᵛ.

sure exerted by the Pope, Philip II of Spain, and Elizabeth of England, all of whom meddled constantly in France's internal affairs. The King of Spain, the Catholic, Italian, and Swiss princes, and, most of all, the Pope, intervened through the "holy League." "Parmy ces guerres s'est mêlé le prextexte & voile de la sainte Ligue, tendant à l'extermination des Heretiques, dont le Pape est chef comme Souverain en l'Eglise. Selon laquelle Ligue on ne peut faire paix ny composition avec les Heretiques." [125] From the start, Elizabeth I had participated, though indirectly, in the wars of religion. In 1560, at the time of the conspiracy of Amboise, her agents were active in Brittany and Normandy, trying to spread rebellion by distributing propaganda pamphlets.[126] She interfered on various other occasions. Her sailors denied to the French the freedom of the seas. In January, 1593, anxious to stop piracy and secure free overseas commerce, Henry IV wrote a letter requesting the Queen to pay damages to a French captain robbed of his vessel and all his goods in an English port.[127] Elizabeth, in turn, made repeated demands on Henry to give her the port of Brest as a base for her troops, but she met with a firm refusal: "Vous me desiréz chose que puisse prejudicier à mon service," wrote Henry IV in the summer of 1592.[128] France, on the other hand, did not wholly refrain from foreign commitments, although in that respect she was greatly handicapped in the period of civil strife. The Guises favored the cause of Mary Stuart and actively intervened in her behalf.[129] The presence of French troops in Scotland guaranteed a balance of power among the aristocracy, the monarchy, and the church. When the troops were evacuated in 1560, the government fell into the hands of the nobles.[130]

Despite the existence of numerous and closely woven international interests, the conception of a community of nations, entertained by several monarchs and statesmen of the period—Henry IV,

---

[125] Coquille, *Oeuvres*, I (*Discours sur les maux presens du Royaume pendant la Ligue* [unfinished work]), 241.

[126] Cf. Thompson, *The Wars of Religion in France*, p. 41. On April 6, Throckmorton wrote to Cecil: "It will be well to make current the proclamation by means of merchants through Brittany and Normandy, to animate the people more against the house of Guise." *Calendar of State Papers, Foreign Series* (1559–1560), No. 954.

[127] Berger de Xivrey, ed., *Recueil des lettres missives de Henri IV*, III, 715.

[128] *Ibid.*, pp. 642–643.

[129] Cf. *Calendar of State Papers*, Foreign Series (1559–1561), *passim*.

[130] Cf. H. T. Buckle, *History of Civilization in England*, III, 86.

Sully, Stephen Batory of Poland and the Polish Chancellor Goslicius, and Sir Francis Walsingham in England—could not make
headway, since the principle of "cujus regio ejus religio" was at that
period finding increasing recognition. National egoism was loudly
trumpeted in different languages in distant places: Machiavelli,
Luther, and More all did so, though in different degrees.[131] Luther-
anism, Calvinism, and Catholicism all divided horizontally the
vertical organization of European states; spiritually, they no longer
shared the same aim. Any conception of international ecclesiastical
organization was quite alien to nationalistic Lutheran Germany.
Calvinism fought on political, not spiritual, grounds. Catholicism
was divided into many national fractions, in spite of the powerful,
all-embracing authority of the Church.

What the closing century had bequeathed with the Edict of
Nantes, and what was much more long-lived, was the body of absolutist doctrines—the result of the prolonged strife and the responsibility, in different ways, of all parties. The manner in which the
Leaguers and the Huguenots behaved, allying themselves first with
the nobles and then with the towns and the corporations, and always
assuming a hypocritical veneer of liberalism, paved the way for the
future triumph of an absolute monarchy.[132] The seventeenth-century
rulers were given a ready-made pattern in a body of doctrines
which had been worked out by numerous schools of thought. Four
broad conceptions of government originated in the epoch of the
Reformation.[133] Two of these structures were absolutist: one was
purely absolutist, as illustrated by the reigns of Francis I and Henry
II, and was defended by the Politiques, notably Pierre du Belloy; the
other was a moderate kind of absolute rule, as envisaged by Seyssel
and L'Hôpital, in which a sovereign ought to respect ancient usages,
justice, religion, and moral duties.

To these two conceptions there were added two more—and opposing—conceptions: one, desired by Bodin, was the royal monarchy,[134] in which the States-General, though not sovereign, were

---

[131] Mesnard, *L'Essor de la philosophie politique,* p. 671.

[132] Accounted for in Ch. Labitte, *De la démocratie chez les prédicateurs de la Ligue,*
p. 364.

[133] Georges Weill, *Les Théories sur le pouvoir royal en France pendant les guerres
de religion,* pp. 276–277.

[134] "Le Monarque Royal est celuy qui se rend aussi obeissant aux loix de nature,
comme il desire les subiects estre envers lay, laissant la liberté naturelle, & la propriété des biens à chacun." Bodin, *Les Six livres de la République,* II, 194.

allotted a certain role in assenting to taxation; against this, Du
Haillan defended a limited parliamentary monarchy, a mixture of
the other types. Bodin denied validity and legitimacy to the latter
system. He thought only in terms of an indivisible sovereignty; a
composite sovereignty was meaningless to him. "Car si la souve-
reineté est chose indivisible, comme nous avons monstré, comment
pourroit elle se departir à un Prince, & aux seigneurs, & au peuple
en un mesme temps? La première marque de souveraineté, est donner la loy aux subiets : & qui seront les subiects qui obeïront, s'ils ont
aussi puissance de faire loy?" [135]

Bodin applied his theories to the conception of the state, which
before his time had never reached maturity. Always careful to devise practical remedies for contemporary France, he investigated
the various fields of state activity, distinguishing among the political, administrative, and economic departments. He was the champion of a strong, centralized power directing all these activities. In
regard to the economic field, the central authority would control
production and exchange, stimulate industrial and agricultural out-
put, and plan the national economy as a whole. The seeds were
thus sown for the *étatisme* of the seventeenth century.

Equally typical of his time was Bodin's failure to define clearly
the legal position of the individual. He spoke only in vague terms
of the "natural liberty" [136] of the subject. He did not state, for instance, as did Althusius, that an individual has rights only as a member of a body politic or corporation, and that he has no right to
stand against absolute power. The neglect of individual rights,
which was characteristic of the age, created the psychological and
doctrinal background for the emergence of absolute monarchy.

This trend was strengthened because Bodin's influence, judging
from the success of his book, was considerable. All those who succumbed to his persuasive, if confused, writings were led to accept
his thesis that pure monarchy is the best type of republic.[137] Sovereignty meant to him the complete absence of any legal restraint. "La
souveraineté est la puissance absolue et perpetuelle d'une République." [138] The sovereign, for the time being, is *legibus solutus*, not
bound by his own laws. Hence the arguments of Bodin had a secu-

---

[135] *Ibid.*, p. 177.
[136] Cf. above, note 134, *ibid.*, p. 194.
[137] Cf. *ibid.*, pp. 674, 678.
[138] *Ibid.*, p. 85.

larizing effect on political theory. For Bodin, the secular power must be unlimited and independent of the spiritual. He isolated the idea of sovereignty, dissociating it from God, and also from the pope or any person within the state. He tended to regard sovereignty as a legal fiction, an attribute of the state to which it owes recognition.

He also secularized the contemporary attitude toward toleration. He rejected toleration as a purely circumstantial matter, and in this his views were typically *politique*. The plea for toleration expressed in *La République* was not merely feeble—it was dangerous. Belittling the issue, he based the case for it on the ground of a choice between two evils—the greater comprising war, chaos, and atheism. Because he started with the premise that dissidence was the lesser evil, he found toleration acceptable. His views undermined the cause of toleration because, while divorcing his treatise from any connection with orthodox religion, he spoke in terms of general moral principles and direct relations with the rules of Christianity. His concept of toleration was essentially negative and, as such, could only retard the day when the idea of genuine tolerance became acceptable.

It was perhaps this question which most clearly exposed the unfavorable effects of the policy of the Politiques. The Edict of Nantes, for which they largely took credit, was self-defeating, because expediency could not provide a lasting basis for any policy of toleration. Later events proved how easily toleration could be dispensed with for reasons just as convincing as those which had caused its acceptance in 1598.

II

THE EDICT OF NANTES

"Même tronqué, ce statut restait une conquête partielle de la liberté."—J. Viénot, *Histoire de la Réforme française,* II, *145.*

"The Church became in the Middle Ages the most dangerous and resolute enemy of this [individual] freedom . . . yet . . . it did in its own way preserve the very principle which it seemed to attack."—R. W. and A. J. Carlyle, *A History of Mediaeval Political Theory in the West, V, 455.*

"A . . . party which is vague about its . . . policy finds an apparent drift among its members to the forces of [another party]."—H. J. Laski, *A Grammar of Politics,* p. *259.*

THE SPIRIT OF THE EDICT OF NANTES

In studying the factors underlying the passing of the Edict of Nantes, one is struck by the confusion of political ideas and party activities that prevailed at the time. The fact that there was a large number of parties and of doctrines is misleading, for no party had a coherent and consistent program. The Huguenots were almost without a consistent political theory, and there was no logical sequence in their rapid changes of doctrine. This lack of coherence in party politics can be accounted for by the fact that the leadership both of the Huguenots and of their opponents changed hands. At first the Huguenot party was largely in the hands of the aristocracy, but toward the end of the sixteenth century it began to shift in the direction of more "popular" [1] elements, particularly the middle-

---

[1] The Huguenot party became less "aristocratic" after 1572; the League, after 1585.

class townspeople. But, leadership apart, there was also a lack of unity of outlook within each party; in fact, as was characteristic of the whole Protestant movement, lively argument was a feature of all the parties. However, the disputations which they held, while bringing together people of widely differing views, did not result in the formulation of any new clear-cut body of opinion which would justify the emergence of a new party. It was much more common to find the theories of one party overlapping with those of another, and there was much interaction of ideas between the parties.

If these were times when it was difficult to go on wearing the same party label, it was even more difficult to keep one's ideas consistent and unchanged for long. Even the great Jean Bodin, who, in his *Methodus ad facilem historiarum cognitionem* (1566), sought to limit the sovereign power, was endeavoring to retract these limitations ten years later in *La République*. With lesser political writers and pamphleteers, plagiarism was frequent—originality was not expected—and the different political groups were ready to adopt any writings which happened to fit in with immediate policy. It is not surprising, therefore, that the same catchwords and slogans were often used by opposing factions, and party programs seemed to have much in common. There would have been practically no dispute between such parties as the Monarchomachs and the Politiques if religious freedom had been granted to the Huguenots.[2]

A striking example of the diffusion of ideas, their common acceptance, and the interplay between them is given by the impact of Duplessis-Mornay and Hotman, the most prominent of the Protestant Monarchomach writers. Hotman was strongly influenced by the opinions of the Politiques; in *Brutum Fulmen,* he expounded ideas "essentially theirs." [3] But this would not have been unusual if he had not in turn influenced the Leaguers, whose ideas opposed those of the Protestant Monarchomachs. The League upheld the ideas of Hotman and Junius Brutus in claiming the right of the "soundest" party to rise in defense of the state, and in granting legislative authority to the States-General.[4]

The Protestant Monarchomach influence reached even the Jesuits, who derived a good deal from the writings of Brutus. The in-

---

[2] Cf. H. J. Laski, Introduction to *A Defence of Liberty Against Tyrants,* by Junius Brutus (pseud.), p. 33.

[3] Cf. *ibid.,* p. 31.

[4] Cf. P. Mesnard, *L'Essor de la philosophie politique,* p. 383.

vestigation of influences and similarities, however striking they may now appear, is somewhat unsatisfactory, because closer examination reveals that the resemblances of doctrine were simply the result of similar conditions and did not necessarily imply that those who advanced them held the same convictions. After 1589 the League played, if less gracefully and with less interest for posterity, the role the Huguenots had played in the years immediately following 1573.

The confusion is increased by the fact that the parties not only had a chameleon-like appearance, but also were split into numerous factions. The Catholics, for instance, as Sandys testifies, were divided into several subgroupings.[5] There were the true *papistes,* who embraced most of the clergy and whose wealth and prestige, backed by the authority of the king and that of the parlements, gave the group its considerable strength—a strength diminished only by the widespread and open opportunism of its members.

But not all Catholics were so uncritical. The "parliamentary Catholics" were fundamentally critical of the Church, its frequent errors and glaring abuses. The "royalist Catholics" were bitterly resentful of the religious changes brought about by the conflict, which was leading, they thought, to the disruption of the Catholic community. There were also the "moderate Catholics," numerous according to contemporary testimony and of no little political importance, who advocated a policy of appeasement.

No picture of the Catholic mosaic would be complete without some mention of the Leaguers, who comprised the most zealous and fiery Catholics. They were "Monarchomach" in the sense of being hostile to absolutism. They claimed, moreover, to have been organized for the defense of a religion which they defined as "true," as opposed to "heretical." They tried to build their theory on an ethical basis, as did their Protestant Monarchomach associates who, being Protestants, were their opponents.

This complexity of the party system makes it difficult to assess the role that each party played in the development of religious and political ideas, and to apportion to each party its just credit for bringing about the Edict of Nantes.

The attempt to determine the attitude of the struggling parties to the problem of toleration reveals a complete lack of sincerity in

---

[5] Edwin Sandys, *Le Miroir de l'Europe* (1599). Cf. J. Viénot, *Histoire de la Réforme française,* II, 5.

their approach. There was certainly no genuine desire for religious freedom.

The Leaguers were dogmatically antitolerant. Even in their purely political conceptions they were not true advocates of popular ideas. The idea of the sovereignty of the people did not mean much to other Catholics, but they contributed to the growth of political ideas indirectly [6] by causing the Protestant reaction.

The Huguenots strove more consciously for freedom of worship, hoping to achieve it through the medium of religious toleration. They seemed to pursue the latter as an end, without understanding its far-reaching political implications. They were not tolerant in the real sense of the word. Indeed, claiming toleration for their own party only, they were by no means magnanimous toward the other Christian churches. Yet they were arrogant enough to advance religious tolerance as an ethical principle.

The Politiques alone had the courage of their convictions; they asserted religious toleration to be an expedient and not an ethical principle. They built up their theory of political activity on the basis of sheer expediency and were not reluctant to declare their intentions and purposes. In the end they succeeded in devising a practical method of action, and their theory contained something beyond immediate usefulness and workability. The Politiques were alone in realizing that the ethical issues at stake were political as well as religious. In a certain sense they fostered the development of later political trends. They were not absorbed purely by religion, but stood above religious controversies, and their preoccupation with practical political solutions anticipated the future dominant role of politics.

The Edict of Nantes, an obvious piece of compromise, was essentially the work of the Politiques, although the part played by the Huguenots must not be overlooked.[7] Without the fearless, aggressive, and provocative attitude of the Huguenots, Henry IV would

---

[6] Cf. Mesnard, *L'Essor de la philosophie politique*, p. 385.

[7] Several prominent personalities who were indirectly or directly responsible for the passing of the Edict of Nantes were either the Politiques themselves or people who sympathized with their ideas. Henry of Navarre behaved like a Politique throughout his political career, both before and after his conversion. Palm stresses that the Edict of Nantes gave a legal basis to what already existed and had been previously secured by the Politiques and the Politique-Huguenot union under the leadership of Henri de Montmorency-Damville. Cf. F. C. Palm, *Politics and Religion in Sixteenth Century France: A Study of the Career of Montmorency-Damville*, p. 242.

never have committed himself to such large concessions as those granted in 1598.

The reason that a Huguenot minority came into possession of such privileges needs closer scrutiny. An explanation in terms of the number of Huguenots in France at the time is unsatisfying; for, however optimistic the estimates of that number, it was never more than a small proportion of the total population.[8] Nor is a full explanation provided by stressing the fact that the Huguenot minority was intelligent, ambitious, active, convinced of its rights, and united in the struggle. The key to the apparent mystery lies in the existence of the Protestant strongholds, *places de sûreté,* the full use of which was granted by the Edict to the Protestants for a period of eight years. That temporary tenure was the only real and effective guarantee of the Edict. In this respect, the opinion of Ubaldini, the papal Nuncio in Paris, is worth repeating. He was a shrewd diplomat and an inveterate enemy of the Reformers as well as of the Gallicans. In his letter to Cardinal Borghese,[9] he made it plain that the best way to destroy the heresy was to requisition the strongholds. Indeed, many of the problems of the age are linked up with that of the Protestant strongholds; the true extent of royal power, for instance, becomes apparent in relation to them. Here was a case of a direct challenge to the sovereignty of Henry IV, and a check upon his powers as King. By the irony of fate, the King of France was himself responsible for giving the Protestants the means to challenge the royal authority, because it was he who subsidized the Huguenot garrisons. He tried to offset this loss of power by assuming supervision over the appointment of governors of the fortified towns, seeking to nominate them before the Protestant "colloquies" could express their opinion on the matter. At first sight, this plan appeared to accord admirably with Henry's wishes, but it soon took an unexpected turn. A decision was made that the governors, although nominated by the King, should be approved by the "colloquies." Ordinarily, according to Benoit, the famous seventeenth-century historian of the Edict of Nantes, it was the

[8] Sandys, *Le Miroir de l'Europe,* estimates 5 per cent of the whole population of France. Viénot's opinion, based on Alexis de Jussieu's *Notice sur les Assemblées Protestantes qui eurent lieu en France à la suite de la conversion de Henri IV,* is more optimistic: his estimate amounts to 8.3 per cent (or one-twelfth of the population), which was equal to 1,250,000 souls. Cf. Viénot, *Histoire de la Réforme française,* II, 2.

[9] Cf. *Archieves du Vatican,* Vol. 115, D. 1775; quoted by Viénot, *Histoire de la Réforme française,* II, 17.

king who accepted or rejected proposals initiated by his subjects; in this case the King had the initiative and the subjects were in a position to refuse.[10]

This was not a common occurrence, in spite of the fact that monarchical power had decreased since the days of the Valois. Some of the contemporaries of Henry IV began to think of royal authority in terms similar to those used in the *République* of Bodin. But the end of the sixteenth century was a period when the influence of the Politiques, who held no uniform views on the nature and extent of monarchical power, was marked. What all members of that party professed was the necessity for toleration and the practicability of compromise. Henry IV himself provided the pattern for the particular brand of limited absolutism commonly favored by the Politiques. His system was that of a benevolent feudal lord who believed in sound monarchy undisturbed by antiroyalist movements, and yet allowed his subjects to live freely. "Rien qui soit si contraire," he wrote in July 1599, "au commandement et au service de Dieu, que de vouloir irriter et esmouvoir les peuples contre leurs magistrats et ceulx auxquels ils doivent porter respect et obeissance, comme nous n'avons que trop esprouvé, à nostre dommage." [11]

Henry's philosophy created the Edict of Nantes, which turned out to be a challenge to the sovereign authority. If strictly applied, the Edict could have been a menace to the way of thinking of the Politiques and a triumph for the Monarchomachs. Henry IV believed, of course, in the policy of compromise—a belief prompted by his strength as well as by his weakness. The Edict was certainly not a complete surrender on his part to Protestant pressure. A policy of compromise was both beneficial and dangerous for the Huguenots. They had less to fear from the King's constant assurances to the Catholic world that he was protecting its interests,[12]

---

[10] Cf. Elie Benoit, *The History of the Famous Edict of Nantes*, I, 288. Hereafter cited as Benoit, *The Edict of Nantes*.

[11] Berger de Xivrey, ed., *Recueil des lettres missives de Henri IV*, V, 149–150. Hereafter cited as Henri IV, *Lettres missives*.

[12] Here instances were abundant. In a circular to the principal towns of the kingdom, his first public act as King of France, on August 2, 1589, Henry IV promised to restore good order "sans y rien innover au fait de la religion catholoque, apostolique et romaine, mais la conserver de [son] pouvoir, comme [il en fera] plus particulière et expresse déclaration." *Oeuvres de Henri IV* (*Lettres et harangues*), pp 14–15. Hereafter cited as Henri IV, *Oeuvres* (*Lettres et harangues*). To Cardinal de Joyeuse, his ambassador in Rome, he wrote on May 8, 1599: "J'ay bien considéré le langage que

than from their own system of fortified towns, which were a real bone of contention. If the existence of these towns was one of the most important factors contributing to the necessity for the Edict, it also made later reactions against the Edict both possible and of vital importance. The towns carried, as it were, a potential explosive charge and served as a constant reminder of the Huguenot problem. Moreover, the strongholds, being an actual and legal guarantee behind the Edict, had real significance only so long as the government was weak. No government could long tolerate the existence of a state within a state, and it was certain that a stronger government, with a respite from long wars and with a more settled international situation, would attempt to raze the Protestant fortresses. Even if it did not do so, the effectiveness of the strongholds as a legal guarantee was bound to diminish, since the Protestant tenure was temporary, and by a simple refusal to prolong it, the government could hit hard at the very basis of the Edict. But in 1598 those strongholds had to be reckoned with. Their importance can hardly be overestimated; their massive presence alone lent weight to the demands of the Huguenots, and at that juncture did them an immense service.

Had there been no strongholds, the Huguenot threat would have demanded less attention, even though the war with Spain had made a speedy settlement of France's internal problems urgently necessary. When the Edict of Nantes was signed (April 13), the treaty with Spain at Vervin (May 2) had not yet been concluded, and Spain was still, technically, not eliminated as a factor in the wars of religion. Thus the religious truce preceded the political conclusion of the wars of religion. In the meantime, new international complications had ensued as a result of the peace negotiations between France and Spain—negotiations which England and the Dutch states resented. Faced with the threat of a new war, urged

---

vous a tenu Sa Saincteté, tant sur le mariage de ma soeur, que sur l'edict que j'ay faict pour maintenir mon Royaulme en repos; et j'espere que le temps luy fera cognoistre que les asseurances que vous luy avés données de mon intention ... sont plus veritables." Henri IV, *Lettres missives,* V, 113. On July 24, 1599, he wrote again: "Je ... loue Dieu que Sa Saincteté commenca à prendre fiance de moy et de mes intentions en ce qui concerne l'honneur de Dieu et la restauration de l'Englise." Henri IV, *Lettres missives,* V, 150. On November 6, 1599, he wrote directly to the Pope: "J'auray tel soing aussy à mesnager l'edict que j'ay faict pour la tranquillité de mon Royaume, que la religion catholique en reçoive le principal et le plus asseuré fruict ... Votre Saincteté cognoistra tous les jours davantage par ce qui s'ensuivra." Henri IV, *Lettres missives,* V, 184.

on by the external allies of the Huguenots as well as by the Jesuits, Henry IV had been obviously under some compulsion to conclude a religious settlement.[13] He was not secure from direct internal threats, as already there were indications that the Huguenots would resort to violence if not given satisfaction. Had it not been for the King's desire for compromise, war would have followed. His policy preserved the peace, prompting him to grant the Huguenots what they desired. Acting as a Politique, Henry IV had the task of solving the delicate and intricate problems involved. Among these was the problem of the fortresses, a highly inflammable matter which had to be handled with care. The King knew that their abolition, even provided he had means to enforce such a decision, would mean an outbreak of revolts, and this he wished to avoid. He also knew that the strongholds were something of a safety valve. They provided an outlet for the separatist tendencies and for the Huguenot spirit of independence. Furthermore, the presence of strongholds demanded official recognition of the Huguenot status.

Henry IV faced the growing revolutionary tension by meeting it halfway. He leased the Huguenots the fortified places that they had held before August, 1598, but limited the validity of the lease to eight years. Moreover, he lessened their importance, making the future suppression of the strongholds easy by not including the clauses relating to them in the Edict but passing these clauses in a separate *brevet* on April 30, 1598. He probably wanted neither the Edict to be "irrevocable," nor the Protestant influence to grow greater. What had been accorded to the Huguenots was a matter of politics, as they were still very powerful, and France badly needed peace, tolerance, and liberty. But Henry's ultimate goal was the religious unity expressed in the formula "un roi, une loi, une foi." Here the preamble to the Edict of Nantes was most significant:

> ... mais maintenant qu'il plaît à Dieu commencer à nous faire jouir de quelque meilleur repos, nous avons estimé ne le pouvoir mieux employer

---

[13] On April 21, 1598, he wrote to the Duke of Pincy-Luxembourg: "La royne d'Angleterre et les Estats, ayant icy envoyé leurs ambassadeurs, se monstrent tres mal satisfaicts de la negociation de la paix. Si nous ne traictons avec les huguenots, il seroit à craindre qu'ils ne se joignissent au desespoir des Anglois et Hollandois, pour susciter en mon Royaulme une guerre plus dangeureuse que celle que nous voulons esteindre. C'est le desseign des [Jésuites] de nous y faire retomber, qui sont plus espangnols que chrestiens, et pour ceste occasion plus violens et ambitieux que charitables." Henri IV, *Lettres missives,* IV, 964.

qu'à vaquer à ce qui peut concerner la gloire de son saint nom et service, et à pourvoir qu'il puisse être adoré et prié par tous nos sujets; et s'il ne lui a plu permettre que ce soit pour encore en une même forme de religion.[14]

The Edict of Nantes, therefore, could be only a temporary measure. One may even assume that it was meant to give to French Protestantism a rigid form that would allow no expansion and no outlet except by way of Catholicism, with which, it was hoped, Protestantism would finally merge.

Although the restrictions imposed by the Edict were by no means excessive, they were nevertheless significant. For one thing, religious practice was seriously limited,[15] public worship being restricted to certain defined places, *lieux d'exercice,* the number of which was to remain constant. There was also a clause forbidding an increase in the number of strongholds. Other limiting rules were of comparatively minor significance, such as the rule barring Protestants from working during holidays and from selling meat on fast days— a rule to prevent unfair competition. But the numerous concessions and rights granted were not free from restrictive limitations. First, the Edict required that liberty of conscience be full and general, and it tried to safeguard this right of liberty of conscience not only within, but also outside, the kingdom.[16] In spite of this reservation, the Edict did not achieve more than limited toleration. Its application was confined to those areas where the Protestant movement had previously existed. The Catholic religion remained the main religion of the state, and the Protestants were tolerated, although not suffered altogether gladly.

Second, the Edict, reflecting the same spirit of tolerance, required that the past should be forgotten. Indeed, it was in part a large-scale amnesty, declaring void all misdeeds committed during the wars and reinstating persons and towns to their previous condition. This aspect, of course, had economic and financial implications. The Protestants were exempted from arrears of taxes,[17] and they re-

---

[14] Henri IV, *Oeuvres* (*Lettres et harangues*), p. 57.

[15] That is precisely where the Edict was most deficient: (1) the provisions for religious worship which it contained were inadequate; and (2) it was far too dependent on the aristocracy—in 1598, out of 951 Protestant churches, 257 were attached to the houses of nobility. Cf. A. J. Grant, *The Huguenots,* p. 70.

[16] Cf. secret (or "particular") Article LIII: "A Collection of Edicts," in Benoit, *The Edict of Nantes,* I, 561.

[17] Cf. Article LXXV, *ibid.,* p. 546.

ceived an assurance that any property lost during the wars would be restored.[18] The previous article concerned also those Catholics who had suffered losses while supporting the Protestant cause. But this "forgetting of the past" had an unforeseen consequence. Because the two religions were given equal rights, towns and even entire regions formerly exclusively Huguenot were thrown open to Catholics, who resettled in over one hundred towns and one thousand parishes or monasteries from which they had been barred for some fifteen years.[19] In practice, while giving equal status to the Protestants, the Edict brought about the full and solemn reëstablishment of the Catholic religion as the dominant creed in the state.

Third, the Edict guaranteed social and political equality. Protestants were declared to have free access to all "Estates, Dignities, Offices and publick Places whatever, either Royal, Signorial, or of the Cities of our Kingdom, Countries, Territories and Lordships." [20] They were given freedom of admission to all councils and assemblies, equal consideration in admission to schools, universities, and hospitals, and equal consideration when applying for public assistance.[21] Financial provisions were not neglected. Large subsidies were granted to maintain Huguenot garrisons and clergy. The Edict included guarantees in case of acts financially injurious; for instance, all the cases of disheritance carried out for religious reasons were to be canceled in the future.[22] The Huguenots were made subject to an equal burden of taxation. Arbitrary taxation was made illegal, and those Protestants who considered themselves overtaxed could present a claim before a judge.[23] On the other hand, a special measure prevented Protestants from profiting unfairly from their religion by working during Catholic holidays, lest they antagonize their Catholic neighbors.[24]

---

[18] Cf. Article LXXXIX, *ibid.*, p. 550.

[19] "L'exercise de la religion catholique fut remis à la Rochelle et en plus de 100 villes closes et 1000 paroisses ou monastères esquels l'edit exercice estoit intermis depuis 15 ans en ça et plus." Gayet, *Chronologie Novenaire* (1529–1598), p. 48, as quoted in F. Garrisson, "Avril 1598–Avril 1948, un trois cent cinquantième anniversaire: L'Edit de Nantes," *Bulletin de la Société de l'histoire du Protestantisme Français*, VC, 42. Hereafter cited as Garrisson, "Avril 1598–Avril 1948," *Bull.*

[20] Article XXVII: "A Collection of Edicts," in Benoit, *The Edict of Nantes*, I, 533.

[21] Article XXII, *ibid.*

[22] Article XXVI, *ibid.*

[23] Article LXXIV, *ibid.*, p. 545.

[24] Article XX, *ibid.*, p. 532.

The clause providing for freedom of access to employment was popular with the Protestants because it could be used to obtain economic power and higher social status. The Huguenots were buying offices and sinecures created by the King and were asking for the creation of new posts. Able, intelligent, parsimonious, and loyal to each other, they soon gave rise to feelings of envy, hostility, and hatred among their religious opponents. Their economic prosperity was no less hateful to the Catholics than were their religious beliefs.

The right of appointments to office became the main point of contention in the parlements, which had strongly opposed the Edict before registering it in 1599 and 1600. In spite of the limitations introduced by the Edict concerning the right to public worship, the Paris parlement had grounds for dissatisfaction, because the ban which the Edict of Poitiers (1577) had imposed on the Protestants within a radius of ten leagues from the capital was now to apply to only five leagues. But the chief stumbling block was the judicial provision establishing the *Chambres de l'Edit,* special courts composed of both Catholic and Protestant members.[25] The parlement of Paris had insisted on a reduction of Protestant representation at court, and until it was agreed that only one Protestant should sit in the otherwise Catholic assembly, the registration (February, 1599) of the Edict was delayed. Provincial parlements were not less obstructive; they needed strong pressure from the King in the form of express orders, or *lettres de jussion*,[26] before they would ratify the Edict. It took two years for the Edict to go through most parlements, except for the parlement of Rouen. Although in practice the parlement of Rouen had accepted in 1599 the consequences of the new act, it refrained from formal registration until 1609.

In this attitude of the parlements, which as a rule represented the interests of the Catholic clergy and of the Gallican elements in particular,[27] the "most weighty opposition"[28] of the clergy was reflected. This opposition revealed the truly progressive character of the Edict and the generosity of some of its principles and concessions. The Edict contained some splendid provisions which the clergy feared and resented: freedom of conscience, complete civil

---

[25] *Chambres de l'Edit* were originally planned to have ten Catholic and six Protestant members in Paris and an equal representation in the provinces.

[26] Cf. G. Zeller, *Les Institutions de la France au XVIe siècle,* pp. 156, 160.

[27] *Ibid.,* pp. 161–162.

[28] Benoit, *The Edict of Nantes,* I, 321.

liberty, the right to ecclesiastical and political assemblies, and a state endowment to the Protestant church. The clergy were probably appalled by the "spirit of tolerance" of the Edict and did not wish to take into account the limitations the Edict actually imposed. Apart from some explicit limitations, such as the reduction of places of public worship to 3,500 castles and some towns, the Edict possessed some further drawbacks implicit in the form given to the treaty. In addition to ninety-two general articles,[29] signed on April 13, 1598, and fifty-six particular "secret" articles, signed on May 2, it contained three secret commissions, or briefs (*brevets*): the first, of April 3, provided an endowment of 45,000 crowns a year to the "Subjects of the So-called Reformed Religion"; [30] the second, of April 30, advanced 180,000 crowns annually to ensure the upkeep of garrisons in the fortified towns, which were recognized as a military guarantee; the third distributed 23,000 crowns to individually named Huguenots.[31] The *brevets* were meant to remain secret and did not require registration by the parlements.[32] Thus, being merely the result of circumstances, and depending entirely on the king's good will, they carried no legal sanction and were by nature revocable.[33]

This does not complete the criticism. As a document of toleration, the Edict was hardly original. It is curious that the clauses favorable to the Huguenots were most indebted to the numerous edicts and treaties previously passed.[34] The Edict contained many rights granted to the Protestants and revoked in the course of the wars of religion. In matters of religious practice, it gave a revised version

---

[29] Not ninety-five, as stated by E. Lavisse, *Histoire de France,* Vol. VI, Part 1, p. 418 n. Cf., in Benoit, *The Edict of Nantes,* I, 526 ff.; full texts of the "general and secret" articles of the Edict and of the *brevets;* the fifty-six so-called "secret" articles were not secret at all, but the *brevets* were.

[30] The purpose was not stated openly; the sum was "to be employed in certain secret affairs relating to them (the Protestants) which his Majesty does neither think fit to specify." Benoit, *The Edict of Nantes,* I, 563. But subsequently the annuity was used for the ministers' stipends. Benoit simply says that the sum was "granted" for the payment of the ministers. *Ibid.,* p. 293.

[31] *Ibid.,* p. 297. This point is usually omitted in the accounts of the Edict.

[32] Cf. Lavisse, *Histoire de France,* Vol. VI, Part 1, p. 418.

[33] ". . . these sorts of Letters are not like a Law, but only continue at the King's Pleasure, who revokes them when he has a Mind to it." Benoit, *The Edict of Nantes,* I, 293. Garrisson also draws attention to the revocability of the *brevets.* "Avril 1598–Avril 1948," *Bull.,* VC, 44.

[34] Cf. Benoit, *The Edict of Nantes,* I, 272 ff.

of the Edicts of 1577, of Nérac, and of Fleix; the sections dealing
with personal rights as well as with general regulations, contained
in the "secret" articles and related to the execution and effects of
the Edict, were also based on old measures. Its legal concessions
were little more than a repetition and collection of older documents.
Why, then, should the Edict have been regarded as an extraordinary measure, evoking the hostility and opposition of the
Catholic camp? The answer is twofold: it was wholly unexpected,
and a genuine effort was made to carry out its provisions. Commissioners, one Catholic and the other Protestant, were appointed
in each province "to act in such a manner as to content both
parties." [35]

The King spared no effort to ensure impartiality. Both commissioners were granted equal authority in hearing petitions and
complaints and were given extensive powers to put the Edict into
effect. The result, however, was disappointing. "The Catholic Commissioner," said Benoit, "had the upper hand almost everywhere." [36]
The realization of the Edict was jeopardized from the very beginning, and despite the good will of its authors, it was never applied
in its entirety because French society proved neither ready to adopt
its principles nor willing to help in their application.[37]

THE EDICT OF NANTES IN
THE LIGHT OF MEDIEVAL POLITICAL THEORY

The epoch which began with the passing of the Edict of Nantes and
closed with the assassination of Henry IV in 1610 was perhaps the
only period in the life of the Edict when it was seriously enforced.

This short period of peace and order was the most solid achieve-

---

[35] Cf. *ibid.*, p. 345.

[36] Cf. *ibid.*

[37] Indeed, the Edict of Nantes loses in comparison with such a generous act as the
Charter of King Edward VI (dated July 24, 1550). The Charter provided for liberal
treatment of foreign Protestant refugees and encouraged material help, which was
subsequently extended to the French exiles by the English community. Cf. D. L. Savory,
"Broadcast on 27th July 1950," *Proceedings of the Huguenot Society of London*, Supplement to Vol. XVIII, No. 4, p. 34.

ment of the treaty. The Huguenots were no longer persecuted, and Henry's prestige and his wish to make good all the provisions of the Edict ensured stability. So long as the King lived to enforce what he had enacted, infringements of the treaty were comparatively unimportant, even if intended to be harmful. Such was the case when the principle of free access to offices was violated by setting limits to the number of Protestants who could be employed in a given profession or institution. These restrictions, at first regarded as an illegal abuse, were later made legal. The next step was to expel the Huguenots from their posts under the pretext that the Edict only claimed that they were capable of holding office, but had never guaranteed that they must do so! The letter of the Edict of Nantes was never sacred. Huguenots were soon excluded from the guild of *arts et métiers*.[38] In many places their children were prevented from attending Protestant schools. The Paris School of Medicine shut its doors to Protestant students. In those localities where the Catholics were in a majority and in power, the Huguenots gradually lost the right to practice their religion. The declaration of June, 1605, ordered the destruction of those of their "temples" in which either mixed-marriage ceremonies had been performed or in which "seditious discourses had been held." [39] The Edict of December, 1606, forbade the erection of "temples" on all sites where Catholics would object to them.[40] The equality of treatment in hospitals promised to the sick and poor Huguenots by Article XXII of the Edict of Nantes left much to be desired.[41] Perhaps the most deplorable aspect was the illegal interpretation of the Edict of Nantes with the aid of the edicts previously passed. These old edicts had been annulled in 1598, and the new Edict forbade all arbitrary interpretation of previous enactments.[42] In spite of this provision, however, the old edicts were often revived, under the pretext that they had never been abolished. The new method was to accept all restrictions found in the old edicts, and apply them to the relevant

---

[38] Cf. Viénot, *Histoire de la Réforme française,* II, 48.

[39] Cf. Ch. Benoist, *Condition juridique des Protestants sous le régime de l'Edit de Nantes et après sa révocation,* p. 188. Hereafter cited as Benoist, *Condition juridique.*

[40] Cf. F. A. Isambert, A. Jourdan, and others, *Recueil général des anciennes lois françaises: depuis l'an 420 jusqu'à la Révolution de 1789,* XV, 307, as cited in Benoist, *Condition juridique,* p. 187.

[41] Cf. Rep. aux cahiers, 18 Sep. 1601, Décisions royales 21, 22, as cited in Benoist, *Condition juridique,* p. 228.

[42] Cf. Article XCI: "A Collection of Edicts," in Benoit, *The Edict of Nantes,* I, 551.

clauses of the Edict of Nantes, while refusing at the same time to apply the favorable stipulations. The favorable clauses found in the royal *cahiers,* given to the Protestants as an extension to the Edict, were disregarded.

Still, it cannot be denied that the Edict, although treated with such contempt and neglect, managed to create appreciably better conditions for the religious minority. The Huguenots felt comparatively safe and contented, and caused no disturbance. They were apparently satisfied with what they had got. Their wants were moderate, and they raised no extravagant claims. The only major request they made before the death of Henry IV was for the prolongation of the lease of the fortified towns, which expired in 1606. That was granted until 1611.[43] Had they asked for more concessions, their chances of success would have been small. It was obvious from the beginning of the century that French society tended to interpret the Edict in terms unfavorable to the Huguenots, that the margin of advantageous interpretation of ambiguous or open clauses would be narrow, and that the King stood isolated in his Huguenot sympathies. In the last few years of Henry's reign, the confidence the Huguenots had placed in him somewhat faded; they became narrowly watchful of his policy, remembering that he had been essentially a Politique.[44] Clearly, the prospects for the irrevocable measure, as the Edict was styled, were not bright.

Other factors were also emerging, which were to have considerable effect on the future of the Huguenot community. Among them was the revival of Gallicanism, which had suffered both a political and a religious defeat in the early days of the reign of Henry IV.[45] Its influence had declined as the Pope asserted his political supremacy over the King and his religious superiority over the General Councils. The higher French clergy, fearing the Huguenot danger, rallied to the papacy, professing orthodox loyalty. But toward 1600 the circumstances changed. The hue and cry of the wars of religion had died down, the internal religious situation in France ap-

---

[43] The lease was to be prolonged three more times; it finally expired in 1624.

[44] Their fears were not unjustified, if one can rely on Ubaldini's account of what the King confided to him concerning immediate suppression of some six strongholds and gradual abolition of the rest. Cf. Letter of Nuncio Ubaldini to Cardinal Borghese of May 13, 1608, *Archives du Vatican,* Vol. 115, D. 1445, as quoted in Viénot, *Histoire de la Réforme française,* II, 17.

[45] Cf. Lavisse, *Histoire de France,* Vol. VI, Part 2, p. 21.

peared more settled, and Gallican feelings were revived. Though progress was slow at first, since Gallican beliefs encountered opposition in the parlements, they continued to gain ground. Gallican ideas, reformulated by Pierre Pithou at the close of the sixteenth century [46] and defended by André Duchesne,[47] were now on the way to winning widespread recognition.[48] The Gallican controversy was to fill the vacuum which religious appeasement had produced. Its influence on the Protestant cause was significant, though indirect.

Gallicanism meant the accentuation of royalist theories and the exclusion of popular doctrines. Gradually, as the royalist tendencies gained wider acceptance, it became clear that the French people on the whole were monarchistic. So long as Henry IV reigned, the Huguenots were natural adherents of the same doctrine. But after 1610 they simply had to drink of the same swift stream of ideas as the rest of the French nation. A unique opportunity arose, unrecognized by both camps, for achieving political unity, when the gulf between them was reduced by such powerful factors as the existence of the Edict of Nantes and the acceptance of common political doctrines. But no party seemed able to grasp the opportunity that was at hand. The Catholics thought the range of liberty given by the Edict to the Huguenots to be too wide. The Huguenots, apprehensive and irritated, had been likely to respond violently ever since their sense of security had been shaken by Ravaillac's assassination of Henry IV. Professing monarchism and not discarding the new notion of sovereignty, which had already taken solid root in their political ideas, they were about to revolt. This new notion of sovereignty had been expressed in the theory of the divine right of kings, which now found complete Huguenot approval.[49] The belief in popular sovereignty, such as could be found in the social

---

[46] Cf. Pierre Pithou, *Les Libertés de l'Eglise Gallicane* (Paris, 1594).

[47] Cf. André Duchesne, *Les Antiquitez et recherches de la grandeur & maiesté des Roys de France.* Hereafter cited as Duchesne, *Les Antiquitez.*

[48] An impetus to revive Gallicanism and Episcopalianism came from many quarters. A rather curious case was that of Emmanuel Rodrigue, who, in his *Quaestiones regulares* (1609), claimed that religious orders are divinely instituted and, as such, independent of bishops' temporal power. Cf. Lavisse, *Histoire de France,* Vol. VI, Part 2, p. 381.

[49] This position was taken officially in 1617 at the synod of Vitré when "le parti tout entier, officiellement, par la voix de ses délégués, faisait adhésion à la doctrine du droit divin des souverains." G. Lacour-Gayet, *L'Education politique de Louis XIV,* p. 252.

contract theory, had been rejected, and a claim for a divinely ordained and independent secular power substituted.

It is strange how little the Huguenots managed to benefit from the adoption of this doctrine, which must have been conceived for reasons of expediency. So long as Henry IV lived, the Huguenot attitude may have been sincere. But what induced them to preserve the incongruous marriage between independent political organization and doctrinal dependence on the monarch? What made them revolt against the King, while professing royalist doctrines? Why were these doctrines proclaimed in all earnestness by nearly every important Protestant writer of the seventeenth century?

So long as they opposed the monarch by advocating popular rights, even though they claimed that in principle they were not fighting him, their position was unambiguous and consistent, and their behavior could be explained in logical terms. But becoming royalist and believers in the duty of obedience meant rejecting the theory of popular rights; and when their theory led them to proclaim allegiance to the King, fighting him became imprudent because it was impossible to deny that such behavior was rebellious. They seem never to have considered the choice between complete loyalty to the monarch and a decisive stand in the name of radical ideas. They provoked wars which they could not control, and on the outcome of which they had little influence. They were full of convulsive agitations, as though anticipating an imminent disaster.

The theory of divine right did not serve them well. By subscribing to it, they only strengthened the position of the King in his fight against the papacy and stressed the similarity of their outlook with that of the rest of the French community. It led them to assist in building up the royal sovereignty at the expense of their own power. Intensified royalism meant the diminution of popular rights, and as the divine right theory became more widely held, the power of the French people was lessened. There was no escape from this predicament. The Huguenots could no more escape from what lay in store than could any other Frenchmen; in other words, they were condemned to a gradual acceptance of strict royalism, which one day was to assume an absolutist form. They were caught up in the midst of a change of ideas as to the proper relationship between religion and politics, between church and state. As Reformers, they contributed their own share to the change, although the ideas eventually emerging were not exactly what they had been aiming at.

The history of the doctrine of divine right at the beginning of the seventeenth century serves to show that, if political practice does not follow political theory, mistakes may be made in the choice of political means, and the consequences may be different from what has been anticipated. The tragic incongruity between Huguenot political theory and practice was measurable by the series of failures the Huguenots had to endure. The success of the Huguenots and their hold on the masses stood or fell by their maintaining their popular principles. Their history in the seventeenth century shows how little they had to say, how few they could convince of the righteousness of their action, and how little justification they could give to their deeds. Until Jurieu started his furious attacks and evoked the reaction of Bayle and his supporters, there was little Huguenot political theory to give impulse to political action in the seventeenth century. Yet the initial period of the functioning of the Edict of Nantes, although uneventful, is of considerable importance and offers some clues to future developments.

The acceptance of the doctrine of divine right by the Huguenots created an ambiguous situation. The doctrine served as a way of escape from the domination of theology, but the Huguenots could not have desired such an escape. If they could have accepted the doctrine without all the consequences involved, it would have suited them better, but this was out of the question. Complete escape from the bonds of theology was neither possible nor desirable, because their Protestantism was based on the tradition of the semi-lay, semi-ecclesiastical Genevan state. The Reformation did not envisage an ecclesiastical system distinct from the state organization. The best solution for the Protestants would have been to reject divine right altogether, although such a move would have had some chance of success only if it had been executed speedily, for every year of the seventeenth century saw a widening gulf between the lay and the ecclesiastical elements of the Protestant communities. The Huguenots' attempts to prevent this breach were fruitless; for while they yearned to preserve the fusion of the two elements, in practice they did everything to destroy it. Their position was a hopeless one. They were part of a general and vast process involving the whole of society, and this they could not escape. They were trying to clarify certain general issues, yet were unable to solve efficiently their own problems of immediate policy. If adherence to the theory of divine right meant escape from theology, it was the irony of fate for the Huguenots that, in order to gain spiritual independence, they fell under temporal domination.

By accepting the theory of divine right, they also drew attention to the doctrine of "two societies," generally ascribed to the Middle Ages, but established in part by the Huguenots.[50] The doctrine of "two societies" seems to be either very modern or very primitive.[51] The threads that link its modern version with the Middle Ages lead to the Reformation, particularly to the organization and activities of the Genevan state. The contemporaries of the Huguenots, watching a clearly set and defined model of society in their communities, were inclined to express the medieval past in terms easily comprehensible to the public, that is, to see the past through the present. Perhaps without the existing Huguenot pattern, our interpretation of medieval society would be different.

Evoking the problem of two societies, the Reformers raised the highly confusing issue of medieval unity. That problem has two aspects: the difference between the medieval and the Reformation unity, and the confusion it involves. Perfect unity existed more in the minds of the thinkers of later generations than in medieval reality.[52] It was conceived ex post facto as a convenient generalization and simplification of a relationship puzzling in its complexity. Although the Reformation had changed that relationship, in many respects it remained the same. In the medieval "unity" there was a good deal of disunity, and in the post-Reformation "disunity" certain elements of unity cannot be dismissed. Moreover, in reality, this unity, though so eagerly pursued, was never actually reached.

What does the medieval unity amount to? The state-church relationship in the Middle Ages owed its complexity to an ambiguous notion of society which "one" but not "uniform." [53] It was not homogeneous, because it comprised two elements: ecclesiastical and lay (*sacerdotium* and *regnum*), which ruled separately,

---

[50] "The organisation of the Huguenots was very important in influencing men's minds. It was so local, so compact, so distinct, that it helped to forward the idea." J. N. Figgis, *Churches in Modern State*, Appendix 1, p. 215.

[51] *Ibid.*

[52] ". . . The spiritual universal state must be regarded as theory rather than reality . . ." George James Bayles, "Church and State," *New Schaff-Herzog Encyclopedia of Religious Knowledge*, ed. by S. M. Jackson, III (Grand Rapids, Michigan, 1950), 107.

[53] "In the thirteenth century Church and State had drawn together as two aspects of one society." F. R. Hoare, *The Papacy and the Modern State* (London, 1940), p. 131.

having separate codes of law—canon and civil.[54] In the medieval world the actual unity was evident in the ecclesiastical system, which was international. Yet it never embraced other spheres of life. It was far more important as an ideal than as a fact.[55] In the evolution which took place between the early Middle Ages and the end of the twelfth century, the ideal had no chance of realization. The Church soon became concerned with political unity, of which the Holy Roman Empire was the expression. But the theory was never fully formulated because there lingered a notion of two supreme authorities—the pope and the emperor.[56] That dualism had to be discarded before real unity could be established, but such a step was impossible during the Middle Ages. Church and state stood too far apart to be reconciled.

In the Middle Ages the ideal of unity was limited and defective; it was a goal pursued but never reached. Only a fraction of unity was achieved. The error of the Middle Ages was to refer it anachronistically to the distant past of the Roman Empire. This retrospection must have caused a rigid and biased attitude. Men in later ages, on the other hand, have been uncertain as to which ideal to choose. Halfway between the Middle Ages and more modern times stood the Reformers. Their merit was that they saw a certain system in the incoherent mass of ideas and detected some traces of unity amid the confusion.

It is also the Reformers who have made us realize that the ideal of the Middle Ages has never been attained—and is in fact unattainable. They tried to preserve the half-formulated medieval ideas and form them into a cohesive, more lasting shape. They saw beyond the Middle Ages, being aware of classical history (of which that period knew little), and they were unfettered by the bonds of the Holy Roman Empire. They possessed real freedom of action, since the Counter Reformation had failed to carry out its full program. Their lack of success was directly proportionate to their failure to understand. The meaning they attributed to the notion of unity would have been opposed by any medieval thinker.[57] Their

---

[54] Cf. J. N. Figgis, *Studies of Political Thought from Gerson to Grotius:* 1414–1625, pp. 184–185.

[55] Cf. C. Delisle Burns, *Political Ideals* (7th ed., Oxford, 1950), p. 104.

[56] Cf. R. W. and A. J. Carlyle, *A History of Mediaeval Political Theory in the West* (London, 1903–1928), I, 287.

[57] Cf. Burns, *Political Ideals,* p. 94.

only achievement was to start a trend in which the medieval separation of the spiritual and secular spheres of life was to disappear. So the division between the ethics of Christianity and natural ethics was to disappear, and consequently each morality was to be deprived of its own separate sphere. Yet unity was not achieved. The modern aspects of unity, which we owe to the Reformation, are purely negative; they consist in the absence of the medieval division into two spheres of life. The medieval disunity (or incomplete unity) possessed at least one positive aspect, because church and state were regarded as departments of the same society, of one coherent whole. The modern unity was doomed when society disintegrated into two independent communities, and the members of state and church began to consider themselves members of two distinct bodies. State and church later became just two associations among many: society changed from unitary to pluralistic. Reducing the power of the Church, the Reformation could no longer attain one of its objectives —unity on the basis of the recognized supremacy of religion over law. It departed from the medieval legalizing of morality, preferring the moralizing of legal behavior. It wanted to achieve an end which was beyond its reach, because Church supremacy was already a thing of the past, and the modern distinction between what is "moral" and what is "religious" had not yet matured.

The Reformation, although in many respects a failure in what it had conceived and in what it achieved, gave a tremendous shock to contemporary and subsequent generations. Provoking vigorous and bold thinking, it provided a momentum to creative speculation in distant and varied fields free from Scholastic bonds. By discussing the issues of preceding ages, it imparted to modern thinkers something of its deep, though often incorrect, insight into their complex problems. Although the Huguenots could help others, they often could not help themselves. They lived up to other people's hopes as Reformers, but practical realities often eluded them: their beliefs and their policy are proof. They could not admit that they were continuing the tradition of the medieval theory of religious unity [58] because such an attitude would have been suicidal. Their attitude to toleration may serve as an explanation. Though in agreement with the Catholic idea of intolerance, they justified it on utterly different grounds: not as a practical necessity, in order to preserve

[58] Cf. Lord Acton, "The Protestant Theory of Persecution," *Essays on Freedom and Power*, p. 104.

unity, but as a political duty, to suppress error. Their justification of intolerance was based on speculation about dogmas, which were more impelling for them than facts—the chief reason for the Catholic theory of persecution.[59] This lack of a realistic approach had its counterpart in their politics—in their gross mismanagement of their affairs as a political party and in their failure as leaders and members of a political party with its own aims.

ROHAN AND THE
POLITICS OF THE HUGUENOT PARTY

The failure of the Edict of Nantes was due to a number of causes, the majority of which were related to the Huguenot party, its character and its activity, and the position in which it found itself after half a century of continuous struggle. After the death of Henry IV in 1610, the struggle for religious toleration took the form of purely internal party strife, intended to achieve a high level of organization. It was partly the hope that the party could retrieve what it had lost by the death of its guardian King which prompted the Huguenots to act in this way. It was partly a desire to regain their former material power which urged the Huguenots to concentrate on the issues of structure and program rather than on ideology. Besides, the Huguenots found themselves in a kind of ideological quandary, and it seemed there was little else they could do at that moment. Ideological disputes were suspended after the armistice imposed by the Edict of Nantes, and the action of Ravaillac had not changed the situation in any way which would justify a radical change of attitude in regard to the question of obedience. Shielded behind their publicly professed loyalty to the monarchy, the Huguenots discovered a new weapon of defense and attack in the form of a party program made more explicit and more coherent than before.

In 1612, in a publication entitled *Discours sur l'état de la France durant les persécutions de Saint-Jean,* Rohan outlined the political

---

[59] "The only instance in which the Protestant theory has been adopted by Catholics is the revocation of the Edict of Nantes." *Ibid.,* p. 109.

program of his party. In this scheme, the role the party had to play
was elevated to a higher sphere. Confronted with the only other
two parties of importance—the Court party, dominated by the
Queen Mother, and the princes' party—he regarded the Protestant
party as the only one able to preserve the country. "Le troisième
parti est celuy de la Religion, lié par la conscience avec tous les
Protestants da la Chrétienté, parti seul capable de maintenir la
France comme il a fait autrefois." [60]

Rohan hoped to serve the glory and power of France by promoting closer relations with the Protestant countries and Protestant
princes and by warning the government against alliances with Spain:
"... contre qui se doit-on gueres fortifier, que contre l'Espagne? De
qui se fortifier que de ses ennemis irréconciliables, & interessés à
notre bien, et cependent nous faisons le contraire." [61] He thought the
role the Huguenot party could play in this respect to be pivotal, and
he also cautioned against the consequences of its alliance with England:

> On se fie peut-être en ce que la partie Réformée ne se peut joindre avec
> le Roi d'Espagne: mais ne voulant se perdre, en se ralliant il peut choisir
> le Roi d'Angleterre, qui seroit l'entiere ruine du Roiaume de France ...
> Et nous serions si aveuglés, que de contribuer notre ruine à l'insatiable
> & immoderée ambition du Pape, & du Roi d'Espagne? Ne voit-on pas
> qu'un tel traictment attire une guerre civile en France, laquelle est plus
> à craindre que les fulminations du Pape de Rome, qui ne pouvant ruiner
> la France par les armes étrangeres, la veut détruire par les naturelles.[62]

The moment was propitious for such a statement, for it nearly
coincided with the extension of the political activities of the
Protestant community, following decisions taken at Saumur.[63] Although those decisions were not fully carried out, the matter was
taken up at La Rochelle, and in 1621 a kind of Protestant republic
was created, following the manifesto *Ordre et Règlement général*.

All these measures seemed to be strangely ineffective. Although
the administrative structure of the party was excellent, it persistently failed to secure its objectives. The power of the party
was dwindling. The reason for this was not the changed balance

---

[60] Henri de Rohan, *Mémoires historiques et discours politiques 1611–1629*, II, 172.
Hereafter cited as Rohan, *Mémoires*.
[61] *Ibid.*, pp. 160–161.
[62] *Ibid.*, p. 170.
[63] Cf. below.

of power and worsened position in relation to other political camps. The weakness was also the party's own. In spite of its relatively higher type of organization, it seemed to have lost some vital source of inspiration.

The party was incapable of putting into practical shape its own plans, which had not been without merit. These plans were given the form of the decisions taken at the Assembly of Saumur in 1611, amid the general feeling of frustration which overcame the Huguenots with the disappearance of Henry IV from the political scene. Had the Saumur declaration been fully realized, its consequences might have been far-reaching, for the work done by the Assembly indicated the highest point of evolution that the party had ever achieved; its political organization found, at least on paper, a final form.

The structure of the Calvinist religious and political organization had been created well before the passing of the Edict of Nantes, which did nothing to improve it; only at Saumur were the final touches given to the representative system.[64] In the religious sphere, the existence of consistories, colloquies, and provincial and national synods was confirmed. In the political sphere, corresponding provincial councils, circle assemblies, and general assemblies were provided. It has been asserted [65] that the provincial councils, although known before Saumur, did not meet regularly before 1611. According to the same writer, it was with Saumur that their continuous history began, to be interrupted only after the fall of La Rochelle, when all political activities of the Huguenots were brought to an end. But even if some minor improvements were made, there was no lasting result. The principles resolved upon by the Assembly found little endorsement in life. Benoit assessed the difficulties involved in carrying them out, when he spoke of them as "very fine Regulations which would have been sufficient to render the Reformed invincible, had it been so easie to put them sincerely in execution as to resolve upon them." [66] No notice was taken of the regulations passed.[67] The high standard in the field of organization was achieved mostly on paper.

The futility of this Huguenot action for self-preservation was

---

[64] Cf. Ch. Weiss, *Histoire des réfugiés protestants de France*, I, 12.

[65] Cf. *ibid.*, p. 16.

[66] Benoit, *The Edict of Nantes*, II, 69.

[67] On this point, cf. G. d'Avenel, *Richelieu et la monarchie absolue*, III, 399.

striking. The death of the King, the same factor which had prompted the Assembly to draw up the plans, made their execution impossible. In 1610 the future existence of the Edict of Nantes was threatened, because no one was available to sponsor it effectively. Strongholds were granted only for a fixed term, and their status was dependent on the King's pleasure. The measures adopted at Saumur could hardly be interpreted as having been contained in the letter of the Edict of Nantes; they were in fact its extension, and no legal means, but only the good will of the late monarch, could have sanctioned them. Doomed from the moment of their conception, they were regarded as a remedy for the fear, which had spread among the Huguenots, that at the death of Henry IV all his projects had died with him. But the feeling was not unjustified. "The Reformed also observed with grief," remarked Benoit, "that all the King's designs were buried with him." [68] There had been no safeguard for the religious liberty of the Huguenots other than the person of the King. This was compatible with the nature of the monarchy, resting as it did on the ruler's personal power and not on the prestige of an institution.

This disappearance of the one stabilizing factor in Huguenot politics meant a sudden worsening of the party's position. Power and influence shifted to its opponents, revealing the true extent of its plight and its relative weakness. The deficiencies of the Huguenot party began to be more conspicuous, although the general pattern of political groups remained the same. They had never possessed the absolute discipline and singleness of purpose of the Jesuits. They never reached the ideals of the *bons Français,* successors to the Politiques, whose policy of expediency was consonant with the good of the country as a whole. The Huguenots were not moderate and not astute enough to advocate toleration other than for their own party. The position of the Protestants was further affected by the increasing number of the *dévots,* zealous Catholics who inherited the tradition of the League. The *dévots* were the hard core of that vast but oscillating Catholic mass which swamped the small Huguenot body. The Catholics were moving in all directions, joining various camps; it was they who formed the bulk of the *bons Français;* they even joined the Calvinist ranks. After 1610, however, their spirit of religious animosity was aroused again, and they

[68] Benoit, *The Edict of Nantes,* II, 11.

became more strongly antagonistic; consequently, the ranks of the *dévots* expanded.

When preparing his party for further struggle, Rohan, who assumed party leadership soon after the Assembly of Saumur, was severely handicapped by the split among the Huguenots. Disunity was recognized by Rohan as one of the main dangers for the Huguenot party. In his account of the elements threatening the future of the party, he mentioned "... le rétablissement des Jesuites, la mort de Henri le Grand, la Regence du Royaume en la Maison de Medici, l'Estat gouverné par les anciens pensionnaires d'Espagne et de Rome ... l'autorité due aux Princes du sang ôtée et la division formée parmi les Réformés." [69]

Indeed the Huguenots had very real cause for alarm, for their disunity was growing. Reassurance, which was obviously needed, came with *Le Réformé,* a publication prepared by several Calvinist writers to refute the reasons for anxiety.[70] The target, however, was missed: no illusions were dispelled; the reasons for alarm were confirmed rather than refuted. The pamphlet repeated the arguments used by one of the Huguenot factions, the so-called Malicious, in its campaign for more members. The publication stated that they were merely a weak minority—an admission which only emboldened their opponents; that there was an organized conspiracy among the Pope, the Jesuits, and the clergy against the Protestants, and hatred of them among some members of the Council of State; that the policy of disruption originated at Court; that the character of the Queen Regent might prove fatal for the future of the Huguenots, as she was easily influenced by their enemies; and that their own fear of strong opposition was equally disastrous.[71] What in fact troubled the Huguenots most was the mistrust they felt toward the Council of State, whose motives they could guess, toward the parlements, which were unjust, and toward the Queen Regent, whom they found unreliable. The pamphlet confirmed the split of Protestant opinion into several distinct groups, which had manifested their presence as early as the Assembly of Saumur: the Malicious, the Zealous, and the Judicious. It revealed the sad truth that none of the groups could be valued very highly: the Malicious

---

[69] Rohan, *Mémoires,* II, 175–176.
[70] Cf. Benoit, *The Edict of Nantes,* II, [37–38] (incorrectly numbered 29–30).
[71] *Ibid.,* p. [37].

were described as purely self-interested, pursuing war in order to gratify their ambitious desires; the Zealous followed them closely, but with somewhat less courage in declaring their aim openly (they wanted to be on the winning side and believed in diffidence as the best policy); the Judicious tried to prevent war and gravitated toward the Court, believing that their obedience would safeguard peace. Huguenot public opinion called the more extreme cases of the Judicious type "les escambarlats" and showed no hesitation in openly declaring its contempt. It was more than an ordinary contempt for moral weaklings. Apprehension and hatred were here intermingled because "les escambarlats" were highly dangerous; still belonging to the Huguenot community and at times passing as orthodox Huguenots, they were often actively serving the other camp.[72]

Benoit's own classification of the Calvinists of that period did not substantially differ; but as one of the three main classes, he included those people of integrity who were suspicious of a Council dominated by the Jesuit influences. His other two classes echoed the division stated in *Le Réformé*: one was the aristocratic group that made use of the rank and file of the Huguenot party for its own purposes; the other was the "timorous" group of those who followed the directions of the Court.[73] It was the Court that widened the split among the Huguenots on the question of which policy should be followed: appeasement or resistance. Both tendencies were strongly manifested in 1616. The party leaders belonged to the first group rather than to the second, but they were not in agreement on the methods to be followed. While Duplessis-Mornay was an uncompromising party man devoted to its interests, Bouillon negotiated with the Queen Mother against his own party, introducing an element of distrust and inviting future dissension.

The Court was looking for other pretexts to accomplish the ruin of the party, and the unusual status of Béarn provided one. Its privileges were regulated by a special edict instead of by the Edict of Nantes, and it was assumed at Béarn that the province was not under the jurisdiction of the latter edict. For these reasons Béarn was represented at Saumur, not as a member, but as a confederate province—a position that created a highly undesirable situation for

---

[72] Cf. "Lettres de deux agents secrets du cardinal de Richelieu," in *Bulletin de la Société de l'histoire du Protestantisme Français*, XXX, 256, 305, 356, 409.

[73] Cf. Benoit, *The Edict of Nantes*, II, [40] (incorrectly numbered 32).

the Protestant camp. It placed a ready weapon in the hands of the enemy: the people of Béarn could be oppressed without any bad consequence for the oppressor, because they were not subject to the same code of laws as the rest of the Protestant community, and any infringement of the privileges of the people of Béarn did not signify an alteration of laws concerning the whole Huguenot body.[74] By making such judicious moves, the government could go ahead with its plans for further disruption of the Protestant body.

Yet the wars which started in the second decade of the seventeenth century were not fought primarily to redress the injustices that the Protestant community suffered from the Catholics and the Court. Persecutions, though not unknown, were still to come; and the period of peace persisted, although among the Protestants there was a feeling of uneasiness as a result of their deteriorating position. The serious political motive of the campaign was to prevent the Spanish marriage of Louis XIII to Anne of Austria, and in this the Huguenots failed. It would seem that Condé and Bouillon had a greater share in fostering war than had the Protestants themselves. Causes for discontent were many, one of them being the financial plight into which the government had plunged the country.[75] On the whole, war was not in the Protestant interest, although it was in the interest of the nobles who made the Huguenot party their victim. But in 1621 the situation radically changed.

By that time it became clear that the reason for the revolt was not political. The Huguenots were left alone by the nobles to pursue their own ends, the external French policy was set on its pro-Spanish course, and there was clearly only one reason for revolt: to protest against the utter disregard Louis XIII had shown for the Edict of Nantes in respect to Béarn. The King had obviously circumvented the law by not applying the letter of the Edict to this particular case. The precedent was ominous. Outraged, the Hugue-

---

[74] Cf. *ibid.,* p. 27.

[75] The Paris parlement grew angry when it became obvious that the millions saved by Sully and deposited at the Bastille had been squandered. Pensions had risen from 1,800,000 livres in 1610 to 4,400,000. Condé and Bouillon led the opposition. Cf. A. Laugel, *Henri de Rohan, son rôle politique et militaire sous Louis XIII: 1579–1638,* p. 66. Hereafter cited as Laugel, *Henri de Rohan.* "[In 1614 the Court] re-established *La paulette* . . . they had been obliged to revoke . . . and the Queen went herself to the Bastille from whence she took 800,000 crowns, which were remaining there of the fourteen millions in ready money, which the Duke of Sully had hoarded there by his management." Cf. Benoit, *The Edict of Nantes,* II, [184]ᵛ (incorrectly numbered 175).

nots rose in defense of their religious liberty. The war was made
more truly a religious one by the absence of political factors.

The variety of motives that played a part in the seventeenth-
century wars should not obscure the fact that these wars were different from the previous ones. In the sixteenth century, wars were
both religious and political. Though now they might be either, the
predominance of the political motive had definitely disappeared. Yet
nothing is further from the truth than the assumption that these
wars were fought for purer ideals simply because they became more
"religious." Their religious character can be discerned because of
the elimination of other motives, such as political ones. By an
irony of fate, when the wars became more purely religious, theology
had already lost its ancient force.

The immediate motive behind the action of the Protestant leaders, with the possible exception of Rohan, was the spirit of gain. The
state of war enabled the leaders and hosts of their subordinates to
mulct the South of its considerable wealth. This was done through
official requisitions, the imposition of taxes, the confiscation of all
goods taken from one town to another without permission, and un-
official looting on an immense scale. The regulations passed in 1621
reflected the extent of the excesses and the desire to curb them. The
lesson of the previous wars had been well learned, and in order to
stop unrestricted war profiteering, the Assembly of La Rochelle
forbade the military leaders and governors to have direct control
over finances.[76] Reckless use of public funds must have necessitated
such a move. The municipality of Montpellier created a central
machinery which, by strict discipline, maintained highly centralized
control over all the inhabitants and the army. This iron discipline
was instituted not only to exact money from the inhabitants but
also to withhold it from the covetous Calvinist soldiers. Regulations
were issued to prevent irregular confiscations as well as ordinary
plunder. Without drastic measures to enforce these rules, the Huguenot administration would have been unable to wage war, as it
would never have obtained the bulk of the money due. Morality
and civic consciousness were low, and few people were reliable.
Money was raised partly by means of loans from rich burghers,

[76] Cf. *Archives de la ville de Montpellier*, VII (*Inventaire de Joffre. Archives du
greffe de la maison consulaire. Armoire C*), ed. by Oudot de Dainville, 179 (fols. 196,
238).

who chose guarantors whom the municipality confirmed to see that the money was repaid. As a rule, men shirked this duty and had to be made to serve as controllers "par la rigueur de l'ordonnance du duc." [77] The countryside was highly unsafe. "L'horloge confisquée, demandée par le duc, lui sera remise à son arrivée. Elle risquerait de se perdre en route," registered the minutes of the Montpellier town council in 1622.[78]

It was not only through the opportunities which arose from the state of chaos that the Protestant leaders enriched themselves: as a rule they profited twice over because, on finally coming to terms with the King, they used to get benefits, lucrative posts, and high pensions as well. As a result of the Montpellier treaty, by which the 1622 war ended, two of the Protestant leaders, La Force and Châtillon, were awarded marshals' batons; in the case of Châtillon, it was for the obvious merit of changing camp and fighting against the Protestants in the last stage of the campaign. Rohan, also, received the governorships of Nîmes, Uzès, and Castres and the continuation of his pension of 45,000 livres a year as compensation for the considerable losses he had incurred during the war.[79]

Accustomed as they were to such a procedure, the Huguenots did not trust Rohan unreservedly and, when he endeavored to put rigorously into practice the articles of the peace treaty, the opposition was so violent that he was not even spared the contemptuous nickname "escamberlat." [80] In the eyes of his followers Rohan was not without blame or reproach. Even his motive for entering on war in 1621 was not unselfish, his reason being almost as much personal as religious: he wished to promote his family interests by making good the right of Béarn to independent sovereignty. There are indications that at Loudun, Father Joseph had secretly worked on him [81] and, although this might not have been known at the time, Rohan's position may have appeared somewhat ambiguous. He was torn between his allegiance to the Crown, from which he held offices and pensions, and his duties to the party. His

---

[77] *Ibid.*, p. 191 (fol. 235ᵛ), relating to June 13, 1622.

[78] *Ibid.* (fol. 234ᵛ), relating to June 11, 1622.

[79] Cf. Lavisse, *Histoire de France*, Vol. VI, Part 2, p. 219.

[80] Or "scamberlat." Cf. *Mercure français* (1622), p. 83, as quoted in Laugel, *Henri de Rohan*, p. 147.

[81] Cf. Laugel, *Henri de Rohan*, p. 73.

attempts to compromise between these two allegiances were always viewed with suspicion by the Protestants.[82]

Another factor may help to explain the opposition he encountered among some members of the party, and his separation from other nobles. The character of the party, based on the *tiers état*, was becoming markedly popular. The princes were no longer on its side, and Rohan was in a strangely isolated position. In his day Rohan was a natural leader and was supported as such, no matter what the changed social aspect of wars meant. As a member of an ancient family, he was accepted by the bulk of the Huguenot party. This is not to imply that the character of the social change was not considerable. Nobles did not cease to play an active and leading part in public life, but they ceased to mingle their religious beliefs with politics. They also refused to express these beliefs in public. The Protestant clergy and the lower classes, on the other hand, were most ardent believers in religious party warfare. They flocked into the ranks of Rohan's followers. This shifting balance of influence within the party meant two things: the growing rift—which the Court was not slow to exploit [83]—between the upper and the lower strata of the party membership; and the estrangement and isolation of the towns, the defense of which had fallen upon the shoulders of the Protestant population of the Third Estate.

To conclude the list of differences between the two periods: the propaganda aspect of the wars lacked its previous vigor, intensity, and efficiency. The radical pamphleteers, numerous in the preceding century, were now so few and constituted such a small danger that no counteroffensive from the opposing royalist camp was required. Only two radical works of any merit appeared: [84] Lescun's *Apologie des Eglises réformées* [85] and Milletière's *Discours*.[86] The former

---

[82] An account of a suspicious attitude of the inhabitants of Nîmes toward Rohan is given in an unpublished manuscript by Anne Rulmann, *L'Histoire secrète des affaires du temps depuis le Siège de Montpellier jusqu'à la Paix dernière* (1620–1627). Nîmes, Bibl. municipale. Hereafter cited as Rulmann, *L'Histoire secrète*.

[83] Cf. Laugel, *Henri de Rohan*, p. 154.

[84] Cf. G. Bonet-Maury, "Le Protestantisme français et la République, 1598–1685," *Bulletin de la Société de l'histoire du Protestantisme Français*, LIII, 366–367. Hereafter cited as Bonet-Maury, "Le Protestantisme français," *Bull.*

[85] Jean Paul de Lescun, *Apologie des Eglises réformées, de l'obéissance au Roy et aux Etats généraux de la Souveraineté du Béarn* (Orthez, 1618–1619).

[86] Brochet de la Milletière, *Discours des vraies raisons par lesquelles, ceux de la Religion en France peuvent et doivent en bonne conscience résister par les armes a la persecution, que leur font les ennemis de l'Etat* ([n.p.], 1623).

was topical, demonstrating the illegality of the edict that Louis XIII has passed in respect to Béarn, on the ground that such an edict contravened both the Edict of Nantes and local custom. Milletière's *Discours* upheld the right to resist persecutions by arms,[87] presenting it against a wider theoretical background which links up with the theories of Hotman and Beza, from whom its author accepted the idea of bilateral contract between the ruler and the people. Legitimacy of insurrection was dependent upon the breaking of contract, the royal authority not being contested in other circumstances.

This lack of direct attack on theoretical grounds against royal authority was significant; coupled with this, in the field of practical politics the Huguenot antimonarchical activity was blunted by a special brand of radicalism that was mainly expressed in the internal party strife. The conflict resulted from the clash of interests between two elements in the Protestant municipalities: the old aristocratic and the newly emerging popular. The latter urged the need for the democratization of the existing institutions. The events at La Rochelle in 1613–1614 show that the call for action had not remained unanswered. The 1613 revolt was the direct result of a violent appeal for reform in the traditional municipal corporations.[88] The next year, changes in organization were introduced by a special charter. The "external" radicalism of the party in its attitude to the King and the state was mild even in 1620, when the King broke his promise to give satisfaction to the *cahiers* voted for by the assembly at Loudun.

The new assembly, which met at La Rochelle in 1621, worked out a plan for a new Protestant organization. According to the plan, entitled *Ordre et Règlement général des milices et finances pour les Eglises réformées de France et de la souveraineté de Béarn,* France was subdivided into eight departments, each to be headed by a governor general (*chef général*) concerned with justice, finances, and the militia. La Rochelle was given a supreme court to play the role of an emergency tribunal. An almost complete pattern for an autonomous organization was created; yet on the part of the revolutionaries there was a persistent claim that this organization was provisional and that they upheld the validity of royal authority.

---

[87] Cf. Benoit, *The Edict of Nantes,* II, 373.

[88] Cf. M. G. Schybergson, *Le Duc de Rohan et la chute du parti protestant en France,* p. 27. Hereafter cited as Schybergson, *Le Duc de Rohan.*

Indeed, it seems more appropriate to take the *Ordre et Règlement général* for the emergency regulation it was than to treat it as a basis for a "republican" constitution.[89]

Tilenus, a contemporary Protestant scholar, however, took a different view in his *Avertissement à l'Assemblée de la Rochelle* (1621). He advocated patience, holding that kings are never bound by their own word or by that of their predecessors. "Nor could the Jesuits themselves write in a more venomous and embittered style," wrote Benoit.[90] Preaching toleration, Tilenus denied that others could hold tolerant views. "Such is many times the Moderation of those that preach up Toleration: they would engross it all to themselves." [91] Tilenus thought the activity and procedure of the Assembly to be rebellious and full of the spirit of faction directed against the royal sovereign. The direct outcome of this book was Milletière's *Discours,* written in a "republican" spirit that the author was soon to reject when he became a devoted follower of Richelieu's policy. Tilenus' bias was particularly significant in his answer to the *Discours.*[92] The Catholic royalist writers were numerous, but among the Protestants, he and Cameron, a sincere preacher of obedience to the king, stood alone as convinced pamphleteers of loyalism; hence his exaggerated opinion expressed in the *Avertissement.* As one of the few writers voicing the beliefs of the Protestant group, he may have regarded it as a duty to condemn the action of La Rochelle as treasonable. The general atmosphere of Huguenot loyalism may also have given rise to the overemphasis of his statement.

Indeed, royalism was so general among Protestants, and had penetrated so deeply into their minds, that radical writers were almost nonexistent. Events and documents seem to confirm the same tendency: among the most significant was the decision reached in 1615 by the Grenoble Assembly to ask for the confirmation of the King's sovereignty and the safety of his life—requests which were included in the articles of the Third Estate in 1614.[93] This was neither an isolated event nor a tactical move. Five years later, when the conflict grew more intense because the King was personally

[89] Cf. Laugel, *Henri de Rohan,* p. 106.

[90] Benoit, *The Edict of Nantes,* II, 308.

[91] Cf. *ibid.,* p. 309.

[92] "It may be said that he had neither sincerity nor judgement." Cf. *ibid.,* p. 373.

[93] Cf. Laugel, *Henri de Rohan,* p. 67.

engaged in the conduct of the campaign involving extensive portions of the Huguenot South, the Protestants remained loyal to their monarch. They only pointed out the role played by the King's councilors and advisers, whom they regarded as guilty of influencing the events of 1620 and responsible for the sudden deterioration of the settled relationship between the Court and the Protestant minority.[94]

In these circumstances, the task of conducting the party's politics was made particularly hard for Rohan. Loyalism would have interfered more seriously with the conduct of the war had it not been for the outbursts of Protestant indignation against the King's troops and the King's representatives. Those reactions were at times so violent that Rohan had to resort even to appeasement. Rulmann describes such an action of Rohan at Nîmes in the summer of 1620.[95] Yet, justifying the expedient of armed action to those Protestants who were not directly harmed by the King's policy, and who considered themselves loyal, must have been an arduous task for the leader. On the other hand, that loyalism would have eased things considerably for Rohan, and would have been conducive to negotiations and to the conclusion of peaceful agreements between Rohan and the Crown, had it not been for the Huguenot dislike of compromise whenever civil liberties were threatened.[96] Indeed, their loyalism was extended to hardly anyone at Court except to the very person of the King; it was to the monarchy, which was still "personal" and not "constitutional." They bore a deep distrust for governors, military leaders, the King's special envoys, advisers, and practically everybody at Court.

Rohan, a man of cool calculation, who, in striving for workable solutions, had always seen matters differently, was eager to compromise, to save what could be saved instead of losing all, to accept a mediocre peace rather than a disastrous war. Desperate because of the Huguenot attitude, he calls his followers "Republicans" to express his disgust,[97] and it seems at times that the loyalism of the Huguenots was running at a low ebb: theirs was an extremely

---

[94] Cf. Rulmann, *L'Histoire secrète*, première narration ff.

[95] *Ibid.*, par. I.

[96] Rulmann describes strong opposition among the inhabitants of Nîmes to letting the King enter the town, which was a condition of peace. *Ibid.*, par. E.

[97] Rohan "leur dit ... qu'ils étaient de Républiquains, et leurs peuples de seditieux et qu'il aimeroit mieux conduire une troupe de loups qu'une fourbe de Ministres." *Ibid.*

lofty notion of obedience only to the King and disobedience to the
makers and executors of his policy. Since Rohan stood close to the
latter, his leadership in the party was often in jeopardy. His loyalism, at least, was genuine and real, deprived of metaphysical flights;
he fought for the cause of the party in a way which at that time was
pardonable. His actions were never treasonable. But grappling with
Huguenot loyalism was a hard and ungrateful task.

Royalism, though on the whole a generally accepted Protestant
policy at that time, was not accepted without opposition. The policy
of the Court, which was reflected in the friendliness of Marie de
Médicis toward Spain and in the brutality of the action of Louis
XIII in Béarn,[98] seriously embittered the Protestants. If these
events were not decisive enough to evoke the dormant radical spirit,
they were important enough to produce, at least for a time, a military confederation of the Protestant churches. Armed uprisings
thus rekindled exhibited much less in the way of theoretical justification than had the wars of religion, their predecessors of the
sixteenth century. Now much of their force was spent. Without an
ideological background, the Protestants became more than ever
the prey of ambitious adventurers like Condé, who dragged them
into his private feud in 1615. Until Rohan inspired them with new
enthusiasm and brought them a temporary success, they suffered
defeat in chaotic and hopeless fights.

It is characteristic that a period so devoid of spectacular military
achievements was on both sides rather arid, ideologically and politically. The Protestant party program could not be a substitute
for political speculations. Although both a party program and the
political theory accepted by a party may be used as a technique for
action, they are not, as a rule, equivalent. In this case the program
was already a part of the party action, as it indicated the practical
political moves to be taken without explaining the ideological motives. The party program, arguing as if from the basic political
and moral issues which underlie political theories, neither tried to
justify an action already taken nor incited people to action. Speculations as to why those basic issues were not referred to, may vary,
but in the case of the Calvinists this was probably due both to their
decreased moral resistance and lack of faith in the future, and to

---

[98] Bonet-Maury speaks of "l'exécution brutale de l'édit de mainlevée des biens
ecclésiastiques en Béarn par Louis XIII." "Le Protestantisme français," *Bull.*, LIII,
365.

their agreement with their opponents on basic principles (as illustrated by their inclination toward monarchism).

What, then, was the relationship between political theory and declining political power? Political theory is usually, a priori or a posteriori, a justification of events. Theory and practice are correlative. If their relationship is vague, indefinite, or nonexistent, both must suffer. The lact of investigation in the field of theory in direct relation to the party's practice was not so much the cause of the loss of power by the Protestant party as it was one of the outstanding manifestations of such a loss.

THE DECLINE OF LIBERAL IDEAS

The beginning of the seventeenth century was no longer a period of pamphlet warfare, but of more serious theoretical work, though its products seldom touched on tolerance. The pamphlets now published were indicative of a marked eclipse of liberal ideas without which the Edict of Nantes could not be enforced.

Since Protestant opposition in the field of political thought was weak, the Catholic royalist writers did not waste time in combating it. Their writings therefore were of two types: either panegyrics extolling the person and powers of the monarch; or attacks directed against the tide of ultramontane ideas. Some of the writings, such as those of Duchesne, were a combination of the two. "Pouvoir [royal] est sacrosaint, ordonné de la Divinité, principal ouvrage de sa providence, chef d'oeuvre de ses mains, image vive de sa sublime Maiesté, & proportionné avec son immense grandeur." [99] "Papes," Duchesne continued, "n'ont aucun pouvoir sur le temporel de la France." [100] And further: "Nos Roys ont donc leur Authorité pour rampart & barriere contre les assauts de la Cour de Rome ... Ils ont l'Appel comme d'abus au futur Concile general contre les indues entreprinses des Papes." [101]

Some monarchist writers of that period have achieved a permanent place in the history of political thought. Indeed, writers such

[99] Duchesne, *Les Antiquitez*, p. 126.
[100] *Ibid.*, p. 134.
[101] *Ibid.*, p. 162.

as Coquille and Loyseau contributed in a remarkable way to the discussion on sovereignty. Starting with the basic argument of Bodin, they restated it with that essentially legal flavor which alone, it seems, may endow a generalized definition of sovereignty with a more universal validity. To Loyseau, sovereignty was inseparable from the form of the state in which it resided. "Elle consiste," he wrote, "en puissance absolue, c'est à dire parfaite & entirere de tout point." [102] Sovereignty was governed by the laws of God, the rules of natural justice, and the laws of the Church. That conception of sovereignty was juristic, issuing from the laws of a limited monarchy, and was much more convincing than the idea of sovereignty based upon the factual supremacy of one political organ over the other. Loyseau's juristic approach led him to a liberal attitude, because no legal superior could be absolutely arbitrary, as he must submit to the rule of law. Yet, in spite of its "legalism," this conception of sovereignty tended rather to strengthen absolutist tendencies than to diminish them.[103] The contribution of the French political philosophers of that period to the development of the concept of sovereignty is important.[104] The significant fact was that in this respect the leading role was played, not by the Protestant thinkers, but by their political and religious opponents. For the Protestants, the period was one of frustration and lost opportunities.

The principle of popular sovereignty (a basis of consent) had much less success. That its tradition survived was due to the ultramontanes, like Bellarmin, who used it, however, merely as a means to ensure the supremacy of the pope over the temporal power. Unfortunately, another legacy of Bellarmin was his intolerance, for he argued that a Catholic prince should be forbidden to suffer the existence of heretics in his kingdom: "Dissipat impious rex sapiens. Porro impios esse heareticos negari non potest." [105] Heresy should be fought not only for the sake of morality but also for that of public peace; [106] therefore it is the duty of magistrates to defend the true religion.

---

[102] Charles Loyseau, Oeuvres (*Traité des Seigneuries*), chap. ii, p. 8.

[103] Cf. J. Maritain, "The Concept of Sovereignty," *American Political Science Review*, XLIV (June, 1950), 343–357.

[104] Cf. C. H. McIlwain, *Constitutionalism and the Changing World*, p. 40.

[105] Cf. Robertus Bellarminus, *Opera omnia*, III (*Secunda controversia generalis de membris ecclesiae militantis* [1615]), 334.

[106] "Libertas credendi perniciosa est etiam temporali bono regnorum, et publicae paci, ut patet primum ex Gregorio lib. 4, epist. 32. ubi dicit, reipub, civilis incolumitatem,

Ultramontanism, however, failed because it was outmatched by Gallicanism. The latter opposed the two ultramontane theses that the spiritual power is superior to the temporal, and that sovereignty belongs to the people; it proclaimed the independence of temporal authority and denied the doctrine of popular sovereignty. Gallican ideas were reflected in practical action when the parlement of Paris ordered the public burning of Mariana's *De Rege et regis institutione* and condemned Bellarmin's *De Potestate pontificis in temporalibus*. By 1614, in spite of comparatively recent anti-Gallican excesses concerning Richer, who two years earlier had been dismissed from the post of syndic at the University of Paris, Gallicanism had reached an assured place in the public mind. The Third Estate voted that the principle of absolute independence of temporal power be made a fundamental law. Resisted by the clergy and the nobles, the article containing this proposal was annulled by the government, only to be upheld again the next year by the Protestants. Again Gallicanism found support from one of the leading Catholic writers of the period, Jean Savaron, who, in his *Premier traicté de la souveraineté du roy et de son royaume* (1615), tried to explain that Gallican maxims are as old as monarchy itself. His argument for monarchism is summed up in the conclusion of the *Premier traicté:* "Que le Roy n'a point de superieur que Dieu, que son royaume n'est subiect à aucune puissance spirituelle et temporelle, en luy rendant tout service, subiection, et obeissance." [107] To illustrate his thesis, he published the same year his *Second traicté de la souveraineté du roy,* and another book five years later entitled *De la souveraineté du roy.* By this time his monarchism had become extreme, the king being compared to "Dieu corporel."

The ultramontane controversy, combined with Huguenot passivity, brought the Gallican issue to the fore, but ultramontanism being much the weaker, and never very popular in France, it was not very difficult for Gallicanism to triumph; the royalist writers could give their attention to issues other than the ultramontane-Gallican controversy. Awareness of broader issues induced some of them to write something more than mere panegyrics, as had Jerome Bignon, who was mainly interested in the glorification of Henry IV. He regarded the King as a miracle of the universe:

ex Ecclesiae pace pendere. Deinde ratione; nam ubi servatur fides et obedientia Deo, ibi etiam servatur principi . . ." *Ibid.*, p. 335.

[107] Jean Savaron, *Premier traicté de la souveraineté du roy et de son royaume,* ed. by Leber, Salgues, and Cohen, V, 464.

"L'occasion me porteroit maintenant à parler de nostre grand Roy Henry IIII miracle de l'univers, qui ne cede ne rien qui soit aux vertus de ses predecesseurs, ny à la gloire de tous les plus grands Princes & Monarques qui furent iamais, s'il ne les surpasse."[108] He tried to prove the independence of the French monarchy and its superiority over all others.[109]

In his treatise *Des ordres* (1610), Loyseau, one of the most remarkable monarchists, found the existing social pattern natural and just; he perceived the bad effects of the new tax, *la paulette* (established in 1604), which had made administrative and judicial offices hereditary and thus deprived the king of his due share of control. A few years later, writers such as Savaron and Montchrétien were more directly bent upon exposing social evils. In 1614, Savaron, as a deputy to the States-General, showed himself desirous of relieving the people's misery. He again gave free rein to an attack on the venality of offices in his *Traicté de ... vénalité des offices* (1615). He was seconded by Montchrétien, an original and serious writer, who, in his *Traicté de l'oeconomie politique* (1615), deplored France's economic and administrative disorder, seeing it for the first time as a clear manifestation of a close union between economics and politics.[110] He also decried the spreading of heresy: "Il ira donc non seulement de vostre conscience et de vostre honneur, mais de la diminution de ceste authorité que Dieu vous a donnée, si Vous souffrez, par connivence ou autrement, qu'il se forme de nouveaux schismes en vostre royaume."[111]

In general, monarchist thought had not yet passed the limits of its milder and more temperate forms, although the time was not unfavorable for more extreme and absolutist trends. When Coquille, writing in 1608, advocated limits in matters of legislation on royal absolutism,[112] France still had a stable and orderly government, and absolutist ideas calling for strong measures were not needed. But the second decade of misrule and chaos could justify tendencies toward such means. Growing Gallican ideas created in

---

[108] P. H. B. P. [Hierôme Bignon], *De l'excellence des roys et du royaume de France.*

[109] Cf. *ibid.,* pp. 255, 256.

[110] Cf. F. Zweig, *Economic Ideas* (New York, 1950), p. 122.

[111] Antoine de Montchrétien, *L'Economie politique patronale: Traicté de l'oeconomie politique, dedié en 1615 au roy* ..., ed. by Th. Funck-Brentano, p. 340.

[112] "Quand les Rois veulent ordonner loix perpetuelles, importantes à l'Etat de Royaume, ils ont accoûtumé de convoquer les trois Ordres de leur peuple, qu'on appelle Etats." Guy Coquille, *Oeuvres,* II (*Institution au droit des Français*), 2.

France a certain uniformity of political opinion—a homogeneity of outlook from which even the Protestant camp, though always isolated, could not escape. This uniformity of thinking created a background suitable for absolute rule and for the disappearance from French public life of those liberal tendencies which earlier had led to the decisions of 1598.

Feeling no longer safe, in 1611 the Huguenots challenged their opponents by extending their own powers and privileges beyond the boundaries set at Nantes. But the results were disappointing, because the Huguenots were crippled by their own loyalism and could not give effect to their resolutions. As the political controversy had been deflected into a channel of Gallican-ultramontane dispute, the Huguenot problems were relegated to the background. The resolutions of Saumur were necessitated by the drawbacks and limitations of the Edict, which had weighed heavily on the Huguenots since the first day of the regency, when there was none of that liberal spirit which for ten years past had protected the Act of 1598.

Thereafter, for the selfsame reasons which made the future of the Edict uncertain, the new decisions were never executed. Still, the prospects were even darker. Whatever faint hopes of success the Protestants preserved in the next fifteen years, they were not to guess that the remedy they had invented in 1611, giving them only a limited amount of freedom and power, was at the same time to present Richelieu with a useful instrument for their own destruction.

III

THE DOWNWARD TREND: THE INFLUENCE OF RICHELIEU'S POLICY AND DOCTRINE

"Le but que nous devions avoir étoit de prendre la Rochelle et ruiner le parti huguenot en France."—Mémoires du cardinal de Richelieu (publiés ... pour la Société de l'histoire de France), VIII (Paris, 1927), 110.

"Il [Father Joseph] essaia de persuader au Connetable de Luines, qu'il falloit combattre l'Heresie par la force des armes."—Abbé Richard, Le Véritable Père Josef (1704), p. 146.

"Plus je travaille à les [Richelieu and Father Joseph] rendre innocens, plus ils sont criminels."—Ibid., préface.

RICHELIEU AND THE END OF THE HUGUENOT PARTY

After 1620, when Richelieu's influence and power were rapidly growing, there were no immediate indications of a forthcoming change. The situation developed gradually together with the slowly developing events, and it is in the latter that most clues to the concept of toleration can be found. Although an empiricist, Richelieu was a careful planner, whose rules, however, were flexible. The political legacy which he left was more a working system than a body of doctrines. His approach to toleration was practical. It is significant that exceedingly little political literature of value, discussing general issues, was written in this period. Richelieu gave himself predominantly to political practice and involved his contemporaries in solving practical problems of the day.

The same political motives which later induced Richelieu to

launch an all-out offensive against the Huguenots, at first urged
him to show good will. He no longer acted as he had in 1614 at the
States-General, when, speaking on behalf of the clergy, he urged
toleration. Indeed, he spoke then for the Protestant cause as if he
were counsel for the defense. Except for a short interlude preceding
his promotion to cardinal in 1622—which explains this period of
anti-Huguenot policy—he undertook no hostile action until 1627.
On the contrary, this was his most liberal period, and it was marked
by his support of the group known as the *bons Français*. His interest in their activity was shown in the help he gave Fancan in
drafting an outline for their policy.

Indeed, so serious was his concern and so close the coöperation,
that the Zealous Catholics accused him of exaggerated toleration,
calling him, ironically if prophetically, the "cardinal of La Rochelle." [1] This spirit of toleration was hardly genuine. Even his
refraining from persecution was not sincere. At this stage he avoided
any direct action against the Protestants; but he used the King for
that purpose, as he had done in 1617, when he advised Louis XIII
to march against the Huguenots. This he did not do out of hatred—
he never felt that for the Huguenots—but in order to win a personal victory over the royal Court, and particularly over the Queen,
Marie de Médicis, whose favors were literally a matter of life and
death to him. That action of his, performed with Machiavellian
cunning, proved, like many others, that he would not shrink from
any measures however stringent. It also marked his first betrayal
of the Protestant cause, which earlier he had seemed to support.
Burckhardt's view—that he betrayed every cause he served—throws
some light on this problem. So also does the contrast between the
prolonged absence of any sustained action against the Huguenots
and Richelieu's occasional anti-Huguenot statements. Surveying
these statements, which reflect the same recurrent thought, one
wonders why the final "betrayal" happened so late. The answer
lies in expediency, which also gives the main reason for his original
leniency and toleration. Naturally, this kind of policy had a dual
effect.

There are indications that from a very early stage he wanted to

---

[1] Cf. *Quaestiones quodlibeticae* ([n.p.], 1626), cited in Petitot, ed., *Mémoires de Richelieu depuis 1610 jusqu'à 1620*, III (Paris, 1823), 16. Also in G. Hanotaux, ed., *Maximes d'Etat et fragments politiques du cardinal de Richelieu*, p. 72 n. Hereafter cited as Richelieu, *Maximes d'Etat*.

destroy the Protestant minority. The idea was not entirely his own, for certainly the influence of Father Joseph was considerable. The earliest indications of Richelieu's designs relate to 1611, when he first met Father Joseph and exchanged promises that a whole-hearted support would be given to the plan for stamping out the Protestant political organization.[2] It took some time for this pledge to be given concrete form. In fact the issue long remained almost dormant. True, Richelieu possessed no real power until he obtained his premiership in 1624. But before that, his attitude to the Protestant question had remained somewhat ambiguous; there are no signs that he conducted any organized action against the Protestants in his public capacity; whatever he did still lacked the iron firmness he developed in later years. Had Richelieu still to be converted to the role of persecutor of the Protestants, the role for which he tried to make his contemporaries believe he was so unfitted? Deception was an important element in his game. When personal considerations mattered, when discredited at Court and anxious to win back power and influence, he tried to secure the help of the highly influential Father Joseph, and he did not hesitate to claim that he had been fighting heresy in his own diocese.[3] Despite all this, he seems never to have had the reputation of an intolerant churchman and oppressor. The question is: Whom had he deceived more—the public or the Grey Eminence? He wrote a topical anti-Protestant polemic, *Principaux points de la Foy de l'Eglise catholique,* as an answer to the defense by four pastors of Charenton against the accusations of the Jesuit Father Arnoux, the royal confessor, who preached the need for the destruction of the Huguenots and for establishing one religion. The four ministers of Charenton: Montigni, du Moulin, Durand, and Mestrezat, wrote their *Défense de la confession des Eglises réformées de France contre les accusations du Sieur Arnould,* dedicating the book to Louis XIII and adroitly soliciting his help. They claimed that their true allegiance was to the King, warning him against the Jesuits, whose allegiance lay elsewhere, and against the temporal pretenses of the Pope: "... nous devons nos vies et nos moyens à la défense de la dignité de votre couronne: surtout à la défense d'un droit que Dieu vous donné et

---

[2] Cf. Gustave Fagniez, *Le Père Joseph et Richelieu,* I, 379.

[3] September, 1617; cf. C. J. Burckhardt, *Richelieu: His Rise to Power,* p. 109. Hereafter cited as Burckhardt, *Richelieu.*

qui est fondé en sa parole. Esperance qu'un jour Dieu vous ouvrira les yeux pour apperçevoir que sous ce nom specieux d'Eglise Romaine, le Pape s'est etabli une monarchie temporelle en terre." [4]

In his *Principaux points de la Foy de l'Eglise catholique,* written during his days of "exile" at Luçon, Richelieu attacked the Huguenot ministers in order to please the King and Luynes, both dominated by strong Jesuit influences. He pleaded submission to the Pope and declared orthodox intolerance: "The Religion Pretended to be reformed is worthy of hatred, because it makes a schisme in the church." [5]

The writing of the *Principaux points* was prompted by opportunism. Richelieu remained curiously noncommittal in matters of tolerance. "La diversité de religion," he wrote in 1617, "peut bien créer de la division en l'autre monde, mais non en celui-ci." [6] It was for Father Joseph to preach (as he did in 1619) that heresy should be fought by means of arms, and that the fire of civil wars should be extinguished in an all-embracing war of religion.[7] But the aim of Father Joseph was primarily religious; politics he used skillfully only as a means to further his ulterior religious ends. The aim of the war of religion that he advocated was, not to put an end to civil wars, but to extirpate the heretics. The destruction of heresy was for him an aim [8] and not a means to further some political end.

Richelieu's plans differed widely from those of the zealous missionary. In 1625 he coined a new slogan—that the Protestants should be ruined by peace: "Que l'on devoit d'autant plus se porter

---

[4] *Défense de la confession des Eglises réformées de France contre les accusations du Sieur Arnould, Jésuite, par les quatre Ministres de Charenton,* préface.

[5] Richelieu, *The Principal Points of Faith of the Catholike Church,* p. 282.

[6] Quoted by J.-B. Paquier, *Histoire de l'unité politique et territoriale de la France,* II, 49. Hereafter cited as Paquier, *Histoire de l'unité.*

[7] "Il essaia de persuader au Connêtable de Luines, qu'il falloit combattre l'Heresie par la force des armes; que ce n'étoit pas assez d'employer les disputes, les prédications et le bon example, si le Roi ne se servoit aussi de ses forces pour vaincre la desobeissance des Huguenots." Abbé Richard, *Le Véritable Père Josef, capucin nommé au Cardinalat,* p. 146. Hereafter cited as Abbé Richard, *Le Véritable Père Josef.* Or in the publication *Archives curieuses de l'histoire de France,* 2ᵉ série, IV (Paris, 1838), 154–155. That the King marched to Guyenne was due to Luynes' approval of the project of Father Joseph to use armed force against the Huguenots.

[8] "Il soutiendra Richelieu dans sa politique extérieure par nécessité politique, mais, quant aux protestants français, il n'a jamais cherché qu'à les détruire." J. Viénot, *Histoire de la Réforme française,* II, 262.

à pacifier les affaires du dedans que l'on avoit même des expédients pour ruiner par la paix le parti huguenot." [9] It had the merits of being ambiguous and of producing later even more disastrous effects for the Religion Prétendue Réformée than the warmongering of Father Joseph. Even if his ultimate designs were already the same as those of the Capuchin, he veiled them carefully with the elaborate ruin-through-peace theory which could have a wide range of interpretation, both favorable and unfavorable, to the Huguenots. Upon his coming to power, he made a promise to the King, declaring that one of his aims was to ruin the Huguenot party: "Je lui promis d'employer toute mon industrie et toute l'autorité qu'il lui plaisoit me donner pour ruiner le parti hugenot, rabaisser l'orgueil des Grands, réduire tous ses sujets en leur devoir et relever son nom dans les nations étrangères au point où il devoit être." [10]

Still, despite an aim stated so clearly and so early, he remained an enigma to those—particularly the Zealous Catholics and the Protestants—who found that his declared intentions and his actions diverged. Both groups wished him to serve their interests; each had grounds to suspect that he served the interests of the other. In fact, he served only his own. Both had reasons for apprehension; both were kept in suspense. The Zealous Catholics were perturbed by the slowness of his action, by the lack of strong measures, by his "fancanism," and by his reluctance to settle decisively the La Rochelle issue. They would have been better pleased if the events of 1628–1629 had occurred five years earlier. Aggressive in their criticism of Richelieu's incomprehensible sympathies with the heretics, they were impatient in their demands to see events take a different course. They probably perceived the divergence between Richelieu's apparent intentions and his real designs.

Perhaps there was really some subtle meaning in the ruin-through-peace theory. Did Richelieu speak his true thoughts on that one occasion? One thing is certain: the machinations inherent in the peace theory, which were meant to bring about the downfall of the

---

[9] *Mémoires du cardinal de Richelieu,* publiés ... pour la Société de l'histoire de France (hereafter cited as Richelieu, *Mémoires*), V (Paris, 1921), 187. And further: "Qu'on ne pourroit plus faire la paix avec les huguenots qu'en ne perdant tous les avantages que l'on avoit sur eux maintenant, et qui sans doute avec le temps causeroient la ruine de ce parti." *Ibid.,* p. 188.

[10] André, ed., *Testament politique de Richelieu,* p. 95. Hereafter cited as Richelieu, *Testament politique.*

party, were of later origin. It was not peace itself which was ruinous for the Huguenots; peace itself was harmless. It was the way in which Richelieu let the Zealous use it; it was the number of infractions occurring in rapidly growing succession. It was the policy of conscious destruction of the freedom established in the preceding century which brought disaster. In peace Richelieu did unobtrusively what he would probably have done openly, had he not "abhorred" bloodshed. Curiously, his "aversion" led him to choose the deadlier weapon, the more effective method. Are we to believe it was mere coincidence? Or are we not rather to believe that his widely advertised likes and dislikes were just another psychological weapon expertly designed to secure his objectives? Considering Richelieu's Machiavellianism and his early collaboration with Father Joseph, one is inclined to believe that this peace formula contained the deadly germ which was to infect the Protestants by disarming them in order to prepare the way for an easy kill afterward.

The conception of an "explosive" peace was implicit in the Plan Codur, presented to Richelieu by one of his ministers in 1624. If this remarkable scheme had not been the Cardinal's first inspiration, it was his guide for years to come. Its cool calculation, its sober tone, the penetrating and detailed analysis of the Protestant opponent, the thorough presentation of the way to fight him most effectively, the completeness of ways and means envisaged, the gripping precision of approach, and the apparent coherence and consistency must have appealed to Richelieu's character. His subsequent attitude toward the plan proved his sagacious tenacity and his indifference to adverse events. He absorbed its content without immediately giving practical expression to it: he knew the time had not yet come. But he meditated on its essence, and this set his policy on its slow-moving course. He accepted some basic advice to the effect that division should be sown among the Protestants,[11] or that discord should be planted between Protestant ministers and their congregations, but he would not yet practice these principles. The plan was shelved for future reference.[12] He certainly behaved as if he

[11] On Plan Codur. See *Bulletin de la Société de l'histoire du Protestantisme Français*, XXXIX, 423.

[12] Later Richelieu made use of the recommendations. Cf. Richelieu, *Maximes d'Etat*, No. CXXXVIII; he devised ways to get Protestant ministers under royal control. Hanotaux remarks that this note was linked with Richelieu's plan to make the Huguenot body disintegrate through a slow process during which Huguenots might be given concessions harmless to the state security. Cf. Richelieu, *Maximes d'Etat*, p. 790.

still held to the notion of the inefficiency of violent measures;[13] he believed this so strongly that even later, when resorting to war during the siege of La Rochelle, he tried to avoid direct persecution.

Thus the attitude of conciliation, the will to compromise, and the spirit of appeasement that Richelieu showed in the disorders of 1625 were the result of theories which suited his character and which he found expedient in political realities. Apparently only a few people thought the same and, to convince others, Richelieu started a propaganda campaign. This was the beginning of an involved literary contest—a violent battle of pamphlets—inspired by Richelieu on the one side and by his opponents on the other, which raged throughout 1625 and 1626. The main impulse came from his opponents, who published a book entitled *Admonitio ad Ludovicum XIII Regem,* probably inspired by the Jesuits and denouncing the policy of Richelieu. Intended as a manifesto of all Catholics, it anticipated those events which were later claimed to be landmarks of radical and sweeping changes, bringing a new period both in external and internal relations. As was noted by the *Mercure Jésuite:*

> L'Autheur (qui ne s'est osé nommer) pratiquant la susdite doctrine contre les Rois et Princes, et leur Conseillers et Officiers, condamne le renouvellement fait par nostre Roi des anciennes alliances de France: dit que la guerre que le Roi fait, est contre Dieu: qu'elle est très-inique, quand bien on ne considereroit la Religion: que c'est pieté de n'obeyr au Roy pour ceste guerre.[14]

On the eve of his change of policy, Richelieu started to mold public opinion in the cast he had devised. The radical change demanded an apology, but all that was forthcoming was a justification, and an anonymous one at that. Richelieu never signed the political pamphlets and libels he inspired or directed.[15] By acting in such a way, he maintained the supremely flexible position of a man of action unhindered by the occasionally misdirected commitments of a man of thought; thus he was free to deny in practice the ideals he professed in theory.

---

[13] As stressed by the Plan Codur: "Il n'y faut point employer des moyens violens ... seulement des doux et qui agissent au commencement sans qu'on s'en apperçoive." In *Bull.,* XXXIX, 423 (see n. 11, above).

[14] *Le Mercure Jésuite,* I, 776.

[15] Cf. M. Deloche, *Autour de la plume du cardinal de Richelieu,* p. 317. Hereafter cited as Deloche, *Autour de la plume.* Deloche gives an excellent account of Richelieu's clandestine campaign by pen.

Richelieu gave the first counterblow when he ordered the prepration of *Le Catholique d'Estat* (1625).[16] This pamphlet started a long series of attacks and libels, not only because of its firm stand on the problems of internal peace with the Protestants and external Protestant alliances, which it claimed to be legitimate, but also because of its attack on Jesuit internationalism. Richelieu wanted it to be not only an argument in favor of the new policy but also an attack on, and exposure of, the Jesuits. He acted in a perfidiously clever manner: while praising the French Jesuits, he contested the doctrine of the order, using the arguments of Jesuit theologians.[17] The pamphlet was successful; the controversy became a national issue and provoked anti-Jesuit feeling. Thereafter never leaving his opponents—real or imagined—in peace, Richelieu, acting through Fancan as his mouthpiece, charged the Jesuits with complicity in the *Admonitio* in another reply to the latter called *Le Miroir du temps passé* (1625), which was an attack on religious orders in general. This was violently refuted in the pamphlet *Quaestiones quodlibeticae* (1626), which urged that the author of *Le Miroir* be punished in the way that the Inquisition dealt with heretics.

Further developments were curious. In the name of the Jesuits, Pelletier disavowed the *Admonitio* with his *Apologie ou Défense pour les Pères Jésuites* (1625), in which Bellarmin's ideas on popular sovereignty were rejected in strongly royalistic terms.[18] The violence of Pelletier's reaction, instead of proving the innocence of the order, betrayed Jesuit complicity in the publication of the *Admonitio*. Richelieu and Fancan responded with *Examen de l'Apologie du sieur Pelletier,* but no reply appeared, and Richelieu could now devote himself entirely to furthering the ideas contained in the *Catholique d'Estat.* He wrote a corollary to the latter, entitled *Advertissement à tous les Estatz de l'Europe* (1625), and he authorized Drion to publish his *Discours au Roy sur la paix qu'il a donné à ses sujets de la R.P.R.,*[19] in which the ideas of the *Catholique d'Estat* were still further developed and a plea was put forward for considering the Protestant rebellion as serving the cause of peace.[20] His chief aim was to turn public opinion in favor of his

---

[16] Attributed to three authors: Jeremie Ferrier, Jean Sirmond, and Father Joseph.

[17] Cf. Deloche, *Autour de la plume,* p. 376.

[18] Cf. *Le Mercure Jésuite,* I, 846 ff.

[19] R.P.R. denotes Religion Prétendue Réformée.

[20] Deloche, *Autour de la plume,* p. 366.

policy against Spain, and for this purpose he promoted an ingenious variety of publications.[21]

Saturated with books on the same recurring theme but from seemingly different sources, public opinion followed the lead of Richelieu; and had it not been for the publication which appeared under the title *Considérations d'Estat sur le livre publié depuis quelques mois sous le titre d'Advertissement au Roy* (1625), it would have seemed that the contest was finished or suspended. But this attack was serious; it was anonymous, though it certainly came from his adversaries. The method it adopted was curious. The *Considérations d'Estat* made a stand against the *Admontio,* and its obvious task was to disparage the order of the Jesuits, which it did in such violent terms and with so little regard for the balance, prudence, and diplomacy in which Richelieu excelled that it must have emanated from circles hostile to Richelieu. It tried to stir up trouble between the Jesuit order and the Cardinal, while incriminating and compromising the latter to the advantage of his enemies. Libelous as it was, the book provoked no response and caused no dispute. It did not lead Richelieu to use less veiled methods in combating the Jesuits, as the authors of the *Considérations d'Estat* had probably hoped.

The anti-Jesuit publication of Drion, *Advis salutaire au Roy sur les affaires présentes* (1625), sponsored at that time by the Cardinal, shows well the tactics of the latter. He carefully avoided all recklessness, even when attacking the Jesuits in an unusually direct way. At the same time, he accused them of being responsible for the religious disunity in France, which was maintained in the interests of Spain. The book also had another purpose: to win the sympathies of the Protestants by flattering them and exposing the Jesuits, their enemies. The latter did not let themselves become involved in argument, but remained silent. Careful not to disclose their identity by an open reply when directly challenged, and weighing their chances of success, they awaited an opportunity for effective action.

This opportunity presented itself with the appearance of the

---

[21] *La France revenant en santé après sa grande maladie* (1625); *La Cassandre française à sa Patrie* (1626); *Pierre de touche politique tirée du mont de Parnasse, où il est traitté du gouvernement des principales Monarchies du monde.* Traduite en français de l'italien de Trajano Boccalini (Paris, 1626).

Cardinalium, Archiepiscoporum . . . Sententia (1626),[22] by Léonor d'Estampes, Bishop of Chartres, who had been officially authorized, in December, 1625, by the Assembly of the Clergy to denounce the *Admonitio*. The *Sententia* proved a failure. Tackling the delicate problem of the relationship between the spiritual and the temporal power in a manner opposed to the Roman doctrine, it was bound to be rejected by the Assembly which had sponsored it. The Assembly disapproved of the doctrine of "régalisme," which the *Sententia* advocated—a doctrine that went far beyond the idea of the sovereignty of kings, expressed in the *Catholique d'Estat,* which the Assembly had, if only implicitly, approved.[23] Its problem became entangled, for it had not only to dissociate itself from the publication issued under its own auspices, but also to resolve its conflict with the parlement which had adopted the *Sententia*.

The *Sententia* also served the cause of Richelieu badly, making him lose the first round to the Jesuits. It was used by their spokesman Cardinal de la Rochefoucauld (Father Phelippeaux) to fight Richelieu on his own ground by applying the method of the *Catholique d'Estat,* which praised the Jesuits while surreptitiously refuting their theories by the use of their own arguments. Rochefoucauld, in his *Raisons pour le désaveu* (1626),[24] extolled Richelieu while "plagiarizing" those passages in the *Sententia* which had been taken from the *Catholique d'Estat* or the *Miroir,* as well as those extracted from the official writings of Richelieu.[25] This was done to show weaknesses in Richelieu's arguments, and contradictions between his recent and his earlier works. Despite all that, the contest was not lost by Richelieu. He exploited other people's inflamed passions for his own benefit, and his painstaking share in the war of pamphlets ended in 1626, when he became a contracting party to three agreements: with the Protestants, with Spain, and with the Jesuits.

This triple alliance was as inconclusive as it was deceptive. The

---

[22] Cf. *Le Mercure Jésuite,* I, 794 ff.

[23] By giving credit to Ferrier, whose authorship it recognized. On the Bishop of Chartres controversy, cf. below.

[24] François Cardinal de la Rochefoucauld, *Raisons pour le désaveu fait par les evesques de ce roiaume d'un livret publié avec le titre: Jugement des cardinaux, archevesques, evesques et autres qui se son trouvés en l'Assemblée générale du Roiaume* (Paris, 1626).

[25] Deloche, *Autour de la plume,* p. 376.

treaty with the Protestants which officially came first in the form of the Treaty of Paris, February 5, 1626, was only a truce to give effect to the ruin-through-peace theory. To reproduce the state of Richelieu's mind will not be an easy task. His conciliatory efforts in the civil war against the Protestants in 1625–1626 were considerable; throughout that period he showed real concern for, and persistently took pains to achieve, a peaceful settlement.[26] Apart from the desire to carry on the war abroad efficiently, his interest in peace was genuine, for he was already responsible for the welfare of the state. Simultaneously, his objections against the Protestants were slowly accumulating, particularly against Rohan, toward whom his feelings had never been friendly.[27] From early days he mistrusted Rohan's sincerity and loyalty,[28] and he was not slow to recognize the danger that the existence of Rohan involved. It was after Rohan and his brother Soubise had joined the rebellion in 1625 that Richelieu endeavored to strangle it.

At that time, Rohan, as a leader of the party, had a different role from that which he had played in the previous decade. He had now to win the following of the large Huguenot masses, who were slower to respond to temptations of vanity and self-interest than were the rank and file of the Huguenot party of bygone decades. At that time the Huguenot upper classes had been able to persuade their followers that their interests were identical. But now the main appeal lay in the domain of religious enthusiasm, which was preserved in a strangely unscathed form. By necessity, the leader's course became one of demagogy, and in this Rohan was not, naturally enough, at his best. His instinctive line was to appeal to human reason; here he had to appeal to human passion. It is no wonder that his goal often eluded him.[29] Because he had to cope

---

[26] The main reason for this was the generally admitted inability of France to wage war on two fronts, both external and internal. But the suggested remedies differed. At Court the majority pressed for peace with Spain out of sheer hatred for the Huguenots. Richelieu thought the contrary: he wanted internal unification for the sake of successful conduct of war abroad. Cf. M. G. Schybergson, *Le Duc de Rohan*, pp. 35–36.

[27] "L'antipathie que Richelieu éprouva toujours contre le duc de Rohan." Avenel, ed., *Lettres, instructions diplomatiques et papiers d'état de Richelieu*, V, 890. Hereafter cited as Richelieu, *Lettres*.

[28] Avenel remarks that the exaggerated tone of praise in Richelieu's letter to Rohan of April, 1617, reflects the Cardinal's diplomatic skill in trying to win over the Protestant leader, whose devotion to the King was not unshakable. *Ibid.*, I, 518–519.

[29] Cf. Schybergson, *Le Duc de Rohan*, p. 32.

with difficulties more formidable than ever before, his activity became more unpredictable; and this Richelieu could not fail to judge as extremely harmful.

There were also less obvious reasons for the Cardinal's dislike and fear of Rohan; for example, the shrewdness in the general design of the latter's policy, which was not always clear because the extent of his secret negotiations with Spain could scarcely be estimated. What Rohan advocated openly as a line of policy to be explored by the government was an alliance with Protestant countries. To argue in this way and to be convincing was easy, because of the self-evidence of the argument that Spain constituted the main threat to France. But the main motive was probably the hope of the almost certain profits to be reaped by the Huguenots from any such arrangements. It was logical to assume that in an international setting of closer coöperation between France and the Protestant powers, the Huguenot problem would receive new consideration which must improve internal relations in France. It was also sound to think that an alliance between the French government and Spain would involve a deterioration of the relationship between the former and the Huguenot party, and would deprive the Huguenots of the possibility of a natural and easily attainable foreign alliance. Hence it was obvious that Rohan would endeavor to prevent the government from entering into closer relations with Spain. This was something which he himself, in spite of his declared policy, hoped to do, and his negotiations with Spain continued until 1629, though a true alliance was never concluded.

Richelieu certainly understood that alliance with Protestant countries meant giving way to the French Huguenots; hence his deep dislike of Rohan. The Duke of Rohan, in his recommendations and suggestive hints, almost anticipated the road that the Cardinal would follow: "Il faut que le roi de France ne se montre pas animé contre ses sujets de la religion, afin que les Protestants ne se jettent pas en la protection d'Angleterre; il ne faut pas aussi qu'il se montre tellement leur partisan qu'il donne soupçon aux catholics, le plus grand corps de son Etat." [30] Richelieu distrusted all able advisers, even the devoted ones who collaborated with him, on whom he temporarily relied but whom he would always betray when a good opportunity arose. What must also have annoyed him was the boldness of Rohan, who was ready to ally the Huguenot party with

---

[30] G. d'Avenel, *Richelieu et la monarchie absolue*, III, 404.

Spain, an ultra-Catholic country—the very technique which Richelieu would use in reverse when contracting external Protestant alliances. There also existed an almost imperceptible competition between the Cardinal and the Huguenot leader: the one wishing to conclude a peaceful settlement with Spain; the other, to obtain her support. It looked as if Richelieu was afraid that Rohan would spoil his game, and so he acted accordingly. He need not have feared Rohan, as superiority of power and resources was always on his own side; yet he dealt with him in a ruthless manner which betrayed both fear and caution—attributes of a dictatorial spirit which Richelieu was bound to develop as time went on. He disliked taking chances or leaving matters open; everything had to be brought to its final conclusion. Without this quality, perhaps his success over his enemies would never have been so complete. It accounts for the ultimate banishment of Rohan from France at the conclusion of hostilities in 1629. It also accounts for Richelieu's dissatisfaction with the peace treaty with Spain, officially concluded at Monçon on March 5, 1626, but in fact signed in January. In principle he approved of the negotiations, but he was offended because it was on Spain's initiative that the talks with his ambassador, Count du Fargis, were held. Moreover, Spain played the leading role, terminating the talks at an early stage when the points agreed on were in the interests of Spain alone, but were in every respect harmful to the relations of France both with her Protestant subjects and other Protestant states. Richelieu detested the inefficiency of the treaty, which was more of a liability than an asset, and which came into being unexpectedly instead of maturing as a product of his will and diplomacy.[31]

For that reason the agreements Richelieu reached in 1626 were confusing and brought no solution. This almost all-round settlement obviously had no solid foundations, because Richelieu had no intention of letting everybody in the long run "vivre dans le repos de sa conscience." [32] Many reasons existed for the general astonishment and confusion. Richelieu himself was uneasy about the Spanish peace; the Catholics were critical of the agreement reached with the Huguenots, although this came much less as a surprise; the Protestants viewed with apprehension the treaty with Spain, and were not pleased that the Cardinal's conflict with the Jesuits, who formally disavowed the *Admonitio,* should come to an end.

---

[31] Cf. Richelieu, *Mémoires,* V, 211.
[32] Cf. Schybergson, *Le Duc de Rohan,* p. 36.

Probably few could have predicted that Richelieu was about to prepare even more shocking surprises: the disgrace of Fancan, and the establishment of a closer relationship with Father Joseph— events which were to seal the Huguenot fate. The policy of deception had so bemused the people that they discarded the more gloomy predictions. If the reshuffle came as a great shock, this was lessened by a disbelief in its seriousness. Richelieu's mastery of deceit had not yet become notorious. True, only the previous year a book had been published at his instigation advocating an anti-Spanish and an anti-Austrian course.[33] But there Richelieu had a double alibi: first, the book's anonymity; and, second, the fact that even if his authorship were suspected, he could point to his negligible role in the Spanish negotiations leading to the Monçon treaty, for which he felt no responsibility. This alibi was hardly needed, for Richelieu was well protected on all flanks. The impression created by the *Response au Manifeste du Sieur de Soubise* (June, 1625), the publication of which Richelieu had sponsored and to which he had contributed, was still fresh in the memory of the people.

The book shows Richelieu's expert ability in spreading the notion that he favored peace and toleration. It is a sample of his brilliance as a pamphleteer and as a diplomat. He alternately menaced and cajoled his readers. He shocked them with his blunt views on royal obligation: "Un particulier est obligé de faire ponctuellement ce qu'il promet, le Roy n'est obligé de le faire que quand il le veut et il ne doit pas le vouloir que quand il le ne peut faire sans préjudicier à son Estat." [34] He tried to persuade them that Soubise and the people at La Rochelle followed different roads, and that their aims did not coincide; that the cause of the nobles, both Catholic and Protestant, was the same; and that therefore it was in their common interest to unite under the King. The problem of toleration was tackled directly, in a passage which uses the words of his own speech of 1614. Further, he reassured the Protestants by saying that a sovereign should be faithful to the heretics.

Did this mean that Richelieu's views on toleration had remained

---

[33] *La Ligue nécessaire* ([n.p.], 1625). Deloche denies that its author was Father Joseph (opinion of Abbé Dedouvres, *Le P. Joseph polémiste,* pp. 112 ff.) or Fancan (opinion of Fagniez, *L'Opinion publique et la presse politique sous Louis XIII,* p. 394). Deloche, *Autour de la plume,* p. 269.

[34] *Response au Manifeste du Sieur de Soubise* ([n.p.], 1625), p. 14, as quoted in Deloche, *Autour de la plume,* p. 267.

essentially unchanged since the States-General? Hardly so: he had had an anti-Huguenot period just before 1622. Just as in 1614, it was internal peace that he desired to obtain through a policy of toleration. His work was now more complete only because at this time he had every means at his disposal. He thus made a thorough job of inspiring Protestant pamphleteers to write in favor of peace.[35]

But certainly his attitude was not the same as that of 1614. He was now temporizing, while at the same time neutralizing [36] the powers of the Huguenots and Spain. According to Eugène and Emile Haag, he already knew his aim; the course of his policy being set, he was only waiting for the right opportunity to start the machinery moving.

> Traité de paix de 5 février 1626 conclu ... Richelieu n'attendait qu'une circonstance favorable pour abattre sans retour le parti protestant. Son projet était bien arrêté de ne plus souffrir dans une monarchie absolue l'étrange anomalie d'une société organisée démocratiquement, et il avoue lui-même qu'il n'avait conclu la dernière paix qu'afin d'arriver plus surement à son but.[37]

Richelieu himself made no secret of his "jeu de bascule," exposing it in an interpretation of his recent policies entitled *Discours sur plusieurs points importants de l'estat présent des affairs de France adressé au Roy*.[38] It was a move made in his own inimitable fashion. However, unlike his other successful operations, it had no single motive, but at least three: to justify his past politics from the point of view of Rome; to warn those who had shown him any signs of opposition, such as Fancan, who was directly threatened because he opposed the English marriage;[39] and to continue his policy of

---

[35] A number of pamphlets appeared as a result of this campaign: *Le Sincère et libre discourse par supplications et remonstrances très humbles au Roy* ([n.p.], 1625); *Le Pacifique ou sommation à Messieurs les Ducs de Rohan et de Soubise de rentrer en l'obeyssance du Roy, pour jouir du benefice de la Paix* (Paris, 1625); *Humble remonstrance au Roy sur les mouvements de la rebellion* (Paris, 1625); *Procès-verbal contre la pernicieuse entreprise et conspiration des perturbateurs de l'Estat* (Paris, 1626). Cf. Deloche, *Autour de la plume*, p. 264.

[36] Deloche, *Autour de la plume*, p. 221.

[37] Cf. Eugène and Emile Haag, *La France Protestante ou Vies des Protestants français qui se sont fait un nom dans l'histoire*, I, lxvii. Hereafter cited as Haag, *La France Protestante*.

[38] Cf. Deloche, *Autour de la plume*, pp. 406–410.

[39] The marriage of Henrietta Maria to Charles I, which, according to Richelieu, Louis XIII regarded as advantageous for France and detrimental to the Huguenot

checks and balances. The last was obviously solidly lodged in the Cardinal's mind. In order to complete the arguments in the *Discours* and to restore the balance in his policy disturbed by his last book, he commissioned Fancan to write *L'Advis salutaire sur l'état présent des affaires d'Allemagne*. The choice of writer was obvious enough. Fancan's natural sympathies for England were well known, and it was logical for Richelieu to accept the services of a man so long as he was useful, no matter what plans he had in mind for the other's future. Richelieu combined to a supreme degree the art of deceit, a remarkable dexterity in dealing with men in his employ, and a complete absence of moral and humane principles when he decided to discard men who had served their purpose.

Fancan was employed to defend and justify to England the Franco-Spanish treaty, in order to prevent the eventual Anglo-Spanish alliance which Richelieu dreaded. Fancan's task was to remind England that competition between France and Spain had not ended, and, as if to strengthen this argument, Richelieu ordered the reissue of several anti-Spanish pamphlets.[40]

That was about the last time Fancan's services were to be used. He became the victim of the very policy which had earlier caused his elevation to the post of the Cardinal's mouthpiece. What Richelieu accepted as a temporary measure, Fancan regarded as a life-long policy. When Richelieu discarded his policy of balancing between the Zealous Catholics and Spain on the one hand, and the Protestants on the other, Fancan had to go, because deflection from this line seemed to him inconceivable. When the final disgrace came, in 1627, Fancan still continued to work in favor of the English alliance and against Spain. Richelieu's attitude had changed completely. He knew that war with England was inevitable because he felt French freedom on the seas to be impaired by the English menace;[41] therefore he tried to preserve good relations with the

---

party: "... si ce mariage se rompoit la religion huguenote étoit fortifiée en France par le secours des Anglois, lequel eût été empêché par ce mariage, et la religion catholique étoit perdue en Angleterre ... Au contraire, si ce mariage se faisoit, la religion catholique recevroit un très grand appui en Angleterre et la religion huguenote seroit ruinée en France." Richelieu, *Mémoires*, V, 12–13.

[40] *La Ligue nécessaire; L'Espée courageuse de Monsieur Frère du Roy contre les ennemis de la France*. Cf. Deloche, *Autour de la plume*, p. 412.

[41] Since October, 1625, England had been at war with Spain. When Louis XIII refused the invitation to join her, English ships began to stop French vessels trading with the Low Countries.

Catholic world. A treaty with Spain duly followed (March 20, 1627). It was for the sake of favors from Rome that Fancan was sacrificed in typical Richelieu-like fashion. A pamphlet was written by Mathieu de Morgues entitled *Advis d'un théologien sans passion,* in which Fancan was defended and praised, but the ideas embodied in his anti-Jesuit and anti-Romish *Catalogue* were exposed and condemned.

It would be absurd, however, to reduce the conflict between Richelieu and Fancan to a single motive.[42] The conflict not only marked Richelieu's drawing closer to the *dévots* and away from the *bons Français;* [43] it also sprang from a deep incompatibility of characters and beliefs, which made it impossible for the two men to coöperate for long. The difference in their characters was so extreme that evidently neither of them could resist some strange, temporary fascination for the other. Fancan combined Utopian ideas and narrowness of outlook with a rigid doctrinaire attitude, lack of knowledge of humanity with inborn pessimism, and an anecdotal manner of speech with a brilliant journalistic style. At the opposite pole was Richelieu: a realist with a flexible mind, open to new ideas, and not immune from that disease common to some outstanding intellects of being only too ready to see the other party's point of view and of being equally able to argue for and against any issue.

If these complementary traits made temporary coöperation necessary, what made it possible were the characteristics they shared in common—pugnacity in argument, zeal and perseverance in politics, lack of scruples in action, and an inclination to opportunism when in trouble.

Their convictions were as different as their characters. Fancan believed in a royal sovereignty under which civil and spiritual powers were kept separate. He was Gallican, though he refused to be kept within the limits of Gallicanism. He had deep sympathies for the Protestant movement, though he disliked its blend of religious and political elements. Richelieu wished to maintain a balance between spiritual and religious power. He accepted political Gallicanism, though he rejected religious Gallicanism; he defended the

---

[42] As was done in Geley, *Fancan et la politique de Richelieu de 1617 à 1627* (Paris, 1884), pp. 300 ff. See Deloche, *Autour de la plume,* p. 430.

[43] "Fancan ... victime du rapprochement de Richelieu et du parti dévot." Cf. Lavisse, *Histoire de France,* Vol. VI, Part 2, p. 264.

power of the state against the reëmergence of the Church. He was for unitary monarchism. He would have approved of the Gallican church probably only if he himself were its head or patriarch. His attitude to the Protestants was seldom genuinely friendly, though often it is difficult to call it hostile.

Was the *rapprochement* of Richelieu with Father Joseph, after he had broken off relations with Fancan, the result of the changed policy toward the Protestant problem, or its cause? The most probable answer, perhaps, would be to say that the long-lasting influence of the Grey Eminence had borne fruit. Richelieu could not have failed to notice certain advantages in an anti-Protestant policy, the notion of which Father Joseph had been persistently implanting in his mind.[44] It is difficult to say which reasons came from Richelieu's chief political adviser and which were entirely his own. Some good reasons for the destruction of the Protestants Richelieu had certainly worked out himself as a natural consequence of his conception of the state.

From the beginning, the Cardinal was resolved to stamp out any center of power in the state outside governmental control; his aim was to create unity of power. This aim explains the deep interest he showed in the Huguenot strongholds during the civil disorders of 1625, when he summarized the causes which had led to the establishment of Huguenot rights to the "towns of bounty." [45] His argument was that, because the Edict had been executed and the surety for which strongholds had been set up was no longer needed, there was no reason to renew the lease, which had expired.[46]

Striving for unity of power, he supported unitary monarchism— an attitude which constituted a special danger for the Huguenot cause. The Protestant movement was a potential enemy of monarchism, as the Huguenot party could theoretically still be used as an antimonarchical ally by the aristocracy. But it was the misfortune of the Huguenot party that it persistently failed to satisfy the interests of any political group; it was useless even in aiding the King to overcome the aristocracy. The Huguenot party had thus become a scapegoat. Its destruction became the Cardinal's *raison d'état*—the term he had in all probability invented and which he

---

[44] Cf. Abbé Richard, *Le Véritable Père Josef, passim.*
[45] Cf. Richelieu, *Maximes d'Etat*, No. XIX, p. 10.
[46] *Ibid.*, No. LXXXVI, p. 44.

applied to those considerations on which rested the public good.[47]
Such an earmarking of the Huguenots as potential victims was even
more serious, because another *raison d'état* scheme of Richelieu's
was the destruction of the power of the nobles and of the remnants
of feudalism—a scheme which fittingly coincided with the extermination of the Huguenot party.

This uniform labeling of the three schemes, on which an equal
degree of importance was bestowed, showed a penetrating understanding of how they were linked. They were, indeed, so closely
linked that an impact of one upon the other became at times inevitable. The survival of Protestantism, in the forms given by the
Edict of Nantes—the 3,500 castles in which the right to worship
was granted—meant a continuation of the dying feudal spirit. Thus
the Huguenot cause was linked, if unwittingly, to the feudal cause.[48]
Without strongholds and castles, Calvinism was doomed, because
these were safeguards that the Reformed religion would be practiced and defended; so it was in the Huguenot interest to perpetuate
their existence. The principle worked well so long as the character
of Calvinism was markedly aristocratic; that is, so long as the
Colignys, the Duplessis-Mornays, the Sullys, the Damvilles, the
Châtillons, the Condés, and the Rohans were numerous and gra-
ciously accepted leadership. But when the soul of the movement,
the aristocracy, deserted the Huguenot cause, the Reformed religion was left in the anomalous position of having feudalism as its
basis for future existence. One of the reasons that the Edict was
bound to fail was this anachronistic anomaly on which the status
of the Protestants was based.[49] Protestantism had become in that
particular instance, in practice, though not in theory, one of those
bulwarks of reaction against the strong centralized power which
Richelieu endeavored to erect. It was antimonarchical in deed, but
manifestly monarchical in word—a discrepancy which had hidden
meaning, but obviously shattering consequences. The realization
that Protestantism could be a potential factor to offset the anti-
centralist and feudal aristocratic tendencies, must, in the eyes of
Richelieu, have predestined it to the same fate as that of the various
other remnants of feudalism he was resolved to annihilate.

[47] Cf. Lavisse, *Histoire de France*, Vol. VI, Part 2, p. 365.
[48] Cf. J. H. Bridges, *France under Richelieu and Colbert*, pp. 18 ff.
[49] Cf. Burckhardt, *Richelieu*, p. 209.

The only hope for the Huguenots lay in a change of the principles on which the Edict of Nantes rested. But certainly this change was not what Richelieu desired. He would not have feudalism destroyed and Calvinism preserved—a situation in which he could not have succeeded without radically altering the Huguenot status, which rested on the right to worship in feudal castles. Even in 1629 he refrained from doing this when, by the Edict of Alais, he deprived the Huguenots of all political rights, leaving them a religious liberty confined within strict limits. Richelieu had earlier refused to renew the lease to the strongholds, lapsing in 1624, and this deprived the Huguenot party of every effective guarantee that their rights would be considered. Now he ordered that all fortifications should be razed. The last blow hit feudalism and Protestantism alike, underlining their common fate. Unprotected and exposed, Calvinism was to follow feudalism, if at a somewhat slower pace, on the downward trend; its agony was heartbreakingly prolonged, but the end was almost certain.

To achieve unity of power for the sake of untrammeled royal sovereignty, to reduce the aristocracy to impotence and insignificance, and to get rid of those nests of reaction which bred feudalism and with some of which the Huguenot party was connected— these were the aims Richelieu had in mind when embarking on his anti-Protestant policy. There were other obvious political advantages, such as improved relations with Rome and Spain and the possibility of dealing in full strength with external enemies, once internal order was assured.

In the mind of Father Joseph, Richelieu's right hand after Fancan was imprisoned in the Bastille, these aims and advantages did not dispose of what was for him the real and only reason justifying the suppression of the Huguenots: the Protestants deserved to be disposed of simply because they were heretics. Father Joseph had worked persistently over a long period to imbue the Cardinal with some of his passionate convictions and with his unflinching faith. He tried assiduously to instill in Richelieu some of his fervent, proselytizing zeal. It seems that at the time he was not entirely unsuccessful: Richelieu's dogged perseverance at the siege of La Rochelle owed much to Father Joseph's persuasion. "Le Père Joseph," wrote Abbé Richard, "organisait contre elle [La Rochelle] une véritable siège théologique, si l'on peut ainsi s'exprimer. On n'a pas peut être tenu assez compte de ce rôle du Père Joseph, ou bien on l'a transporté à Richelieu." [50] After 1630, Richelieu let himself be guided even more by the Capuchin. He fought all unorthodoxy, as exemplified in the movements of Richerism, Quietism, and Jansenism, and he planned a wholesale conversion of Protestants. His proselytism never reached the high tone of enthusiasm that emanated from the Grey Eminence; it was never an all-devouring flame; yet the will of Richelieu had transformed it into a kind of restrained but devastating force.

RICHELIEU AND TOLERANCE

It is in the light of this proselytizing spirit that the value of the Peace of Alais (1629) should be assessed. Otherwise that passionate yet restrained intensity of conviction Richelieu had imbibed from Father Joseph presents a grossly distorted picture when confronted with Richelieu's acts at the time of the negotiations which concluded the hostilities, and later. It is possible that an inadequate emphasis on the change wrought by the Grey Eminence on the mind of the Cardinal led historians to accept Alais at its face value. It led to a widespread but fallacious belief that what followed was a period of religious toleration of the Protestants, that only their political freedom was abrogated.

True, in 1629 the Huguenots were given freedom of religion; or, to be more precise, being deprived of their political freedom, they were left to practice their religion without restriction. But did they obtain any assurance that freedom of conscience was left as their inalienable right? Far from it; Richelieu had no intention of giving long-term recognition even to a purely religious sect. Furthermore, the new Edict was the last enactment before the Revocation to contain any substantial number of clauses favorable to the Calvinists. The Edict itself made no pretense to being another instrument of toleration; it was simply a royal pardon generously extended to the

---

[50] Abbé Richard, *Le Véritable Père Josef,* p. 208 n. The inspiring role played by Father Joseph at La Rochelle is also shown in the unpublished manuscript of Lherminier, *Supplement à l'histoire de France 1624–1638.* British Museum, Bibl. Egerton, MS 1673, fols. 49, 51.

Huguenot party, whose sins were forgiven, yet whose back had to be broken lest the party should again revolt, even in self-defense. The letters Richelieu wrote at this time show how completely he was in accord with this view. His immediate aim was a ruthless suppression of the rebellion: "terminer à la rigueur la rebellion des huguenots" [51]—a rebellion for which he could never forgive its leader, a sinner against the King and a destroyer of the state's established order. "Je n'eusse pas creu ... qu'après la prise de la Rochelle on eust esté capable de pardonner à M. de Rohan qui a tant faict du mal à la France." [52] As soon as the Edict was signed, he gloried in his subjects' humiliation. "Je m'asseure que Vostre Majesté aura une extresme joye, non seulement de ce que le roy a donné la paix à ses subjets, mais de la façon avec laquelle elle est faite. Le roy n'a point fait de paix avec ses subjets, comme il avait esté fait par le passé, mais il leur a donné grace." [53] He reveled in their submission and helplessness. He repeated with obvious satisfaction that the Edict was not a treaty, but an act of mercy, and that it was highly advantageous for the King, because Rohan would leave the kingdom and all rebellious towns would raze their fortifications. "Jamais il n'a esté fait une paix sy advantaguese, veu qu'oultre que leurs députez généraulx l'ont acceptée soubz le nom de grâce, ils ont obligé touttes les villes rebelles à razer entièrement leurs fortifications." [54] He was particularly proud of the last decision, which indeed had no precedent; it gave secure foundation to the restored peace and marked a spectacular end to the Huguenot party, which, leaderless and illegal, could not exist even as a clandestine organization.

The treaty of 1629 closed the long series of wars of religion, but it was scarcely the laudable event it is sometimes claimed to be. Even the Protestants of later ages saw in it only a reflection of Richelieu's justice and clemency,[55] in which he of course wanted

---

[51] Richelieu à Condé, Usez, 14 juillet 1629. Arch. de Condé. Richelieu, *Lettres*, VII, 639.

[52] Richelieu à M. Le Prince [Condé], 8 juin 1628. Arch. de Condé. Richelieu, *Lettres*, VII, 616.

[53] Richelieu à la Reyne, 29 juin 1629. Paris, Bibl. Imp. Fonds Béthune, MS 9323, fol. 76. Richelieu, *Lettres*, III, 359.

[54] Richelieu au prince de Condé, 30 juin 1629. Archives des Affaires éstrangères France, L. In Richelieu, *Lettres*, III, 362–363.

[55] Cf. *Bulletin de la Société de l'histoire du Protestantisme Français*, XI, 377.

them to believe. It represented for them the last visible sign of toleration; yet it was in fact more like the beginning of the end.

Richelieu spoke hopefully of the prospects for lasting peace because he had seen that Rohan was disposed of, the Huguenot power crushed, and the "Protestant Republic" at an end; he could even indulge in the wish that Protestant hearts, particularly those of Rohan and Soubise, might be won by gentle treatment.[56] He could reasonably hope for a period of tranquillity because he had left the Huguenots to enjoy liberty of conscience and religious practice. He also induced in them a sense of guilt for having seriously trespassed upon the rights of dutiful subjects—not an unduly hard task when the monarchist concept was a generally accepted rule of political behavior. Leaving them to remorseful speculations, he was careful not to make the terms too hard, because that might have brought a dangerous reaction. He planned to stun them, not to awaken in them the sense of mortal peril; he could not yet anathematize their religion! He would not have troubled about such niceties if he had not been afraid that the Huguenots, if goaded to desperation, might attempt to regain some of the power they had once enjoyed. As shown also in the case of the Jesuits, Richelieu was always careful not to awaken the resentment of any social group.

Here he acted wisely, recognizing that since the Huguenots had had a strong party organization,[57] they might be capable of resuscitating it and thereby bring about a change in the Protestant status; that ignoring them meant increasing this possibility. In this case the power of Richelieu's political diagnosis revealed itself in those ambiguous and apparently irreconcilable traits of character which led to his highly enigmatic and contradictory behavior,[58]

[56] Cf. Richelieu à Mazuyer, 1 juillet 1629. Arch. Aff. étr. France, LI. Richelieu, *Lettres,* III, 364.

[57] Bonet-Maury maintains that the liberal character of the Edict of 1629 was mainly due to the powerful Protestant organization. Cf. G. Bonet-Maury, "Le Protestantisme français et la République, 1598–1685," *Bulletin de la Société de l'histoire du Protestantisme Français,* LIII, 381.

[58] Paquier, describing the character of Richelieu, shows symptoms of a state of mind dissatisfied with the evidence given, anxious to find the truth, yet reluctant to pronounce the verdict, and ultimately lost in vain speculation over the pronouncements of biased witnesses and age-old untruths: "Il [Richelieu] eût à un haut degré l'universalité et la liberté d'esprit. Prince de l'Eglise romaine, il voulut que le clergé fût national; vainqueur des calvinistes, il ne frappa que la rebellion et respecta les droits de la conscience; enfant de la noblesse et imbu de son orgueil, il agit comme s'il eût reçu mission de préparer le règne du Tiers-Etat." Paquier, *Histoire de l'unité,* II, 48.

puzzling those who look for too simple and too straightforward explanations. Was the Edict of Alais a measure of toleration or was it not? The Edict reflected both the positive and negative aspects of Richelieu's policy and of his qualities. It meant a limited degree of freedom, but it was also conducive to a climate in which Calvinism was left to wither.

Of course, to speak of pure expediency when referring to the policy of Richelieu means to be looking for an easy solution; yet the risk of doing so is even greater if the oversimplified theory that Richelieu was liberalism incarnate is adopted. The nineteenth-century historians who were responsible for the incomprehensible and unmerited "rehabilitation" of the memory of Richelieu, and who treated him as if he were a real father of the nation, failed to appraise his Machiavellian character. The present-day plea for "debunking" [59] him is unusually reasonable, because it does not mean the destruction of views held for centuries but simply the elimination of certain distorted notions to which some writers, especially in the latter part of the last century, succumbed.

The view that Richelieu was tolerant can scarcely find any confirmation in fact. He created a fairly strong impression of being tolerant—an impression that persisted during his lifetime because events moved against his proselytizing plans, which he did not pursue to the end. But to an acute contemporary observer, these plans probably did not constitute an insoluble enigma; doubtless Richelieu's duplicity, which accounted for a good part of the dislike, and indeed open hatred, with which he was commonly regarded, later led to a good deal of confusion, which is largely responsible for the defects of modern interpretations.

His duplicity shows at every stage how greatly he was ruled by expediency, of which his quasi-toleration was a weak offspring; he had destroyed the Protestants politically, not in order to assure their survival in the religious sphere, but in order to make their religious practice at a later stage difficult, and much later, impossible. The process was to be painstakingly slow; it had to avoid violence,[60] but doubtless the destruction of the Calvinist religion

---

[59] Put forward in Edmond Préclin and Victor L. Tapié, *Le XVII**e siècle* (Paris, 1949), p. 182.

[60] "Il était convenu de n'agir dans cette affaire que par des voies de douceur, et de n'y employer que des moyens de persuasion." M. M. Tabaraud, *Histoire critique des projets formés depuis trois cents ans pour la réunion des communions chrétiennes*, p.

was envisaged as the ultimate aim and as the last stage of a long-term plan for the dissolution of Huguenot society. This plan, which was never set forth in detail, permitted a good deal of flexibility; but within the limits of the principle of gentle oppression on which it rested, it was carried out assiduously and relentlessly.

Evidence which may serve to dispel the common illusion that Richelieu intended to deprive the Protestants only of their political rights is to be found in the period immediately following the treaty of Alais. The case of David Ligonnier, an inhabitant of La Rochelle, who in 1631 was expelled from his native town in spite of his oath of loyalty to the King and his rights as a burgher, is testimony that the administration was resolved not to tolerate the Huguenots either as members of a political party or as believers in an unorthodox creed.[61] In 1634, Omer Talon, the Advocate General, "affirmed openly that the Reformed were suffered only by Toleration and Connivance, as men suffer a Thing which they had rather be without." [62] Although Richelieu did not commit himself openly to an anti-Huguenot policy either by statement or by letter, his was more than a tacit agreement with those who pursued such a policy. He must have acted, if not as a source of inspiration and encouragement, at least as a ready recipient of views and plans to that effect.[63]

---

199. Cf. also C. C. de Rulhière, *Eclaircissemens historiques sur les causes de la révocation de l'édit de Nantes et sur l'état des Protestants en France.* Hereafter cited as Rulhière, *Eclaircissemens historiques.*

[61] Cf. "La liberté de conscience à Le Rochelle en 1631," *Bulletin de la Société de l'histoire du Protestantisme Français,* XXXVII, 417.

[62] "From which dangerous Principle," continues Benoit, "he drew a Consequence much worse: that what concerned the Religion of the Reformed, was not to be reckoned among Things favourable, for which the Terms of the Law are wont to be favourably interpreted; but that in their cases the Rigor of Expression was to be observed." Elie Benoit, *The History of the Famous Edict of Nantes,* II, 510. Hereafter cited as Benoit, *The Edict of Nantes.*

[63] "... par la force de vostre courage et très généreuze conduite, il [Dieu] a entierement estainct la faction des huguenots, il vous donnera la rezollution de les convertir à luy ... j'ozeray vous dire, Monseigneur que vous cognoissant autant qu'en ma bassesse je puis cognoistre la grandeur de vostre Eminence, je me suis promiz pour la fin de ceste oeuvre la conversion de tous les heretiques du Royaume, lesquels après des miracles si manifestes, n'auront plus bezoin que du commandement du souverain pour retourner en giron de leur mère." De Laubardemont à Richelieu, Loudun, 20 Août 1634, *Catalogue des Autographes de la collection Morrisson,* III, 97, as quoted in E. Griselle, ed., *Louis XIII et Richelieu, lettres et pièces diplomatiques,* p. 41.

It is to the ostensible attitude of benevolence which masked his little-known hidden activity that Richelieu owes his reputation as an enlightened and generous ruler; but this appraisal does not take into account the "benevolence" which let loose on the Huguenots the malice and ill will of the governmental agents whose activity the Cardinal condoned.[64] At the same time the Council of State was allowed to pass special *arrêts* restricting the exercise of Calvinist rites or forbidding them altogether in various localities, in direct contradiction and violation of the Edict of Nantes.[65]

The struggle with the Protestants was continued underground, and contained little spirit of tolerance; there was also no sign that as such it ever troubled the Cardinal's heart; it had scarcely interfered with the period of organized peace within the framework of the strong monarchy he was slowly erecting. It was his *raison d'état*, and therefore any sinful action which it entailed had obtained in advance his full absolution. There ensued a period almost unfettered by overt expression of religious passions and hatred, which in itself was a remarkable achievement. This was the long religious armistice he had been so anxious to see realized, yet equally eager to undermine by his unobtrusive methods. The times certainly did not signify a revival of legal toleration, dormant since 1610. Hence, revisionist opinions representing Richelieu as an enlightened absolutist who intended that the Huguenots should be left to the full enjoyment of their rights, even those redefined in the newly restated codes, are erroneous. He intended nothing of the kind. He was truly totalitarian in his pursuit of an absolutist way of ruling. His treatment of various institutions, social groups, and sects, as well as of the people surrounding him, was symptomatic of his authoritarian outlook and behavior.

He defended the indivisibility of royal power against the encroachments of popular assemblies and the claims of social groups. He considered the States-General useless, and that of 1614 in particular as entirely futile—an opinion which was fairly commonly shared.

---

[64] Cf. Haag, *La France Protestante*, I, lxix (Pièce justificative No. LXXXIII, "Vexations exercés contre les Protestants depuis l'édit de 1629 jusqu'à la mort de Richelieu," *Pièces justificatives* [unnumbered volume], p. 354).

[65] See Viénot, *Histoire de la Réforme française*, II, 319–320, where he gives a survey of oppressive measures.

Ainsi ces Etats se terminèrent comme ils avoient commencés. La proposition en avoit été faite sous de spéciaux prétextes, sans aucune intention
d'en tirer avantage pour le service du Roi et du public, et la conclusion en
fut sans fruit, toute cette assemblée n'ayant eu d'autre effet sinon que de
surcharger les provinces de la taxe qu'il fallut payer à leurs députés et de
faire voir à tout le monde que ce n'est pas assez de connoître les maux si
on n'a la volonté d'y remédier.[66]

Acting consistently, he never convoked it. Of the parlement which
succeeded the States-General he was equally defiant, and he was
equally careful to exclude it from the sphere of indisputable and
unrestricted royal authority,[67] although he recognized its necessity:
"Parlement," he said, "en beaucoup d'occasions importantes est
nécessaire à la manutention de l'Etat." [68] He fought it with perseverance, but was never quite so successful as he was with the
States-General, which had disappeared completely. Reluctant to use
outright force against the parlement, he first tried gentle means;
by calling the assembly of notables in 1626, he hoped to run the
country while preserving a constitutional façade. But the assembly
ruined his good intentions by discussing the problem of the independence of the States-General from the king, and he felt bound to
dissolve it instantly. A prolonged struggle followed; the parlement
was duly subdued and "honorably overpowered," though never entirely defeated. It was revived after Richelieu's death and continued
to gain considerable political power until it was reduced to insignificance by Louis XIV soon after he attained his majority.

No social class was left uninfluenced by the ideas of Richelieu;
his conservatism, though dynamic, meant retrogression. Though
able to reshape French society and secure the interests of the
monarchy, his conservatism put shackles on various social groups,
particularly the Third Estate and the aristocracy. Only the latter
was able to shake off those shackles, not without considerable pain,
and only temporarily, during the Fronde. His revolutionary conceptions, though destroying the feudal fabric, were not truly progressive; for he was determined to keep the Third Estate at the bottom
of the social scale in a state of perpetual poverty and in conditions

---

[66] Richelieu, *Mémoires*, I, 367–368.

[67] "... il est important d'empêcher que les officiers de la justice n'empiètent sur
l'autorité du Roi." Richelieu, *Testament politique*, p. 247.

[68] Richelieu, *Mémoires*, V, 236.

incapable of improvement,[69] and at the same time to preserve the aristocracy at the top of the social scale,[70] amid plenty, but in a state of semiservitude, and with its activities restricted to military duties. Richelieu's measures against the aristocracy not only affected its future, but indirectly injured the Protestant movement, which was still connected with powerful families, though in a much looser way than in the previous century. Thus Calvinism, against which a separate plan was already operating, found itself under a flanking fire, and in a particularly vulnerable position. In consequence, the Calvinists sank lower, though less rapidly than the nobility taken as a whole; and whereas the latter rose again under Mazarin, the Protestant organization and society were reduced to a level from which they had no chance of revival under the *ancien régime*.

The relationship of Richelieu with the Catholic clergy, oscillating between extremes, shows his absolutist tendencies in practice. His consideration for the clergy as a consequence of his *esprit de corps* slightly lessened his impatience with the clergy's split into the Gallican and the ultramontane groups. Because he believed only in political Gallicanism, he could not give wholehearted support to either group. He was prepared to give the clergy its due, but he was on guard when the order of the state was at stake, or when the monarchy was threatened by being involved in a controversial dispute. The latter was the case in the conflict between the parlement and the clergy over the *Cardinalium, Archiepiscoporum . . . Sententia* of the royalist Bishop of Chartres, written on December 13, 1625.[71]

Kings not only are ordained by God, the *Sententia* insisted, but are themselves Gods: "Reges a Deo esse, praeter publicum omnium gentium, atque saeculorum consensum, etiam Prophetae denuntiant, Apostoli confirmant, Martyres confitentur, neque tantum a Deo, sed etiam Deos." [72]

The report of the Bishop of Chartres was approved by the

---

[69] "Tous les politiques sont d'accord que, si les peuples étoient trop à leur aise, il seroit impossible de les contenir dans les règles de leur devoir." Richelieu, *Testament politique*, p. 253.

[70] "Divers moyens d'avantager la noblesse pour la faire subsister avec dignité." *Ibid.*, p. 218.

[71] Cf. *Le Mercure Jésuite*, I, 794.

[72] *Ibid.*, p. 799.

parlement, which forbade the clergy to assemble again lest it change anything essential in the text. But the Assembly of the Clergy, disobeying the order, disavowed the report and worked out a new statement.[73] It condemned Sanctarellus' doctrine of the pope's absolute rights [74] as rendering the pope's dignity odious, opening the way to a schism and abrogating the royal sovereignty, which depended on God alone. The parlement then ordered the Assembly to dissolve. The Bishop of Chartres appealed to the clergy to sign his declaration that rebellion against the king is forbidden, that all subjects should obey the king, and that none may depose him.

But there was a lack of unanimity among the clergy on this issue.

> Le clergé étoit divisé. Le Parlement s'animoit contre l'Eglise, et la matière de la dispute touchoit l'autorité et la personne du Roi. Il falloit empêcher le schisme, réunir le clergé, maintenir l'autorité de l'Englise, et ne pas violer celle du Parlement ... Le Cardinal, intéressé en ces deux corps par la dignité qu'il a en l'Eglise et par la qualité de premier ministre de l'Etat ... par un sage temperament les mit d'accord.[75]

From the Bishop of Chartres, Richelieu extracted a written statement that his declaration of December 13, 1625, had in view simply the safety of the King. Seeing the majority of the clergy united against the Bishop of Chartres, he made a deliberate concession to the ultramontane point of view, though he would not depart from political Gallicanism. With a firmness which brooked no opposition, he rebuked the parlement for the role it had played in the conflict with the clergy,[76] and he managed to restore order.

As a corollary to the controversy, there followed what may be regarded as a comment on the events of 1626 put in doctrinal form by a man who was responsible for writing an outstanding apology for the rule of Richelieu: *De la souveraineté du Roy*. The controversy revolving around the Bishop of Chartres was reflected in Lebret's opinion that the clergy owed submission to the secular justice. "Aussi nous voyons que la pluspart des plus celebres Conciles

---

[73] "Facultas improbavit et damnavit doctrinam his propositionibus et horum capitum corollariis contentam, tanquam novam, falsam, erroneam, verbo Dei contrariam, Pontficiae dignitati odium conciliantem, schismati occasionem praebentem, supremae Regum auctoritati a Deo solo dependenti, derogantem." *Censura sacrae facultatis Theologiae Parisiensis. Le Mercure Jésuite*, I, 897–898.

[74] Cf. below.

[75] Richelieu, *Mémoires*, V, 236.

[76] Cf. *ibid.*, p. 237.

de l'Eglise ont esté confirmez et publiez au nom des Empereurs et des Roys ... Pourquoy ne fera-t'il pas iuste de les intimer en leur nom, comme l'on fait tous les autres Juges." [77]

Conversely, the change which had occurred in a decade from Lebret's mild monarchism to Marca's acute absolutism [78] was representative of the road which Richelieu himself traveled in the realm of practice: his authoritarian rule grew larger and vaster, as if it aimed at embracing the totality of life—an aim Richelieu never reached, but toward which he was well advanced. What were the factors holding back this process, continuous in his lifetime and expanding after his death? They were, first, the natural opposition of powerful elements, like the clergy, which Richelieu was unable to control completely, and second, his prudent policy, which in pursuit of surer though slower results made him avoid acting rashly.

His attitude to the Jesuits was typical. He treated them in a much gentler way than might have been expected of him, and always avoided oppression and violence, through fear of their revenge. He desired to break their force and bridle them, but he never planned any annihilatory coup, because then they would be no longer useful but only dangerous in their desperation.[79] He defended the Jesuits against the parlement when in 1626 it sought their expulsion after the publication of Sanctarellus' *Tractatus de haeresi* (1625), in which the Italian Jesuit proclaimed the absolute power of the pope over temporal rulers. "Principes omnes sunt subiecti potestati spirituali Romani Pontificis," wrote Sanctarellus.[80] The treatise asserted very bluntly that the pope exercises controlling and corrective powers over princes; that he can annul and revoke those laws made by princes which are contrary to custom; that he can brand incompetence; that he can also punish heretic rulers in the temporal sphere by deposing them and by freeing their subjects from allegiance. By divine law the pope has both spiritual and temporal power: "In summo Pontifice iure divino est utraque potestas spiritualis & temporalis." [81] Over spiritual matters he exercises direct, supreme, and absolute control. "Romanus Pontifex in administra-

---

[77] Cardinal Lebret, *De la souveraineté du Roy*, pp. 79–81.

[78] Cf. below.

[79] Richelieu, *Maximes d'Etat*, pp. 74–75.

[80] Antonio Sanctarellus, *Tractatus de haeresi, schismate, apostasi sollicitatione in sacramento poenitentiae, et de potestate Romani Pontificis*, p. 290.

[81] *Ibid.*, p. 298.

tione rerum spiritualium directe supremam habet potestatem, tempo-
ralem vero nonnisi indirecte, nempe quatenus necesse est uti gladio,
& potestati temporali ad defendendam & conservandam potestatem
spiritualem." [82] His indirect control in the temporal sphere provides
safeguards for his spiritual powers. "Summus Pontifex propter
potestatem, quam habet in Principes, potest etiam in temporalibus
eos dirigere ad finem spiritualem." [83]

The Jesuits complied with the order of Richelieu, rejecting the
doctrine contained in the *Tractatus,* and thus saved themselves
from expulsion. With frankness Richelieu himself gave the King
the reasons for his defense and toleration of the Jesuits, his primary
argument being the usefulness of such an action. Such an argument,
of course, could be applied to other religious groups.

> Le Cardinal dit au Roi qu'il y a certains abus qu'on abolit plus aisément
> en les tolérant qu'en les voulant détruire ouvertement; que bien qu'aucuns
> fois on sache des opinions être mauvaises, il est dangereux de s'y opposer,
> principalement quand elles sont colorées du prétexte de religion. La
> raison de ce conseil aboutissoit à ce qu'il falloit réduire les Jésuits en un
> état qu'ils ne puissent nuire par puissance, mais tel aussi qu'ils ne se
> portassent pas à le faire par désespoir. [84]

Despite similarities in form, his attitude to various religious
groups differed in content. Richelieu might treat with an assumed
magnanimity both the Jesuits and the Protestants, but his motives
and his purpose varied in each case. The Jesuits were left in relative
peace because they were powerful, influential, and useful; Richelieu
conceived no plan for their complete destruction, though he entertained the idea of curbing their extensive powers. They had to be
tolerated, as did some of their dangerous moves and beliefs directed
against the independent secular powers; in respect to this opposition,
Richelieu's toleration was merely a ruse to ensure results, but it was
because of the real power of the Jesuits that such a ruse was necessary. The Calvinists had no such asset; they were only a threat and
were doomed to perish just as other groups, weaker and less dangerous to the state, had perished at the hands of Richelieu. The Richer-
ist movement was destroyed for its aristocratic conceptions of the
Church, which the Cardinal feared might be translated into the
skeleton of a civil government; the Quietists (1623–1636) were

---

[82] *Ibid.,* p. 300.

[83] *Ibid.,* p. 291.

[84] Richelieu, *Mémoires,* V, 245.

destroyed for their false spirituality, their negation of civic and moral virtues, and consequently for the deleterious effect on society and the state; the Jansenists, for their mixture of Calvinism and stoicism, were reduced to a narrow "libertine" basis.[85] Having ordered the arrest of Abbot Saint-Cyran, the leader of the Jansenists, Richelieu uttered the following significant words: "Quoi qu'il en soit, j'ai la conscience assuré d'avoir rendu service à l'Eglise et à l'Etat. On aurait remédié à bien des malheurs et des désordres si l'on avait fait emprisonner Luther et Calvin, dès qu'ils commencèrent à dogmatiser." [86]

This passage is most revealing. It shows Richelieu's bent for unscrupulous authoritarian action, supposedly in the public interest, which he justified from the standpoint of *raison d'état*. It reveals his deep concern for the problem of subduing all uncontrollable elements, the Protestants in particular, which for the sake of the state could not always be dealt with radically. It reflects his conviction that he would allow himself more stringent measures than before; the day was not long past when he had promised the King not to negotiate any longer with the Huguenots. "Qu'il [Richelieu] avoit supplié le Roi de l'excuser des négociations que, par le passé, il avoit faites avec les huguenots rebelles, protestant n'y en vouloir plus à l'avenir." [May, 1629.] [87] Manifest, too, is his passion for strong, decisive measures to solve the urgent needs of government [88]—a passion which was always restrained, of course, by some ulterior motive. It throws light on the discrepancy between his tyrannical attitude toward his entourage [89] and his apparent "toleration."

---

[85] Cf. Fagniez, *Le Père Joseph et Richelieu*, II, 73.

[86] Richelieu à Hardouin de Beaumont de Péréfixe, 14 mai 1638, as quoted in Fagniez, *Le Père Joseph et Richelieu*, II, 73.

[87] Richelieu, *Mémoires*, IX, 209.

[88] Among these the Protestant question and its relation to absolute rule was always one of the most important issues. Richelieu had stressed it previously on several occasions: "... tant que les huguenots auroient le pied en France, le Roi ne seroit jamais le maitre au dedans ni ne pourroit entreprendre aucune action glorieuse au dehors." [1625] Richelieu, *Mémoires*, V, 29. "Que c'étoit chose certaine que tant que le parti des huguenots subsisteroit en France, le Roi ne seroit point absolu dans son royaume." [1625] *ibid.*, p. 182.

[89] "Nous vivons ici dans la plus étrange servitude du monde et nous avons affaire au plus grand tyran qui fut jamais," wrote Chévret, Richelieu's secretary. Tallement des Réaux, *Le Cardinal de Richelieu*, Collection des Chefs-d'oeuvre méconnus (Paris, 1920), p. 100.

The principle of a *raison d'état* which would justify any arbitrary action, if expedient and in the public not a private interest, was defended by Balzac in his *Le Prince* and by Gabriel Naudé: "la considération du bien et de l'utilité publique passe ... par dessus celles du particulier."[90] In the eyes of Richelieu, reasons of state also justified pretense and concealment in the form of a pseudo-toleration. Doubtless he went further than intended by these two exponents of the principle he himself practiced extensively and successfully in actual politics. He was successful because his rule possessed many suggestions of toleration. One of them was his reputation as a man of toleration, which he earned primarily through the lack of certain qualities which make a man intolerant: he disliked bloodshed and all violence, although he often used force. He betrayed in the sphere of international relations those characteristics that one would emphatically deny him in respect to his own subjects; he would quite gladly suffer Protestant foreigners, provided they remained abroad.[91] By paving the way to the Treaty of Westphalia, which was to create, after his death, a balance between the two religions in Europe,[92] he was prepared to give to other nations what he was withholding from the French; he was thus constructing abroad what he was destroying at home.

What cannot be denied, however, was his refraining from petty oppressions. Endowed with a sense of justice, he was not blind to social wrongs,[93] and he never stooped to the small vexations which were still locally inflicted on the religious minority. Indeed, central government in those days greatly surpassed local authorities in the matter of toleration.[94]

Richelieu was concerned with the maintenance of the validity of legal rules and, within their limits, he was even of some help to the Reformed church.[95] The annual subvention of 200,000 livres

[90] Gabriel Naudé, *Considérations politiques sur les coups d'Etat,* pp. 100–101.

[91] In March, 1634, the parlement of Paris made a decree that no foreign minister should perform his functions in France. Cf. Benoit, *The Edict of Nantes,* II, 503.

[92] Cf. Bridges, *France under Richelieu and Colbert,* p. 152.

[93] He was, for instance, a partisan of a more equal system of taxation than the existing *taille* and the *gabelle* from which the nobility and the clergy were exempted. Cf. *ibid.,* p. 61.

[94] "Il est plus facile aux réformés de devenir conseillers de parlement que maitres tailleurs ou contrôleurs des gabelles." D'Avenel, *Richelieu et la monarchie absolue,* III, 407.

[95] According to d'Avenel, the help received by the Protestants from the state under Richelieu equaled the assistance they received in the nineteenth century. Cf. *ibid.,* pp. 408–409.

was for some time paid regularly, and the Calvinists in the South, endowed with considerable church property and other sources of revenue, could provide for the needs of their less fortunate brethren in other provinces. The result was that Protestant ministers were to a considerable degree more highly remunerated than their Catholic counterparts—a fact Richelieu did not deplore, because winning over the Huguenot clergy was part of his scheme. "Il est plus facile," he said, "de ruiner les huguenots en gagnant les ministres que par les armées." [96] Understanding the great truth that persecutions are economically detrimental,[97] he gave the Huguenots full economic freedom, of which they made all the better use now that they were debarred from the benefits of full political freedom.

Unwittingly directing them into new tasks and giving them no alternative but to excel in their new industrial and commercial specialties, he gave French industry and commerce a vital if brief impulse. Moreover, he pushed the Protestants toward the acquisition of material wealth and practical skill, the basis of those capital assets which, increasing from generation to generation, made the life of Protestant *émigrés* abroad in the days of Louis XIV both bearable from their own point of view and desirable from that of their countries of exile.

Finally, the contemporaries of Richelieu were under a constant fire of propaganda, which, while describing his tolerant intentions, was intended to divert public attention from the real design that could be pieced together by a sober observer. Hidden by the propaganda agitation, the behind-the-scenes action of Richelieu was furnishing those precedents which pushed the Edict of Nantes on its downward course.

The Protestants were maneuvered into a position in which they believed that their loyalty and strict obedience would ensure religious liberty. The Edict of Alais had played an official part in an action designed to trap the Huguenots by reassuring them that their

---

[96] Quoted *ibid.*, p. 417.

[97] This aspect of Richelieu's thought and activity had never been given adequate and proper attention until the publication of H. Hauser's *La Pensée et l'action économiques cardinal de Richelieu*, which seems to do him justice. Hauser dismisses the view in which the Cardinal appeared as an irresponsible statesman, ignorant of economic issues and particularly incapable of understanding finances. Richelieu's attitude to the Protestant minority, his appeasement in the religious sphere after 1629, and his quasi-toleration were certainly not unconnected with his work of laying the foundations for the country's economy, which was to be expanded brilliantly, if with less vision, by his successor in the economic sphere, Colbert.

freedom of conscience would be left intact; the series of subsequent moves aimed directly at that right was the beginning of a process which was to prove fatal because it found the victim powerless and only half-aware of what was at stake. The stealthy and secretive character of those moves should be noted. When Richelieu finally succumbed to the fanatic missionary zeal of Father Joseph, and made him Minister for Conversions and the Restoration of the Catholic Faith, the door was left open for further action designed to destroy the Huguenots. Although excesses of persecution were rare, the gradual long-term plan must have come from Richelieu, who put into operation the counsels of the Plan Codur, which he had adopted in its entirety.[98]

The execution of this plan had every chance of success, for Richelieu combined assent to Codur's belief in the effectiveness of withholding the yearly grant to the Huguenot church, with an innate faith in the power of money.[99] In fact, the annual subvention of 200,000 livres, suppressed in 1627, became a reduced grant of 60,000 livres in 1631.[100] At the same time, he spared no expense in winning to his side the individual ministers, thinking this to be a direct road to the ruin of the Huguenot church. He approved of subsidized conversions, both individual and collective, hoping that they would become general. The Congrégation de la Propagation de la Foi, founded in 1632 by the Capuchin, Father Hyacinthe, often resorted to force in conducting its activities, but Richelieu hoped that a general conversion might be effected peacefully. He expected to achieve it as a result of a monster congress he was carefully preparing. Piloted by a certain number of the Calvinist clergy previously won over by Richelieu and Father Joseph,[101] the congress was meant to be a spectacular declaration of union of the Protestant and the Catholic churches. The trial congress undertaken at the provincial synod of Charenton, in September, 1631, was a failure. The thirty influential ministers, though "converted" to the

---

[98] Cf. Richelieu, *Maximes d'Etat*, No. CXXXVII, as cited in Fagniez, *Le Père Joseph et Richelieu*, I, 431.

[99] "Sans argent on ne fait rien ..." Richelieu, *Mémoires*, VI, 321.

[100] Cf. E. Arnaud, *Histoire des protestants de Provence, du comtat venaissin et de la principauté d'Orange*, I, 387.

[101] According to Benoit, eighty Protestant ministers were won over by Richelieu: "And there are Memoirs that shew the number of the Ministers thus gained to be about fourscore." Benoit, *The Edict of Nantes*, II, 475.

cause, could not cope with the majority of the other representatives. Possibly their number was too small, or perhaps the move was premature—an opinion held by the papal Nuncio.[102]

Although success eluded Richelieu at Charenton, the synod gave him the opportunity of exercising pressure in many directions and of prying closely into the affairs of the Protestant church. Its freedom was impaired by that strict administrative control of all proceedings, to which Richelieu, by bearing the cost of the assembly,[103] had acquired the title. On the whole it was mainly through administrative channels that Richelieu's intolerance found expression, rather than through open persecution.[104] It was impersonal, less obviously cruel, and better suited to the atmosphere of semiofficial oppression practiced by the higher ranks of administration. Of this, the occurrences at the national synod of Alençon, in May, 1637, are a particularly incriminating testimony: the royal commissioner made a point of forbidding criticism of and blame for any action of the government and its magistrates, even if the action seemingly impinged on the liberty of conscience. The use, both oral and in print, of words such as "torments," "martyrs," and "persecutions" was forbidden. This move was a prelude to a marked deterioration of the Huguenots' liberty to practice their religion.[105] It probably suited Richelieu's more pious disposition after the death of Father Joseph, in 1636, when he started to write his *Traitté qui contient la méthode la plus facile et la plus asseurée pour convertir ceux qui se sont séparez de l'Eglise.*

The *Traitté* was a theological treatise with a political significance. Laboring during the last years of his life over the *Traitté*, Richelieu had in mind the execution of the second stage in the process of stamping out heresy; the rebellion being already quelled, it was the conversion of the heretics which was still unfulfilled. "Comme l'heresie qui attaque l'Eglise incessamment employe contre elle deux sortes d'armes: l'erreur pour combattre ses véritez, et la rebellion

---

[102] Cf. Fagniez, *Le Père Joseph et Richelieu*, I, 433.

[103] On the Charenton synod see Benoit, *The Edict of Nantes*, II, 480 ff.

[104] "Ce fut encore Richelieu qui établit pour maxime dans le gouvernement de n'accorder aux Réformés les grandes dignités de la Cour et des Armés que dans des cas extraordinaires ... On érigea en principe d'Administration l'exécution rigoureuse de cette clause." Rulhière, *Eclaircissemens historiques*, pp. 17–18.

[105] Cf. S. Beaujour, *Essai sur l'Histoire de l'Eglise réformée de Caen* (Caen, 1877), pp. 217–218.

pour resister à la puissance legitime qu'elle trouve contraire a ses desseins ... le cardinal de Richelieu ... arrachait ces deux sortes d'armes à l'heresie." [106]

In spite of occasional, local incidents of intolerance, this disposition never pushed Richelieu to open persecution. He might have approved of some stronger means now and then, as he had done before,[107] but the plan of conversions never became an extreme measure. The general impression it creates is that of a series of half measures very carefully and somewhat timidly executed. Except for the Charenton mass-conversion scheme, which miscarried, emphasis was never put on speed. Carefully laid plans were never rushed, in order that their effectiveness could reach more widely and deeply. Furthermore, it was easier to proclaim in public, with truly Machiavellian ingenuity, the principle of toleration. By 1638 the lifework of Richelieu as a statesman may be said to have been finished. The Huguenots were left, it would seem, almost unhurt, even thriving. Indeed the Cardinal did not require violent measures or Huguenot martyrs. The prey was already half-strangled, and the kill was only a matter of time.

The absolutist doctrine was on the ascendant.

THE ASCENDANCY OF THE THEORY
OF ABSOLUTISM: LEBRET, MARCA, RICHELIEU

The problem of how the idea of toleration was reflected in the policies of Richelieu has been dealt with in detail because it found in them its main expression. The toleration controversy disappeared from the doctrinal stage as completely as the dispute over the problem of sovereignty. The concept of sovereignty indeed reappeared in the prevailing royalist doctrines, but, as the latter were generally accepted, it caused no dispute. It was only reasserted

---

[106] Richelieu, *Traitté qui contient la méthode la plus facile et la plus asseurée pour convertir ceux qui se sont séparez de l'Eglise,* advertissement.

[107] Fagniez stresses that a letter of Father Joseph in 1629 indicates that Richelieu sponsored conversions and was in favor of separation of Protestant children. Cf. Fagniez, *Le Père Joseph et Richelieu,* I, 423.

now and again. But the concept of toleration was hidden in deep silence. It obviously needed the background of wider political dispute which the problems of sovereignty and of obedience to the ruler had provided earlier. The possibility of disobedience being now ruled out, there was no logical need to start a dispute over toleration. The political doctrines of the day formed only a side issue, and were not immediately related to the religious policies. The latter represented the slow and steady progress of Richelieu's absolutism, which both prevented religious controversy and jeopardized the future of the Protestants.

The system was created by an elaborate plan which coped with the enormous problem of giving France a new political form. It did not spring up overnight. The whole life of the Cardinal was devoted to this single aim. The determination to find a solution of the Protestant problem was a single but necessary element in the whole pattern. It was mentioned by the Cardinal in the oft-quoted phrase, as one of his four main designs: "... ruiner le parti huguenot, rabaisser l'orgueil des Grands, réduire tous ses sujets [ceux du roi] en leur devoir et relever son nom dans les nations étrangères au point où il devoit être." [108] As a problem of such magnitude, the Protestant question could not have been summarily dismissed. Although formally the Huguenot party was destroyed within five years, the Cardinal's preoccupation with the Huguenot problem filled all his years in office. It was solved only temporarily. In fact, when his life was nearing its close the problem was still virtually unsolved.

But technically the solution of the Protestant problem was ready when the rule of Richelieu ended. This solution was to be found in the very system which the Cardinal had created. It was from the spreading absolutist doctrine that twilight finally descended upon Protestants. The manner in which it was done and the speed of performance are in direct relation to the manner and tempo of the development of the absolutist theory of the state. Subsequent developments under Louis XIV provide obvious evidence in favor of such an assertion: every outburst of triumphant monarchism, limited in the time of Mazarin and almost unlimited under Louis XIV, marked a further step toward the extinction of the Protestants. Finally, with absolutism reaching its climax after the revocation

---

[108] Richelieu, *Testament politique,* p. 95.

of the Edict of Nantes, the silence of the Huguenots was broken, and the toleration controversy was begun again in the form of doctrines and schools, much like the disputes at the time of the first wars of religion.

In the days of Richelieu there was no toleration controversy. The ostensible tolerance of Richelieu was perhaps the main reason for its absence. But there were also no great philosophical defenders of absolutism, and there was little dispute around the latter issue.

Richelieu was a great man of action who built up a system and created a working organism with very little theoretical background. But alongside his creative work in the field of political practice, he encouraged a host of writers to expound the subjects he had given them, which justified, amplified, anticipated, commented upon, or otherwise aided his course. Still, the body of doctrines was limited. There was more of absolutism in the air than justification for it in written form.

Perhaps only the writings of the jurist Lebret pretend to independence and originality. His was the best doctrinal account of Richelieu's political practice. He gave a serious comment on the nature of sovereignty, to which he ascribed divine right and which he regarded as total and unrestrained ("parfaite et accomplie"). It is to be taken for a constant factor, he argued, that the French kings recognize no superior but the Divine Majesty which makes them fully sovereign.

Starting with that assumption, Lebret endeavored to find a recipe for the best government in the legislative sphere, to which he desired royal sovereignty to belong. His views can be summarized in the formula that the king belongs to God [109] and that laws belong to the king—an essentially Gallican doctrine. On the basis of divine right, lawmaking was vested solely in the royal sovereign, to the exclusion of all other bodies or persons in the state; for participation in lawmaking would mean sharing in sovereignty—an inadmissible situation because sovereignty is as indivisible as a point in geometry. Obedience to the prince is unconditional, because subjects have no right to judge his legislation. Law is enforced by compulsion. The alternative—disobedience—is ruled out. The prince can equally make and unmake law. He can abrogate, change, limit, or interpret

---

[109] "On ne doit attribuer le nom et la qualité d'une Souveraineté parfaite et accomplie, qu'à celles qui ne dépendent que de Dieu seul, et qui ne sont subjectes qu'à ses loix." Lebret, *De la souveraineté du Roy*, p. 9.

it,[110] as it is all a matter of his sovereignty. In short, he can do with legal rules anything he pleases.

Although Lebret did not admit it, the *lex regia* principle in fact led straight to absolute power. But Lebret, though a monarchist, was not ostensibly a partisan of unlimited absolutist power. His Gallicanism found expression in his opinion that the clergy owed submission to the secular justice in the "appels comme d'abus," [111] that is, against abuses of ecclesiastical courts, but he did not push it a step further and link the independence of temporal power with the dogmas of absolutism. The spirit of his *De la souveraineté du Roy*, when it was published in 1632, was in agreement with the political spirit of Richelieu in that it expressed no extreme principles.

By fostering political pamphlets or learned treatises, Richelieu created opportunities for testing out his projected plans. If the reaction they caused provided justification for his actions, well and good; if not, he would assert his authority without it. When, in 1640, Richelieu asked Marca to answer Optatus Gallus, the author [112] of *De Cavendo Schismate*,[113] he was no longer leading a war of pamphlets, as at the outset (1625–1626), when he had been fighting for power. He was now popularizing some of his conceptions on monarchical power which had matured and which were a part of the legacy he left.

The book that provoked the discussion was the compilatory work inspired by Richelieu and written by Dupuy, *Commentaire sur le traité des Libertez de l'Eglise Gallicane de Pierre Pithou* (1639), which contained his three principal rules of Gallicanism. Dupuy claimed, first, that the popes have no temporal power: "Les Papes ne peuvent rien commander, ny ordonner, soit en général ou en particulier de ce qui concerne les choses temporelles." [114] Second, he asserted that in France, although spiritually sovereign, the pope is limited by the canons of past councils.[115] The third rule was that the kings of France, having no temporal superiors, are endowed

---

[110] Cf. *ibid.*, chap. ix.

[111] *Ibid.*, p. 80.

[112] His real name was Charles Hersent. Cf. F. Gaquère, *Pierre de Marca (1594–1662)*, p. 85.

[113] Optatus Gallus, *De Cavendo Schismate, ad illustrissimos ac reverendissimos Ecclesiae Gallicanae Primates, Archiepiscopos, Episcopos, liber paroeniticus.*

[114] Pierre Dupuy, *Commentaire*, p. 13.

[115] Cf. *ibid.*, p. 20.

with executive power with respect to the canons.[116] Having described the maxims of the Gallican church, Dupuy devised means which would serve as a guarantee that its liberties would be preserved. Among them he mentioned amicable conferences with the pope, confirmation of papal bulls by the king, appeals to future councils, and checks on ecclesiastical power by "appellations précises comme d'abus." [117]

Dupuy's book was condemned by the clergy of France. Optatus Gallus' reply, *De Cavendo Schismate,* was also used by its author to "reveal" Richelieu's design to assume the role of a patriarch of the Gallican church. The author was condemned by the parlement in 1640; whereupon Marca was engaged by Richelieu to make a reply.

Marca was not, like Lebret, a solitary philosopher, thinking out long-term solutions expressed in political doctrines which reflected an anxiety to secure the most stable government. At the instigation of Richelieu, he was prepared to extemporize a defense for any extreme doctrines and to refute them if necessary. His book, *De Concordia sacerdotii et imperii, seu de libertatibus ecclesiae gallicanae* (1641), was an extremely able and bold attempt to find a common basis for the spiritual and temporal powers. By declaring identical the sources of the two powers, he created a reason for the further assertion that their sovereignty is equal.

But later Marca made a reservation which carried him outside the range of most Gallicans. Describing political power as derived from God, he maintained that this power comes to the king directly, not through the intermediary of society. To Marca, the notion was untenable that a power may be diffused or made conditional at the intermediate stage through some sort of social compact with a body politic. Such a process he saw as a direct attack on the liberty and authority of the king.[118] He insisted, therefore, that the royal power is conferred by God immediately on kings: "Unicuique Regum potestatem Regiam immediate a Divino numine conferri." [119]

---

[116] Cf. *ibid.,* pp. 36–37.

[117] For the four guarantees, see *ibid.,* pp. 181, 183, 185, and 187, respectively.

[118] "Quae sententia libertatem Regum aliquo pacto imminuit, dignitatem violat, factionibus vires subministrat, imo & in ipsas scripturas sacras peccare videtur, quae Deo imperium uniuscuiusque Principis ascribunt." Petro de Marca, *De Concordia sacerdotii et imperii,* p. 147.

[119] *Ibid.*

Dispensing at one stroke with the concepts of the people and of the social contract, Marca created a precedent for thinking in terms of absolutism. Though the vehemence of the argument may have been his own, the main responsibility for the book was certainly Richelieu's, for the Cardinal had commissioned it. The comprehension of the existing links between independent and absolute temporal power was essentially the Cardinal's, rather than the author's.

Richelieu, as has been said, found his main preoccupation in shaping political events, and throughout his life his actions gave strength to his ideas. From the former, in addition, he drew certain conclusions which were scattered in his *Maximes,* the bulk of which was left in the form of his political will, known as *Testament politique.*

The *Testament politique* showed some flaws in the absolutist theory of Richelieu. It was not a book expounding a pure doctrine in its final form, but, like the *Maximes,* written earlier, a companion to his political action. Voltaire, obviously not ready to accept the absolutist view, detected a number of contradictions and fallacies, and argued therefore that Richelieu could not have been its author. The *Testament politique* was not meant for publication [120]—a fact of profound significance. The full sense of the doctrine which it contained had meaning only for the new ruler trained in the spirit of absolutism.

The first edition of the *Testament politique* appeared in 1688, in Holland, from the press of a Protestant exile publisher.[121] The fact that it was published at the height of the absolutist rule of Louis XIV had a peculiar effect. Ruthless authoritarianism had advanced so far, compared with the milder forms introduced by Richelieu, that it was possible for the *Testament politique* to be published by a Protestant and used by his coreligionists in support of their own cause after the Revocation!

The first publication of the *Testament politique* registered another, if posthumous, triumph for Richelieu, but the appeal made to his memory had a false tone. An uncalled-for meaning and an exaggerated importance were attached to the bloodless measures of which the Cardinal spoke when referring to conversions.[122] The

---

[120] Cf. Richelieu, *Testament politique,* préface, p. 11; introduction, p. 36.

[121] Henry Desbordes, a native of Saumur, emigrant in 1682, later librarian in Amsterdam.

[122] Richelieu, *Testament politique,* p. 323.

fact that his policy was quoted as a remedy for the ills caused by Louis XIV had a touch of irony. The first publishers of Richelieu's "will" were unaware of the absolutist legacy he left, of the King's acceptance of it, and of the way in which it condoned and justified decisive action against the Protestants.

Voltaire's refusal to accept the *Testament politique* as a genuine work of Richelieu must have followed, in part, from his reluctance to accept Richelieu as a champion of a limited toleration, which the publishers desired to imply. However, it was not that Voltaire found the book an antiabsolutist work, which in his view Richelieu would never have written, but that he considered the contradictory and false statements unworthy of a great statesman.

The book is certainly no plea for popular government. It is a prescription for good ruling, given on the assumption that the interest of a monarch is in line with the public interest and identical with that of the state. The monarch's supreme power was considered by Richelieu, in his address to Louis XIII, as a remedy for all ills: "Connaissant ce que peuvent les Rois lorsqu'ils usent bien de leur puissance, j'osai vous promettre, sans témérité à mon avis, que vous trouveriez remède aux désordres de votre Etat." [123] Further, the king is above law and not bound by legal measures. It is advisable for him to resort to special commissions to maintain discipline.[124] Royal power has no limits. Though the liberties of the Gallican church must be preserved, royal power should prevail over that of the church. It must, however, be imposed with moderation, as Richelieu explained when discussing the use of the *parlements* as courts of appeal in case of "appels comme d'abus": "Il sera d'autant plus avantageux à V. M. qu'en contenant la puissance de l'Eglise dans ses propres bornes, elle éteindra aussi celle des parlements dans la juste étendue." [125]

All public assemblies and public bodies were ruled out by the author of the *Testament politique,* since they obstructed royal power. The States-General had been scornfully rejected elsewhere as useless.[126] Parlements, being judicial bodies with no knowledge

---

[123] *Ibid.,* p. 95.

[124] Cf. *ibid.,* pp. 245–246.

[125] *Ibid.,* p. 168.

[126] "La trop grande corruption des siècles n'y apporte pas d'empêchement." Richelieu, *Mémoires,* I, 368.

of government, should be deprived of political power.[127] The leading principle in politics is the *raison d'état,* which means equating the public good with the interest of the king as the personification of the state—a principle which takes little account of the good of the individual. Not being greatly interested in the improvement of the life of his subjects, Richelieu found in his main political principle reasons for abstaining from social reforms which might have been detrimental to the public good as he understood it.

The *Testament politique* was absolutism in a nutshell. As such, it was not meant for circulation, but was designed primarily for the Dauphin and was to achieve its aim later in circumstances ripe for royal absolutism. It was not intended to bring absolutist theories to public notice, although actually they did already form part of the general current of opinion at the time.

A leading representative of the absolutist doctrine, Richelieu cleverly contrived to prevent the controversy over toleration from reappearing, in spite of his destruction of the Huguenot party; while at the same time he postponed the dispute about absolutism, which he had so successfully established in the practical field. Richelieu refrained from blunt statements of absolutist doctrines. Even the ideas of Marca led to absolutism only by implication. In his own writings Richelieu used his absolutist vocabulary sparingly. But he took care to create an atmosphere of absolutism in which he deemed it necessary for the new monarch to be educated. In the hands of Louis XIV, the maxim of Richelieu that "la perte des particuliers n'est pas comparable au salut public" [128] became the basis for a formula applicable to the Huguenot case. That maxim was reinforced by the statement from the *Testament politique* [129] concerning the duty of all sovereigns to encourage conversions, but it was divested of those mellow qualifications which the manuscript contained. The spirit of "douceur" in conversions, with which, according to the *Testament politique,* a monarch is to act, has been, since 1688, repeatedly attributed to the action of Richelieu himself—an attribution leading to fundamental misconceptions about his religious policy.

---

[127] Cf. Richelieu,*Testament politique,* p. 248.
[128] Richelieu, *Maximes d'Etat,* No. CXXV.
[129] Cf. Richelieu, *Testament politique,* p. 323.

IV

MAZARIN: THE TRIUMPH
OF MONARCHISM

*"Les Reformez ne demandoient qu'à vivre en repos: trop
contens si on les eût laissé jouir tranquillement de ce qui
leur étoit accordé par les Édits."*—Elie Benoit, *Histoire
de l'edit de Nantes, III, 6.*

*"La maxime fondamentale de la Politique nouvelle étoit
que les sujets ont toujours tort; et qu'ils ne peuvent être
innocens quoi qu'ils fassent, quand le Souverain veut qu'ils
soient coupables."*—*Ibid., p. 14.*

THE HUGUENOTS UNDER MAZARIN

Although it seemed obvious that the future of the Huguenots must
be precarious, the likelihood might have been less certain of ful-
fillment had not the policies of Richelieu been strictly pursued by
his successors.

It is puzzling that a man so universally hated—a man whose
death occasioned a sigh of relief from many,[1] including Louis XIII
—was so faithfully obeyed when the terror of his absolute rule was
no longer present. His political will was executed with amazing
accuracy. Mazarin entirely, and Louis XIV to a large degree, continued his policy; the work of a host of statesmen, including Colbert
and Louvois, fits well into one structure resting on a foundation of
which Richelieu was the architect. Louis XIII, although he barely
outlived Richelieu, had time to sanction the continuation of the
latter's policy.[2] It was natural for Mazarin, who was the protégé

---

[1] Guy Patin wrote fourteen years later: "Le cardinal de Richelieu n'en avait que 57
et n'a vécu que 30 ans plus qu'il n'étoit besoin pour le bien de la France et même de
toute l'Europe." Quoted in Pierre Pic, *Guy Patin*, p. 169.

[2] "... la mort de Monsieur le Cardinal. Quoique le Roi en eût une joie incroyable, il
voulut conserver toutes les apparences: il ratifia les legs que ce ministre avait faits des

of Richelieu, to continue on the same track; he was not a man to break away. He continued where Richelieu had left off, rigidly keeping to the course already set. The same *raisons d'état* remained valid under his rule. The parlement, the nobles, and the Huguenots continued to be, in his estimation as they had been in Richelieu's, the main threats to the central government.[3] Anxious to protect the power of the monarchy against encroachments from these quarters,[4] he was particularly aware of the Huguenot problem, insisting on that complete Protestant obedience which he regarded as a condition of all royal favors and concessions.[5]

To reassure the Huguenots and create good will, Mazarin declared himself a lover of peaceful measures and tranquillity.[6] In 1646, by stressing the King's impartiality in the treatment of his subjects, he refuted rumors circulating in the United Provinces to the effect that the government had promised the Pope to massacre the Calvinists.[7] His dislike of violent action was even more pronounced than Richelieu's, and he remained more true to his nature

---

charges et des gouvernements; il caressa tous ses proches, il maintint dans le ministère toutes ses créatures ..." Cardinal de Retz, *Mémoires*, ed. by Maurice Allem, p. 39.

[3] "Il parlamento, li principi, li governatori di provinzie, ed il partito di Ugonotti et altri procurano disfare, sotto altri pretesi speciosi, quello si fece in tempo del re defunto per lo stabilimento dell' assoluta authorità sua independente da tutti, e vogliono ridurre le cose come nel tempo che la Francia, benche in apparenza governata da un re, in effecto era republica." 2ᵉ "Carnet," to Anne of Austria, pp. 43–44, as quoted in P. A. Chéruel and G. d'Avenel, eds., *Lettres du Cardinal Mazarin*, I, cxix. Hereafter cited as Mezarin, *Lettres*.

[4] "Se S. M. non vi prendre remedio, il parlamento et li grandi havranno troppa authorità." 2ᵉ "Carnet," p. 10. In Mazarin, *Lettres*, I, cxix.

[5] "Aussy vous et tous les autres de vostre religion, vous devez vous asseurer que vous trouverez tousjours l'esprit de la Reyne très disposé à vous proteger et a vous faire ressentir les effets de sa bienveillance proportionnés au zèle que vous tesmoignerez au service du Roy son fils." Mazarin à MM les officiers de la Religion de la Chambre de l'Edit de Castres, 19 nov. 1643. Bibl. Mazarine, MS 1719, I, fol. 137ᵛ, in Mazarin, *Lettres*, I, 457.

"La bonté de la Reyne embrasse generalement et sans distinction tous les vrais subjects du Roy, son fils, et la preferance qui se peut gagner dans son esprit despend du degré de la passion et de la fidelité qu'on aura pour son service ..." Mazarin à MM de la R.P.R., 12 sept. 1644. Bibl. Mazarine, MS 1719, III, fol. 350ᵛ, in Mazarin, *Lettres*, II, 62–63.

[6] "Et pour moy ... je vous proteste que je contribueray tousjours comme j'ay fait jusques icy mes conseils et mon credit pour faire fleurir cette concorde et regner cette tranquillité." Mazarin, *Lettres*, II, 63.

[7] Mazarin to Brasset, December 21, 1646, Mazarin, *Lettres*, II, 341–344.

than had his predecessor. Eager partisan of Protestant conversion though he was, he never resorted to force in carrying out his plans, as Richelieu had done. Like the latter, he had not that innate proselytizing zeal which comes from a deep religious spirit, such as Father Joseph's. But, while Richelieu had the Capuchin to guide his proselytism, Mazarin had only the example of the political teacher in whose steps he was following scrupulously and faithfully; it was that which helped him to create an impersonal standard of behavior, based on the pattern of Richelieu's policies. His intentions were formed in the same spirit; his carrying out of the scheme of conversion had accordingly this characteristic predominance of the political over the religious motive.[8]

This almost perfect understanding of the designs of the deceased Cardinal does not fully account for the way in which Mazarin treated the Huguenot problem. What made his task easier was the sense of security so deeply ingrained in the Huguenots that even the Fronde did not present itself to them as an opportunity to avert danger by an armed uprising. In 1650 the Calvinists were royalist to the core. They believed that the promises of Richelieu were still valid, that the intentions of Mazarin were sincere, and that the continuation of an autocratic government was harmless. Richelieu was, of course, entirely responsible for that state of mass hypnosis; it was mainly owing to him that they were lulled into an illusion of security. He knew how to make them believe he had meant no harm in destroying their political liberty. His success lay in his power to persuade his contemporaries of what he wanted them to believe. Such was his immense influence that the spirit of the Huguenots remained dormant until Louis XIV revoked the Edict of Nantes. The triumph of Richelieu was not only that he destroyed the Huguenots' physical force, but that he paralyzed their will to resist. Had he not succeeded, they would have started a new revolt under Mazarin or Louis XIV before final systematic oppression began. By not trying to regain their political autonomy, they helped Mazarin to execute Richelieu's design. Moreover, they helped create conditions which later provided their enemies with natural arguments that their legal suppression was necessary and the revocation of the Edict of Nantes inevitable.

---

[8] "Du reste ces conversions, plus politiques que religieuses, ne furent jamais violemment imposées." Mazarin, *Lettres,* I, cxxi.

The political atmosphere remained essentially unchanged, and its main tendency was even further emphasized, as if to mark a permanent trend—the hardening of French society into an absolutist cast. This process was continuous, and everything seemed to work in its favor. Since 1629 the Calvinists had remained invariably faithful to the King—a loyalty for which they had a very good reason: the King's word was their sole guarantee of religious liberty, and in the absence of any material guarantees, such as strongholds and political assemblies, they were naturally inclined to side with the royalists in opposing political unrest and agitation. In their polemics they missed no opportunity of asserting their monarchist sympathies, as was the case with André Rivet [9] and Pierre Dumoulin, writing in reply to the Jesuit Petra Sancta.[10] Like Pastor Philippe Vincent, they praised and extolled the clemency of Louis XIII. Finally, to prove that their fidelity was not mere bravado, in 1636, "the year of Corbie," when the Spanish invaded the North of France, the Huguenots in Paris rushed to the King's colors, while their preachers Jean Daillé, Charles Drelincourt, and Jean Mestrezat stirred the rest of the Protestant population in Paris to even more active fidelity.[11] When the English Civil War shook French public opinion in 1642, uncertainty and excitement in France led to a sudden outburst of political writing in which the Protestants were particularly anxious to assert their unchanged royalism.

But they were not very well disposed toward Charles I, an Anglican and anti-Presbyterian. The Calvinists sympathized with the Presbyterians, mainly because the latter's views resembled those of the early Calvinists, unspoiled by the doctrine of resistance which the Calvinists accepted later. During the English Civil War the

[9] "Quicquid sit de Monarchia absolute considerata, quam praestantissimum omnium Regimen omnes censemus ... nos sumus omnes, Gallorum ingeniis Monarchicum Regimen esse optissimum, nec posse diu stare sub aliam gubernandi forma." André Rivet, *Jesuita vapulans*, p. 472.

[10] "La monarchie est le seul gouvernement civil qui invite le gouvernement du monde universel, où il n'y a qu'un maistre." Pierre Du Moulin, *Hyperaspistes ou Défenseur* ([n.p.], 1634), pp. 554–556, as quoted in A. Galland, "Les Pasteurs français Amyraut, Bochart, etc., et la royauté de droit divin, 1629–1685," *Bulletin de la Société de l'histoire du Protestantisme Français*, LXXVII, 106. Hereafter cited as Galland, "Les Pasteurs," *Bull.*

[11] Jean Daillé, *Mélange de sermons* (Amsterdam, 1658); Jean Mestrezat, *Sermon fait ... le 21 Aout, 1636* (Quevilly, 1936); Charles Drelincourt, *Sermon ... célébré à Charenton, le jeudi 21 Aout, 1636* (Quevilly, 1636).

Presbyterians remained "half-hearted rebels" [12]—an attitude which endeared them to the Calvinists and made it easier for the prominent Calvinist pacifist Bochart to justify their position in the war.[13] The Presbyterians saw nothing iniquitous in a rebellion initiated from the floor of Parliament. But they never fully sanctioned regicide, leaving that to the Independents, from whom the Calvinists dissociated themselves officially at the national synod at Charenton in 1644. The Independents used violence, which was regarded by the Calvinists Bochart and Amyraut as an unacceptable remedy. If the king commits violence, according to Bochart,[14] it is best to submit to the judgment of God. Amyraut likewise advised passive resistance and reliance on God in cases of oppression.[15]

The Independents had little in common with the Presbyterians, except their Calvinist theology. They were the mainstay of republicanism in England, while the Presbyterians were monarchists as were the Huguenots. The Presbyterians desired a reform of the church accompanied by royal support, rather than by hostility; the Independents desired church and state to coexist as two societies in an atmosphere of noninterference and toleration. The Huguenots preserved the traditional medieval notion of church-state unity, which they—like the Anglicans—were unable to put into practice. Like the Presbyterians, they ceased to form a separate enclave within the state. The Independents excluded the alternative of a national church, while the Calvinists were not hostile to Gallicanism.

The main bone of contention between the Presbyterians and the Huguenots on the one hand, and the Independents on the other, was the attack on the sovereign, which culminated in his brutal extermination. According to Amyraut, writing in 1654, all Europe condemned the rebels for their attack on the King, allegedly carried out to preserve the liberty of the people and in the interests of religion.[16]

---

[12] G. H. Sabine, *A History of Political Theory* (New York, 1950), p. 444.

[13] *Lettre de M. Bochart à M. Morley* (Paris, 1650), pp. 104 ff.

[14] "... les Rois sont absolus et ne dependent de nul autre que de Dieu seul; ... Il faut supporter les maux qui ne se peuvent corriger sans grande prejudice ..." *Ibid.*, pp. 101–102.

[15] Cf. Moïse Amyraut, *Discours de la souveraineté des Roys*, pp. 148 ff.

[16] "... La pluspart de l'Europe croid que ç a esté une rebellion contre la Puissance souveraine." Amyraut, *Du Regne de mille ans ou de la prospérité de l'Eglise*, pp. 316 ff.

As early as 1647, Amyraut gave expression to antirevolutionary and antirepublican convictions, stating that he would not defend an insurrection against the prince in England, no matter what the cause for which it might be undertaken.[17] He condemned the very thought of reducing the authority of a monarchy.[18]

With the execution of Charles I, the apprehension of the Huguenots reached a climax. With redoubled energy, they asserted their position, fearing that their compatriots, shocked by the regicide, would look at them as suspect antiroyalists and at the Calvinist church as a nest of revolution harboring a pernicious doctrine.[19] Condemnation of the regicide came from the pens of a host of writers, such as Saumaise,[20] Bochart, Maximilien de l'Angle, Amyraut, and Dumoulin.[21] They were all trying to protect their brethren with the shield of political theory—a design in which they were spurred on by external political action and by the fear of internal political reaction. In their publications and sermons [22] they showed the validity of the relationship between political theory and political practice. The emphatic defense of the monarchist principle by Louis Hérault,[23] pastor of Alençon, culminating in his conclusion that there is no sovereignty except in a monarchical state, not only marked the earnestness with which the royalist theory was proclaimed, but also brought out clearly how closely political theory followed external events. The events of the Fronde were to prove

---

[17] "Je ne veux nullement entreprendre la défense de la prise d'armes contre son prince pour quelque cause que ce puisse estre." Amyraut, *Apologie* (Saumur, 1647), p. 71, as quoted in Galland, "Les Pasteurs," *Bull.,* LXXVII, 112.

[18] "Mutine et criminelle pensée de secouer l'authorité de la monarchie." Amyraut, *Apologie,* p. 94.

[19] "Nous craignons mesme que l'atrocité de ce crime commis par ceux que le plus part croyent estre de mesme religion que nous, n'attirast un blasme sur nos Eglises que le temps n'effaceroit jamais, et que les vices de personnes ne l'imputassent à la doctrine." *Lettre de M. Bochart à M. Morley,* p. 113.

[20] Claude Saumaise, *Defensio regia pro Carolo I.*

[21] Pierre Dumoulin (the Younger), *Défense de la Religion Reformée et de la Monarchie et Eglise Anglicane;* Pierre Dumoulin (the Younger), *Clamor regii sanguinis adversus parricides anglicanos [published anonymously].*

[22] The activity of royalist Protestant preachers increased significantly in the period from 1651 to 1655. Among the most illustrious were Drelincourt, Amyraut, and Daillé. Cf. *20 sermons de Jean Daillé* (Genève, 1653); *15 sermons de Jean Daillé, 1653–1654* (Genève, 1669); *Mélange de sermons* (Amsterdam, 1658).

[23] Louis Hérault, *Le Pacifique royal en deuil* (Saumur, 1649), pp. 116–143, 256–272, 296, as quoted in Galland, "Les Pasteurs," *Bull.,* LXXVII, 111.

that the reverse was equally true, the actual policies often being recast by the theories previously and contemporaneously expounded.

The undisputed victory that the period of the Fronde brought to the royalist cause meant not only Protestant nonadherence to the insurgent camp but also such a thorough permeation of the whole of society by the same ruling idea that even the revolutionaries of the Fronde could not help being mildly monarchistic. The latter also held strong antiabsolutist views; the cause for discontent had been present since the days of Richelieu, who had initiated the free use of *lettres de cachet* and thus had violated the constitution. The apologists of the Fronde, particularly its most prominent spokesman Claude Joly, appealed to the need for restoring the constitution, the integrity of which, indeed, found in them true champions. Although ultimately the revolt was aimed at Mazarin,[24] against whom public feeling was aroused, it was equally directed against Richelieu. It was clearly realized that Richelieu was primarily responsible for undermining the constitution,[25] and the Constitutional Instrument of July, 1648, presented an opportunity to demonstrate against Richelieu's intendants, contemporary "Inquisitors," whose abolition was desired.[26]

The Fronde, anathematizing all absolutism, made the name of Richelieu the butt of a hatred which had grown over the years and which was intensified by the moves of Mazarin that were reminiscent of the action of his predecessor. The despotism of Louis XIV, however, outshone that of Richelieu, and, consequently, the feelings of anger and revenge against the new absolute ruler were more widespread among the people. More despised than hated, Mazarin was never feared in the way his predecessor had been. Claude Joly did his best to slander the name and the rule of Richelieu, whose government he called unbearable and whose memory was "odious to posterity." [27] This feeling had long persisted, although it was not due solely to the Fronde. It was predominantly the rule of Mazarin that united public opinion against the memory of Richelieu.

Yet Richelieu won a curious victory from the grave. He meant his absolute rule to give a basis to the already flourishing monarch-

---

[24] J. Denis, *Littérature politique de la Fronde,* p. 4.

[25] P. R. Doolin, *La Fronde,* p. 157.

[26] C. C. de Rulhière, *Eclaircissemens historiques,* p. 43.

[27] Claude Joly, *Recueil de Maximes véritables ... pour l'institution du roy,* pp. 389–390. Hereafter cited as Joly, *Recueil de Maximes véritables.*

istic principles with which he had deeply indoctrinated society. The Fronde, by violently opposing absolutism and by professing monarchistic tendencies, however discreetly, was in a dilemma, because the good of the monarchy and that of authoritarian rule were one. The Fronde was thus subject to doctrinal confusion—a posthumous triumph for Richelieu. The result was its defeat in almost every sphere and an ultimate strengthening of absolutism.

The Fronde started with the tradition of the revolutionaries of the sixteenth century, using as its source of inspiration sixteenth-century writers, particularly the Huguenots, such as the author of the *Vindiciae* and Hotman, but also others, such as Bodin and Boucher. Its pamphleteers, who, with the exception of Claude Joly, were somewhat lacking in originality, tended simply to reproduce ideas borrowed from the writers of the preceding century. Taking some rather timid liberal doctrines, which had scarcely influenced sixteenth-century political thought, the Fronde strengthened and expanded them, since it was seriously concerned with social ills and financial troubles. The doctrine of the sovereignty of the people began to acquire a new meaning, embracing the totality of the nation; it was desired that political equality—an outcome of such a restated doctrine—be extended to the realm of public administration, in which all Frenchmen should be allowed to participate.[28]

Another aspect of the new attitude to the doctrine of sovereignty was the desire that parlement be given control over royal authority. Claude Joly, who was said to embody all the ideas of the revolutionary camp, later maintained that absolutist tendencies should be checked by public assemblies—the parlement, the States-General, and the commissioners nominated by the States-General and responsible for supervision in the intervals between sessions.[29] Fighting absolutism, the pamphleteers of the Fronde were deeply anxious not only that parlement retain the liberty it had gained, but that civil liberties be defended; the acquisition of the right to a free press was put forward as the first aim worthy of the assembly. "Il faut demander pleine liberté d'escrire ou faire imprimer de bon advis ou autres choses profitables au public," declared the *Prompt et Salutaire avis* (1649).[30] Claude Joly wished to safeguard individual

---

[28] Cf. F. Bouchez, *Le Mouvement libéral en France en XVII⁰ s. (1610–1700)*, p. 74. Hereafter cited as Bouchez, *Le Mouvement libéral*.

[29] Joly, *Recueil de Maximes véritables*, chaps. viii, ix.

[30] C. Moreau, ed., *Choix de Mazarinades*, I, 519.

liberty by assuring the right to property, freedom of the press, and freedom of conscience. Although not in favor of unqualified freedom of conscience, Joly was tolerant. The influence of L'Hôpital on his writings was remarkable. He deplored the conversion of heretics by force and decried all flagrant cases of violence, severity, and injustice against the Huguenots.[31] In criticizing the policy of the Valois,[32] he had the courage to declare that one should not treat the Huguenots unjustly. Despite a reprimand from the public prosecutor, he continued to argue that to persecute the Huguenots was to act against the royal interests, and to arouse the enmity of a powerful party.[33]

This historical diagnosis of Claude Joly could be, perhaps, applied with less justice to his own days, for the revolutionary spirit was certainly no more than dormant in contemporary society.[34] Even among the "frondeurs" it was not strong. It was tempered by a strange mixture of liberalism and monarchism, which was to be enforced through a revolution that was neither preached nor executed with excessive fierceness. The idea of popular government, sapped by ubiquitous monarchistic tendencies, had no chance to grow deep roots. Circumstances deflected the channel through which the anticipated contribution of the Fronde to posterity had flowed; its hopes for a more equalitarian and just social system and its fear of radical opinions were derided, but, what was of more lasting importance, its conclusions began to be at fault. Though able to formulate satisfactorily the story of the beginning of societies—explaining it in terms of natural law—the pamphleteers of the Fronde were strongly biased in favor of monarchism, and their description of the origins of monarchy in France was marred by the pretense that the monarchy had always been democratic.

This opinion betrayed the new spirit of adulation which usually accompanies and follows an authoritarian rule. It revealed the atmosphere necessary to those pamphleteers of the opposition in whose thoughts the royalist undercurrent was ever present. It was

---

[31] "La grande rigueur et sévérité que les Valois avaient exercé contre ceux de la R.P.R." Joly, *Recueil de Maximes véritables*, p. 552.

[32] Cf. *ibid.*, pp. 552–553.

[33] Cf. Joly, *Lettre apologétique pour le Recueil de Maximes véritables*, published with *Recueil de Maximes véritables* (1663 ed.), pp. 20–21. Cf. below.

[34] "L'esprit révolutionnaire et républicain fait complètement defaut." Denis, *Littérature politique de la Fronde*, p. 5.

the result of subconscious motives, since they were all essentially loyal to the monarch, although they cared more for the monarchic institution than for the person of the king.[35] The disparity between their attitude and that of the Huguenots was apparent. The monarchism of Huguenot writers could often be identified with the sympathies they showed for the individual ruler whose favor they were anxious to win. That attitude, with its human touch of expediency, lacked the sternness—bordering on ideological fanaticism—which led the Fronde to the crossroads, made its writers utter appeals that had little bearing on their real convictions, and stimulated wild and unpredictable action.[36]

That rather vague disparity in the theoretical sphere is worth noting, though it could have no ultimate influence upon the Calvinists' nonadherence to the revolution; in 1650 theirs was a religious group with a realistic political sense that was less prone to lapse into doctrinaire thinking. Perhaps remembering that, two decades before, they had fought the King while believing in the institution he represented—an inconsistency between theory and practice at the time of the final party decline—they avoided joining the Fronde, although the offer was made. Perhaps they declined to throw in their lot with the rebels because they believed these discrepancies within the Fronde to be too serious, monarchistic feelings too formidable, or the odds against revolutionary action too great.

Of course, their nonparticipation in the revolt was not without repercussions on their future. The Fronde, like the Huguenots, could not muster popular support; it would have greatly welcomed Protestant participation, as that might have changed the character of the rebellion. It would then have been nearer to achieving its aim by delivering a strong blow to absolute rule through a general civil war. As it was, the Fronde failed to shake absolutism, but was serious enough to arouse the instincts of self-preservation. Strong counteraction from the Government, based on Lebret's defense of the rule of Richelieu, but reinforced with the more radical

---

[35] "La justice n'est pas avec le Roy, mais avec la royauté." Dubosq-Montandré, *Le Point de l'Ovale*, p. 3, as quoted in Bouchez, *Le Mouvement libéral*, p. iii.

[36] "Alarmons tous les quartiers, tendons les chaines, renouvelons les barricades, mettons l'espée au vent, tuons, saccageons, brisons, sacrifions à notre vengeance tout ce qui en se croisera pas pour marquer le parti de la liberté." Dubosq-Montandré, *Le Point de l'Ovale*, pp. 1–2.

convictions of the pro-Government Fronde pamphleteers, ultimately strengthened absolutist tendencies.[37] Furthermore, when the Fronde's plea for action could no longer be heard, its demand for a limited monarchy could have no consequences. The words of the pamphleteers alone carried too little weight to evoke any echo, and they did not outlast the conflict between the parlement and the King. When the former failed, its political ideals had no further application.

The reaction that followed was intensified by fear and suspicion of Mazarin. The plea for civil liberties postulated by the parlement became a dead formula. The problem of religious toleration was not directly affected, because the Protestants had stayed out of the last conflict. Indirectly, the victory of Mazarin over the Fronde made him even more rigid in his conception of society, and this attitude helped him to pursue a stiffened policy toward the Protestants, from which he thereafter never departed. This policy did not involve increased signs of intolerance. On the contrary, the events of the Fronde, in which the Huguenots had not participated, made any future interference of Mazarin with the Huguenots unnecessary; he acted as if he did not consider the Protestants a political problem. As he had little time for religious problems,[38] silence on Protestant affairs followed.

That did not mean that Mazarin was blind to the existence of political issues involved in the Protestant question; he was well aware of these; his silence was a sign of his success. After the Fronde he was to follow the same policy that he had adopted in principle when he came to power—a policy which is illustrated by his two letters of 1643.[39] This policy, however, was to be even more

---

[37] Cf. Doolin, *La Fronde*, pp. 91, 109.

[38] "Mazarin, tout occupé d'affairs politiques ne mettoit qu'un intérêt médiocre à celles de la religion." M. M. Tabaraud, *Histoire critique des projets formés depuis trois cents ans pour la réunion des communions chrétiennes*, p. 203.

[39] "Je suis de vostre avis ... de les maintenir [les Huguenots] inviolablement dans les avantages dont ils jouissoient à la mort du feu Roy." Mazarin to M. de Lauson, Intendant of Guyenne, December 24, 1643. Bibl. Mazarine, MS 1719, I, fol. 146ᵛ, in Mazarin, *Lettres*, I, 515–516. "... l'inviolable dessein qu'on a icy de maintenir les choses en l'estat où elles estoient durant la vie du feu Roy ..." In the same letter Mazarin refused to let the Protestants at Montpellier install church bells because, he argued, although this was not contrary to law, the royal acquiescence might push Calvinists to further demands. Mazarin to M. Baltazar, Intendant of Justice in Languedoc, December 24, 1643, Bibl. Mazarine, MS 1719, I, fol. 146ᵛ, in Mazarin, *Lettres*, I, 516–517.

strongly accentuated. Its basic tenets were to maintain the Protestants in the rights which they possessed at the death of Louis XIII, and, in order that these should not be enlarged, never to accede to Protestant demands for privileges. Mazarin's fear that the Huguenots might again become a political issue—though lessened in the civil war [40] by the Huguenot neutrality, which made conspicuous their indifference to internal and foreign influences [41]—was reawakened by the advent of Cromwell. This worry, however, never seemed to become unduly serious: the behavior of the Huguenots during the rebellion convinced the Cardinal of their loyalty to such an extent that he planned to use Protestant troops against the Protector, a self-styled champion of all Protestants, in the event of his invasion of France.[42] Mazarin advised prudence in relations with the Protector,[43] but openly declared his resentment at any intervention from abroad, affirming that it was no business of Cromwell's to meddle with Huguenot affairs.[44] He took a firm stand in 1655, when Cromwell intervened in the case of the Vaudois massacre, urging the King of France to use his authority over the Duke of Savoy, who was guilty of an outrage which, in fact, did not possess the character of a religious persecution since both denominations were victims.[45] The *démarche* of Cromwell delayed his peace negotiations with France for a treaty against Spain, but produced no other effect. The Huguenots did not come within his sphere of influence. Cromwell bargained as long as he held the keys to the Spanish alliance, threatening France and simultaneously endeavoring to interfere with her internal problems. But, as a treaty with France against a mounting Spanish menace was paramount, he had

---

[40] When Mazarin was able to say: "Je n'ai pas à me pleindre du petit troupeau; s'il broute de mauvaises herbes, du moins il reste fidèle au Roi." Quoted in G. Bonet-Maury, "Le Protestantisme français et la République, 1598–1685," *Bulletin de la Société de l'histoire du Protestantisme Français*, LIII, 382.

[41] There was an English plan to set up a Calvinist republic at Bordeaux in 1653, a temptation to which the Huguenots had not succumbed. Cf. Victor Cousin, *Madame de Longueville pendant la Fronde*, II, 464 ff.

[42] Mazarin to Baron de Baas, May 8, 1654. Archives des Affaires étrangères Angleterre, LXIII, fol. 382. In Mazarin, *Lettres*, VI, 158.

[43] Mazarin to M. de Bordeaux, October 30, 1654. Arch. Aff. étr. Angleterre, LXIII, fol. 576. Mazarin, *Lettres*, VI, 333.

[44] Mazarin to M. de Bordeaux, August 20, 1654. Arch. Aff. étr. France, LXIII, fol. 526. Mazarin, *Lettres*, VI, 286–287.

[45] Mazarin to M. de Bordeaux June 19, 1655. Arch. Aff. étr. Angleterre, LXVI, fol. 71. Mazarin, *Lettres*, VI, 490–491.

to drop his plans for undermining France from within. Obviously the Huguenots could not receive effective support against their own government from a country anxious to win its favors.

Mazarin regarded with suspicion the merest trace of foreign influence. He had to be constantly on his guard, for Cromwell's interest in the Huguenots never seemed to slacken.[46] It was a hard task to keep Cromwell off and yet preserve their alliance, as well as the Swedish, Dutch, and German Protestant alliances essential to his foreign policy, which was patterned after that of Francis I, Henry II, and Richelieu. The result of this policy was to bring the end of the Habsburg epoch and advance the cause of the Bourbons.

Mazarin "protected" the Huguenots against a conflict, trying to preserve their *status quo*. He never consented to any concessions which would in the slightest degree extend the Edict of Nantes. As early as 1643, he showed that he would not agree to the Calvinists' being given anything not actually included in the Edict.[47] Although the Edict of Pacification[48] brought him wide repute as a tolerant statesman, his administrative policy barely justified it. As a severe administrator of the Edict of Nantes throughout his whole rule, he paved the way for future abuses resulting from a too strict interpretation of its clauses. His "toleration" only meant warding off the Protestants, lest they cause any trouble; he was obsessed until the end with fear of their least activity. Only after a close scrutiny of the situation, which assured him that he risked nothing,[49]

---

[46] "Il est arrivé quelque chose dans une ville du Languedoc, nommée Nîmes. Je vous prie que tout s'y passe sans effusion de sang, et le plus doucement qu'il se pourra," Cromwell wrote to Mazarin in 1657. Cited in Lettre de l'archevêque de Toulouse aux Etats de Languedoc, Bibl. de Nîmes, MS, as quoted in Ch. Weiss, *Histoire des réfugiés protestants de France,* I, 256.

[47] "Sa Majesté ... desire-t-elle tenir soigneusement la main à ce qu'ils [les Huguenots] n'entreprennent rien au delà de ses edits, et ne passent point les bornes qui leur sont prescrites par l'autorité du prince; ce qui est mesme la pensée des plus sages ... de cette religion." Mazarin to the Bishop of Poitiers, October 2, 1643. Bibl. Mazarine, MS 1719, I, fol. 121ᵛ, in Mazarin, *Lettres,* I, 400. "... Sa Majesté est resolue de maintenir exactement l'estat des choses." Mazarin to M. de Lanson, December 24, 1643. Bibl. Mazarine, MS 1719, I, fol. 146ᵛ, in Mazarin, *Lettres,* I, 515–516.

[48] "[nous] voulons et nous plaît que nos-dits sujets de la R.P.R. soient maintenus et gardés ... en la pleine et entière jouissance de l'edit de Nantes." From the declaration of May 21, 1652, confirming all previous edicts of pacification, as quoted in Cousin, *Madame de Longueville pendant la Fronde,* II, 288–289.

[49] Ruvigny, Protestant Deputy General since 1653, promised him that the synod would consist of well-intentioned people and that it would deal only with matters of

did he advise the King, in 1659, to let the Protestants have their national synod. He won an exaggerated reputation for toleration/ through his conciliatory attitude to the Protestants, whose champion/ he has become in the eyes of many historians. It is true that he has never been appraised so highly as Richelieu; nevertheless, his portrait has seldom been unflattering. This is so because his activity has not been judged in conjunction with the will of Richelieu, which means that the facts alone have been interpreted, while the motives and undercurrents of action have been ignored.

True, Mazarin confirmed the Edict of Nantes,[50] annulled the decrees against it,[51] and showed disapproval of the frequent disregard of the edicts favorable to the Protestants.[52] It is also true that, although he revoked his declaration of 1652 under pressure from the clergy, in 1656 he made a new one creating mixed commissions to answer complaints and watch over the execution of the edicts.[53] Moreover, while he was in office the Calvinists lived in peace and enjoyed political equality, being admitted to civil and military posts. But it is equally true that Mazarin made the Huguenots harmless in the face of absolute rule by his scrupulous execution of the will of Richelieu.

During the later years of Mazarin the Huguenot question was relegated to the background when Jansenism—"le calvinisme reboulli" [54]—became the important issue. Jansenism professed to introduce a new reform of the Catholic Church. Shifting the emphasis to the spiritual side of religious life, it was marked by indifference to such sacraments as baptism; by disapproval of the secularization

---

the internal discipline of the Calvinist churches. Cf. Mazarin to M. de Ruvigny, July 29, 1659. Arch. Aff. étr. France, CCLXXIX, fol. 472, in Mazarin, *Lettres*, IX, 207–208.

[50] Mazarin induced the Regent (Anne of Austria) to confirm the Edict on July 8, 1643. Elie Benoit, *Histoire de l'edit de Nantes*, III, "Recueil d'Edits," 3–4. Yet this declaration "étant plutot donnée pour amuser le monde que pour être executée; et pour ne donner point de defiances aux Alliez Protestans, que pour faire justice aux Reformez du Royaume, elle n'empêcha pas qu'on ne les traitât partout comme on avait commencé." *Ibid.*, p. 8.

[51] "Ils [les Huguenots] obtinrent de lui non seulement une confirmation nouvelle de l'édit de Nantes et la cessation de tous les arrêts qui y étaient contraires." Eugène and Emile Haag, *La France Protestante*, I, lxx (Pièce justificative No. LXXXIV).

[52] As in the case of Toulouse. Cf. Mazarin to M. de Fieubet, President of the Toulouse parlement, May 15, 1654. Bibl. Nat. MS fonds fr. Mélanges de Colbert, tome XLI. Mazarin, *Lettres*, VI, 160–161.

[53] Pièce justificative No. LXXXV. Haag, *La France Protestante*, I, lxx.

[54] E. Lavisse, *Histoire de France*, Vol. VII, Part 1, p. 93.

carried out at Rome; by vigorous disciplinary yet individualistic routine and a simple piety allowing, in cases of doubt, direct appeals to God without the intervention of the clergy; and finally by a critical spirit akin to that of the Reformation—pessimistic and deriving some morbid satisfaction from innate human ineptitude and helplessness. The doctrine of Jansen, expounded in his book *Augustinus* (1640), in which he gave his own interpretation of the theories of St. Augustine, was condemned by Popes Innocent X and Alexander VII. The Jesuits, who feared that one day the new sect might take their own place, were its declared enemies. The remnants of the Fronde joined the Jansenist ranks, seeking refuge and peace, and conspired abroad through their agents to induce the banished Cardinal de Retz to start a new revolt. All these factors explain why the Government devoted itself to the persecution of the Jansenists. Mazarin was concerned with that issue up to the last days of his life, and at his death he left the King a strongly expressed recommendation that the Jansenists not be tolerated. He prepared the way for the recommendation of Louis XIV, in 1661, upon which the Assembly of the Clergy condemned Jansen's teachings.

This act was in line with the policy of the late Cardinal; it marked the ascendancy of the clergy, against whom his policy had proved ineffective, as it had against certain religious groups. He desired neither the existence of the intolerant Company of St. Sacrament, which he had forced underground but was unable to suppress effectively, nor the increase of Jesuit power.

The success of the Company of St. Sacrament was probably not unconnected with the new ascendancy of the Jesuits.[55] Both aimed at the revival of the Catholic spirit;[56] but while the Jesuits were a powerful, influential group whose efforts were directed toward promoting the cause of the Catholic Church and toward purifying its members through higher spiritual and intellectual attainments, the

---

[55] "Certains gens [de la Compagnie du St. Sacrement] ... se mêlaient de la politique et avaient dessein de faire mettre l'inquisition en France ... c'était une machine poussée par l'esprit des Jesuits." Gui Patin to Falconet, September 28, 1660, as quoted in A. Brette, *La France au milieu du XVIIe s. d'après la correspondance de Gui Patin*, pp. 336–337.

[56] Cf. N. Weiss, "A propos des annales de la Compagnie du Saint Sacrement," *Bulletin de la Société de l'histoire du Protestantisme Français*, XLIX, 94. Hereafter cited as Weiss, "A propos des annales," *Bull.*

Company of St. Sacrament was a kind of clandestine religious police at its worst, spreading the contagion of intolerance against religious minorities. The Company was the spirit of intolerance itself. Created in 1630, according to the original idea conceived by the Duke of Ventadour three years earlier, it was dissolved in 1666, but its influence lingered until the end of the century.[57] In the period from 1640 to 1655 it was notorious for its interference with all Protestant enterprises,[58] which was designed to bar Protestants from professions and trades. It was responsible for outbursts of anti-Huguenot fanaticism.[59] Aimed directly at the extirpation of heresy, the company stirred up those important and growing sections of public opinion which did not later oppose either the closing down of the Port Royal or the revocation of the Edict of Nantes, and which were blind to the disastrous impact of these events on the liberties previously gained during many decades of argument and struggle.

Mazarin acted for various reasons as an indirect instrument of intolerance. The anti-Jansenist Act of the Assembly of 1661, of which he was a spiritual father, did not yet involve the Calvinists, but the fact of the removal of the errant sect carried grim prospects for other religious groups, including the R.P.R.

His declaration of 1656, creating commissions composed of men of both religions to remedy infractions of the Edict in the provinces, was well meant; yet it never materialized in his lifetime, and as soon as it was used after his death it made for the Huguenots' ruin.[60]

No final assessment of the character and value of the activities of Mazarin should be made without taking into account his blind passion for the policies of Richelieu. They had for him such compelling force that even Richelieu himself could not have hoped for better results. Indeed, this passion made Mazarin a faithful executor of the inherited policies. His eagerness to hand over to Louis XIV the well-integrated system of institutions his predecessor had conceived almost submerged that sense of vision and imagination

---

[57] Cf. Zivy, "Compagnie du Saint Sacrament," *Bulletin de la Société de l'histoire du Protestantisme Français,* LII, 186.

[58] Cf. *ibid.*

[59] Cf. Weiss, "A propos des annales," *Bull.,* XLIX, 97.

[60] Cf. Rulhière, *Eclaircissemens historiques,* p. 19.

which Richelieu had detected in him. He preserved intact the legacy he had received from his master, and it was owing to him that Richelieu's ideas were tried out under the new sovereign.

THE TRIUMPH OF MONARCHISM

It is strange that the Fronde not only failed to upset the prevailing absolutist system but even contributed to its reinforcement. The Fronde was not popular enough and was altogether too weak to promote and enforce liberal ideas that could change the religious policy of the rulers of the day. All that happened during the first phase, or Fronde of the Parlement (1649), was the decrease of monarchistic tendencies and the emergence of an antiabsolutist and liberal movement, which slowed down in 1651.

It became obvious during the Parliamentary Fronde that the Protestants had little chance of success. Dissociating themselves from the rebels, they only earned dubious approval from Mazarin. Notwithstanding their attitude, had the Parliamentary Fronde been victorious, the Huguenots would have benefited from its liberal ideas; but it soon became evident that the so-called "constitution" of 1648 was doomed to failure. The declaration of the parlement of Paris, of July, 1648, was rightly termed a "constitution" because its extensive reformatory clauses were permeated with a liberal spirit extended to the spheres of public administration, taxation, justice, finance, commerce, and, most of all, of individual liberty.

These proposals for reform were almost too far-reaching to be acceptable and successful. The response which they evoked in the country was meager; political freedom, which the constitution had so anxiously propagated, was still a revolutionary principle. The people were not yet quite able to grasp its meaning, and its underlying ideas were not acceptable to the monarchy. Further, these principles, in spite of the innumerable pamphlets called *mazarinades*, were not clearly integrated into a systematic doctrine.

It is true that in the mass of purely occasioned literature, in most cases personally abusive and pertaining to day-to-day politics, certain pamphlets contained ideas of a more general character and of some permanent value. In the few pamphlets which stand out from the rest, one may distinguish certain ideas characteristic of the Parliamentary Fronde, and still alive in the Fronde of the Princes (1650–1652). The underlying feature which, so to speak, cemented the two Frondes into one movement was respect for monarchism, in the name of which the popular demands were made. The pamphlet *Les Souhaits de la France à Monseigneur le duc d'Angoulesme* (January 11, 1649) breathed this spirit when it exposed the difference between the activities of the League and the present revolt:

> La Ligue avoit pour but l'usurpation de la monarchie; et elle vouloit esteindre et coupper la racine de la Maison Royale. Mais dans cette fatale et cruelle conioncture, on ne respire que le bien général; on ne travaille qu'à maintenir l'authorité souveraine; on ne cherche que la félicité publique; et on ne demande au ciel que le bonheur de tous mes suiets; et la Cour est en cela d'accord avec le Palais; et tous les François crient unanimement: Vive le Roy![61]

Equally monarchistic was the *Lettre d'avis à MM. du Parlement de Paris, escrite par un Provincial* (March 4, 1649), a pamphlet which aroused perhaps more praise and criticism than any other *mazarinade*. "La France est une pure Monarchie Royale," claimed the *Lettre d'avis*. It distinguished sharply between seigneurial and despotic power, between a royal and a despotic monarchy:

> Il y a bien de la différence entre ces deux propositions: le Prince peut prendre et disposer de nos vies et de nos biens à sa fantaisie; et nous devons employer vies et biens pour le Prince. La première suppose une puissance despotique et seigneuriale; et la seconde une suggestion dans le subiet qui l'oblige à servir son Prince aux dépens de son sang et de ses biens, quand la nécessité est grande. [In a royal monarchy] le Prince est obligé de se conformer aux lois de Dieu, et où son peuple obéissant aux siennes demeurera dans la liberté naturelle et dans la propriété de ses biens; au lieu que le Despotique gouverne des subiets come un père de famille ses esclaves.[62]

By an appeal to the King and to monarchistic ideals, the Fronde desired to avoid rebellion against a true monarch. But it was the declared enemy of absolutism, an attitude which was revealed by the antiabsolutist nature of some of its comments and by a certain

---

[61] Moreau, ed., *Choix de Mazarinades,* I, 83–84.
[62] *Ibid.,* pp. 387–388.

awareness (betrayed by some pamphleteers) of contractual theories and of the nature of popular government.

This dislike of absolutism was given expression in the pamphlet entitled *Catéchisme des Partisans, ou Résolutions théologiques touchant l'imposition, levée et emploi des finances* (February 19, 1649). The king, although a "living image of God," according to the *Catéchisme*, was not the master of either the lives or the property of his subjects.

> D. Le Roy est-il le maistre de la vie de ses subiects?
> R. Ouy, mais non pas en la manière que l'entend le Politique de Machiavel, mais en celle que nous apprenons de l'Evangile ...
> D. Le Roy n'est-il pas le maistre de tous les biens de ses subiects?
> R. Nullement. Ce sont des maximes impies, damnables et abominables ... qui n'ont esté inventées que depuis quelques années par des sangues populaires ... pour servir de prétexte aux vols et aux violences qu'ils ont faites à l'oppression de tout le monde, qui sont cause des troubles et des mouvemens que nous voyons a nostre grand regret.[63]

Similarly, Cardinal de Retz, a defender of liberalism during the first Fronde, claimed that the despotism which had triumphed since the days of Richelieu engendered an anarchy and lawlessness which meant ruin to the royal authority.[64]

By the *Maximes morales et chretiennes pour le repos des consciences* (March 15, 1649), the revolt against absolutism was reduced to an attack on ministers and royal favorites as usurpers of power. As a rule, the *mazarinades* never attacked the King but were full of invectives against Mazarin. The *Maximes* urged that no obedience was due to such a minister: "Cette obéyssance et les respects n'obligent point les peuples à l'endroit du conseil des Ministres et des Favoris." [65] As for the King, the author of the pamphlet regarded him as bound by considerations of justice, divine laws, and the prescriptions of the Church. Outside these limits the people could use their right of resistance. "Tant que les Roys commandent des choses qui ne choquent point le salut, les subiets sont tenus d'obéyr." [66] Disobedience was legitimate if the king were an obstacle to salvation.

---

[63] *Ibid.,* pp. 278–280.

[64] Cf. Feillet, Gourdault, and Chantelauze, eds., *Oeuvres du cardinal de Retz,* I, 279–281. Hereafter cited as Retz, *Oeuvres.*

[65] Moreau, ed., *Choix de Mazarinades,* I, 426.

[66] *Ibid.*

The doctrine of limited monarchy also found expression in the statements reflecting the contractual theory, to which some pamphleteers occasionally referred. "Ainsi devons nous dire de la Maiesté et du pouvoir qui appartient à chaque peuple pour se régir, maintenir et conserver. Ils en ont donné la principale fonction à leurs chefs; mais ils ne s'en sont pas privez totalement," [67] declared the *Manuel du bon citoyen ou Bouclier de défense légitime contre les assauts de l'ennemi* (March 22, 1649).

The concept of the social contract was even more directly tackled in the *Lettre d'avis à MM. du Parlement*, although again the term itself was not used. "Quand les Roys viennent à la couronne, ils jurent ... qu'ils maintiendront l'Eglise ... qu'ils observeront les loix fondamentales de l'Estat, et qu'ils protégeront leurs subiets selon Dieu et raison ... et moyennant ce sermont, les peuples sont obligez de leur obéyr comme à des Dieux sur terre." A formulation of the right to disobedience followed:

> Si les Roys ne protègent leurs subiets selon le droict et la raison, conformément aux Lois de Dieu et aux Ordonnances des Estats ... les subiets sont exempts de l'obéyssance; et bien d'advantage, s'ils sont opprimez iniustement et avec une violence tyrannique, qui ne peut compastir avec la Monarchie Royale, où les subiets ne s'obligent aux Roys que pour en estre protégez contre ceux qui pourroient troubler leur repos. [68]

In the *De la Puissance qu'ont les rois sur les peuples et du pouvoir des peuples sur les rois* (1650), probably written by François Davenne, [69] it was clearly stated that the obedience of subjects rests on the meaning which the prince gives to the contract he had undertaken to uphold. Davenne firmly believed that princes had been made by the people, and not conversely. He asserted forcefully that obedience must be conditional.

Yet these writings formed neither a consistent nor a complete doctrine. No one tried to integrate them. Consequently there is no major controversy to be recorded in the history of political thought during the period 1649–1652. The defenders of the legitimate government just kept on repeating, almost sullenly, that obedience was required of subjects.

An ideological vacuum followed the constitutional proposals of

---

[67] *Ibid.*, p. 451.
[68] *Ibid.*, pp. 398–399.
[69] Cf. G. Lacour-Gayet, *L'Education politique de Louis XIV*, p. 231.

1648. The actual strife of the Parliamentary Fronde brought no change in this respect. The parlement had no authority to enforce its decisions; it was utterly deprived of its last vestiges of power in unsuccessful armed encounters. The campaign being lost, the chances for constitutional change were also lost.

The downfall of the constitutionalists was the first step in re-enforcing renascent absolutist rule. In 1651, with the Fronde of the Princes, the liberal movement started to decline, and monarchistic tendencies, which had never been completely eliminated, made a forceful reappearance.

The factors which helped the monarchist system to gain strength were manifold. During the second Fronde and later, a strong personal rule was preferred to other types of rule. This new situation was partly due to the ill-fated Fronde of the Parlement, which had missed its aim. As the Fronde of the Princes failed in 1651 to find a compromise with its predecessor, it provoked both a sudden revival of monarchism and a twilight of popular ideas. The latter were associated with the first phase of the revolt, and their importance diminished during the chaos which ensued. Public feeling, not on the whole favorable to the cause of revolution, turned against the uprising. Not only was the Fronde unable to fulfill its aims, but, losing its foothold and uncertain of its convictions, it did not hesitate to betray the original cause. A typical case was that of Cardinal de Retz, who at first served the popular parliamentary cause, but after 1651 sided with the aristocratic and determinedly monarchistic party. The new Fronde undermined the cause of the revolution by upsetting the code of ideals recently established. Some pamphleteers still continued to write in the spirit of the original revolution, but the power and influence of the writers lay elsewhere.

Certain conceptions of the social contract still lingered in pamphlets such as *Le Raisonnable Plaintif sur la dernière Déclaration du Roy* (August 19, 1652). "La royauté française," it declared, "est issue de l'élection." [70] By breaking the contract, the prince disrupts the social system: "Le Prince s'estant dépouillé de toute charité et ne rendant plus iustice ny protection, la liaison mutuelle est dissoute; il n'y a plus ny Prince ny subiets; et les choses sont réduites à la matière première." [71]

---

[70] Moreau, ed., *Choix de Mazarinades*, II, 458.

[71] *Ibid.*, p. 454.

Anxious to prove that the concepts of sovereignty and limited monarchy were not incompatible, the *Instruction Royale ou Paradoxe sur le gouvernement de l'Estat* (1652) stressed that all sovereignty must be referred to the source of power.

The consequences of absolutism were rejected outright by *Le Guide au chemin de la liberté* (1652), which described servitude as being against nature. Dealing with the fundamentals of political organization, the *Guide* prudently denied the right of existence to the theory of divine right.

The author of *Le Raisonnable Plaintif* expressed similar views, except that he appealed to custom instead of nature when defining the incompatibility of absolute power: "Revenons à cette puissance absolue et disons qu'elle n'est pas compatible avec nos moeurs, soit chrestiennes, soit françoises." [72] Consequently he urged its rejection: "Je soustiens que la puissance absolue doit estre rejettée, et que les loix fondamentales de l'Estat n'authorisent point les Rois de dépouiller leurs suiets de biens et d'honneurs, pour affermir leur puissance." [73] It should be noted that, although so markedly anti-absolutist, he showed strong monarchist sympathies: "Je regarde mon Roy; je le choye et le respecte, comme une personne sacrée; mais j'ay en horreur le barbare officier qui me tyrannise." [74]

Coadjutor Paul de Gondi, later Cardinal de Retz, stated in his memoirs of July, 1651, that the Fronde was directed against Mazarin. He repeatedly stressed that, in his opinion, it should serve the royal cause: "Notre principal soin est d'empêcher que ce que le salut du Royaume nous a forcés de faire contre le Ministre ne puisse blesser en rien la véritable autorité du Roi." [75] The beliefs of the second Fronde and those of Retz appeared crudely opportunist. But whatever his motives, Retz exerted a powerful influence in molding the policy of the revolt with his "monarchist" memorandum presented to Gaston of Orléans in July, 1651: "[Son Altesse Royale] fait connoître à tous les esprits sages et modérés qu'il ne veut pas souffrir que, sous le prétexte de Mazarin, l'on continue à donner tous les jours de nouvelles atteintes à l'autorité royale." [76]

---

[72] *Ibid.*, pp. 460–461.
[73] *Ibid.*, p. 464.
[74] *Ibid.*, p. 452.
[75] Retz, *Oeuvres*, III, 411.
[76] *Ibid.*, p. 412.

In his *Défense de l'ancienne et légitime Fronde* (1651), Retz wrote of the monarchist attitude of the soundest party in the rebellion; he denounced absolutism in general, and the lack of reverence which the party of Condé had shown to royalty:

> Toute sorte de tyrannie nous est odieuse, nous n'avons point combattu pour le choix des tyrans; et quand la plus saine partie de la France s'est opposée aux desseins du cardinal Mazarin, et que vous aviez communs avec lui, ce n'a pas été pour élever votre puissance, mais, au contraire, pour soumettre à notre jeune monarque celle que vous usurpiez dans la faiblesse de son gouvernement.[77]

It was in 1652, shortly before the end of the revolutionary disturbances, that promonarchist feelings reached their highest level. The *Requeste des Peuples de France affligez des présens troubles à Nosseigneurs de la cour du Parlement séant à Paris* (September 24, 1652) urged everybody to defend the royal authority: "L'authorité Royale estant attaquée comme elle l'est maintenant, avec tant d'excès et de scandale, tous les suiets du Roy indifféremment sont obligez de s'armer pour la deffendre." [78] The pamphlet granted to the kings of France the highest authority over their subjects: "Les Roys de France sont les seuls Pères véritables et les seuls Juges Souverains de leur Suiets." The monarchical authority makes the authority of the parlement "limitée et soumise à un plus haut ressort." [79] Royal sovereignty is indivisible: "Le point qui ferme la couronne de France est indivisible ... les Roys ne doivent et mesme ne peuvent partager le droit et la gloire de l'Empire avec qui que ce soit." [80]

When the Fronde of the Princes was drawing to its close, the new doctrinal trends were clearly established. Toward the end of the unsuccessful revolt, the spokesmen for the Fronde became more monarchist. Again, the Fronde was serious enough and lasted long enough to inspire in the ranks of the defenders of the government the fear that a period of unrest might recur. In consequence there ensued a movement toward a strong centralized government. The partisans of the governmental camp turned to the idea of absolutism as a remedy against the ills of civil war and

---

[77] *Ibid.*, V, 180.

[78] Moreau, ed., *Choix de Mazarinades*, II, 465.

[79] *Ibid.*, 466.

[80] *Ibid.*, 468.

internal chaos. Their pamphleteers revived and carried further the doctrines of Lebret.

Thus the *Response chrestienne et politique aux Opinions Erronées du Temps* (1652) placed the king above the civil law;[81] in this it followed the opinion of Lebret. The right to resistance against unworthy rulers had been made acceptable by Lebret in certain cases, such as that of an action of the king in contravention of the divine law. That right was now, as a rule, sternly rejected; the only concession, granted by several pamphleteers, was some degree of disobedience limited to special circumstances relating to *cas de conscience*.[82] The only kind of resistance allowed was a passive one.[83] The king was the embodiment of the sum total of all civil power. It is clear that the Fronde had provoked an unambiguous and blunt assertion of those ideas which the original revolt had tried to push into oblivion.

With liberal ideas receding into the background, it was only natural for the Protestants to stand apart during the Fronde of the Princes and to follow the same policy of neutrality as before. This line of policy seemed best under the circumstances; they had little faith in a movement led by a social group rendered powerless by Richelieu.

In spite of their neutrality, however, the Huguenots were accused of being responsible for some of the strong monarchistic views pushed to extremes by excessively zealous anti-Protestant writers. This issue was constantly arising out of the lingering conviction that the Protestants were planning to set up a separate republic. An accusation to that effect was brought forward by *Le Raisonnable Plaintif*:

> Nous n'avons pourtant pas faute d'Escrivains, qui par le titre de leurs offices, et pour se monstrer excessivement fiscaux, portent cette authorité absolue au delà de toutes bornes ... ç'a esté par un zèle de party; les uns pour refuter les premiers Huguenots qui vouloient mettre l'Estat en République; les autres pour s'opposer aux attentats et pernicieuses maximes de la Ligue.[84]

---

[81] Cf. Doolin, *La Fronde*, p. 93.

[82] Cf. *Bandeau levé de dessus les yeux des Parisiens pour bien iuger des mouvemens présens et de la partie qu'eux et tous les bons Français y doivent tenir* (19 février 1649), Moreau, ed., *Choix de Mazarinades*, I, 228 ff.

[83] Cf. *ibid.*, p. 233.

[84] Moreau, ed., *Choix de Mazarinades*, II, 461.

It was particularly unfortunate for the Huguenots that the rumors about the projected republic at La Rochelle began to circulate at a time of pronounced monarchism. Serious damage was inflicted on the reputation of the Huguenots. Mazarin, and later Louis XIV, in whose memory the horror of revolution was deeply imprinted, always regarded the Protestants as a potential threat. No demonstrations of loyalty could change that distrust. The fear that civil disorder might spread widely in French society caused this distrust of every move of the Huguenots, although the latter were insignificant politically.

The advocates of the Huguenot cause could do little. The most prominent was Claude Joly. He put the case for toleration when answering the lawyer Châtelet, who had attacked his *Maximes*. Among other things Châtelet had derided the sentence attributed by Joly to Catherine de Médicis: "C'est malfaict d'avoir chassé les Huguenots." [85] In the *Lettre apologétique*, Joly explained [86] the meaning of his earlier statement, giving it a wider scope by rejecting all persecution, and not merely the expulsion of the Huguenots. He displayed a genuine interest in the Protestants, desiring that they be allowed to live in peace. The reasons which he suggested the king should take into consideration in adopting a policy of toleration, however, were utilitarian:

> Au reste un Advocat du Roy ne devoit pas mettre cet article en jeu pour faire condamner un livre; puisque le proposition contradictoire de celle qu'il condamne sçavoir est celle-cy, C'est bien fait de chasser les Huguenots: choque directement l'interest de S. M. détruit ses Declarations et les Edicts de pacification & remet les armes à la main a un puissant party, pour empirer nos maux & renforcer nostre guerre civile.[87]

Claude Joly was a true representative of halfhearted liberal reaction—the outcome of halfhearted revolution. He was a prudent liberal, careful not to suggest any control over monarchistic government other than by the parlement. In theory he advocated the sovereignty of the people. He believed France was not a pure monarchy because of the limiting role played by the States-General. He distinguished between a despotic and a royal monarchy.[88] He rejected divine right and displayed an unflinching faith in the limited

---

[85] Joly, *Lettre apologétique pour le Recueil de Maximes véritables*, p. 20.
[86] Cf. *ibid.*
[87] *Ibid.*
[88] Cf. *ibid.*, p. 24.

character of royal power: "Jusques à présent je n'avais pas douté de cette vérité [que le pouvoir des Roys est borné et fini] & j'avais creu qu'il n'y avait que la puissance de Dieu qui fût sans bornes & sans limites." [89] Yet he lacked vision and the ability to make his doctrines applicable. Desiring to check a power that had unduly expanded, he had no clear notion of political liberty. Too ready to compromise, he was vague in his statements and ambiguous in his arguments. Thus, defending before Châtelet his assertion that the authority of the king came from the people, he stressed that it was also derived from God: "Les deux propositions ne se choquent donc point; les Roys tiennent leur autorité de Dieu; et les Roys tiennent leur autorité des peuples." [90]

Joly's spirit of toleration was at least growing, but here as elsewhere his views were restrained, fettered by the opinions of the day. True, he was shocked by oppression and persecution, but he did not admit the idea of full philosophical tolerance or suggest any political machinery which would establish a system favorable to legal toleration.

Joly was an outstanding exception. In the later years of Mazarin, silence had settled around the Protestant problem. The conflict between the churches was kept alive, not in the clash of political doctrines, but in the theological sphere. Political thinkers sought the remedy for the conflict between the Huguenots and the state through monarchism, professed in the hope of reconciliation. That policy could not ultimately provide any remedy at all, for indeed there was no remedy against absolutist rulers.

---

[89] *Ibid.*, p. 21.
[90] *Ibid.*, p. 30.

V

THE CLIMAX

"Les acteurs sont nouveaux, la farce est toute pareille."—
Gui Patin [*1665*].

*"La révocation de l'Edit de Nantes fut l'exagération de
la pensée de Richelieu."*—*"L'Edit de Nantes en Bourbon-
nais,"* Bulletin de la Société de l'histoire du Protestantisme Français, XII, 375.

THE ABSOLUTIST THEORY: LOUIS XIV, BOSSUET, MERLAT

Louis XIV was determined to set up a system of "seigneurial monarchy," which the pamphleteers of the Fronde opposed in the hope
that the system might not be put into effect if the Fronde were
successful. Subsequent history shattered their hopes. Not only was
the revolt unsuccessful, but it created in the King a lasting aversion
to the state of confusion which it had caused. He wanted to provide safeguards against a new Fronde; he discarded any idea of
adopting the concept of "royal monarchy," which had been advanced by some pamphleteers of the Fronde. He sought both a
remedy for disorders and a guarantee of a peaceful, untroubled
reign, in an extreme absolute rule employing despotic methods.
He had a high opinion of his status as a supreme ruler and of the
ideals of his mission. He desired that his motives for any action
be supposed as his consideration for the good of the state, and
not be ascribed to revenge on the spirit of revolutionary faction.
He was anxious to deny the rumors which had emanated from the
palace that in his childhood he had been seriously alarmed by the
events of 1649–1652.
    To his son, he made this appeal: "En toutes ces choses et en
plusieurs autres que vous verrez ensuite, qui ont mortifié, sans
doute, mes officiers de justice, je ne veux pas que vous me donniez ...

des motifs de peur, de haine et de vengeance pour tout ce qui s'était passé durant la Fronde." [1]

Psychologically the case was a simple one: his concept of absolute rule, which came naturally to him, partly because of his mental structure and partly because of his education, was strengthened by the great shock from the Fronde that he had received as a child. A reasoned justification of absolutism soon followed. Regarding the state as part of his own personality, he quite naturally believed that the good of the state and his personal unlimited rule were one. When he came to the throne the original fear caused by the Fronde still remained; and that fear was responsible for his endeavors to stamp out all trace of the Fronde. Like Richelieu, he thought less of the interests of his subjects than of the state, which in fact meant his own interest. Though never a profound or even a precise thinker, he left a set of consistent principles reflecting his deep conviction that no limits should be set to the full enjoyment of royal authority.

If one takes divine right—as Louis XIV did—for granted, the king is the source of all discipline: all subjects owe unquestioned obedience to him, and they are perpetually kept in readiness by the constant vigilance ensured by his personal rule.

According to Louis XIV, the necessity for personal rule was ineluctable: "Car vous devez savior que cette indépendance sur laquelle j'insiste si fort ... relève plus que toute autre chose l'authorité du maître, et que c'est elle seule qui fait voir qu'il les gouverne en effet, au lieu d'être gouverné par eux." [2]

Louis XIV understood that royal rule, though personal, cannot always be direct. To keep his own office safe and to set it above all others, the king must maintain the hierarchical system; he must act through his officers. But he must maintain personal supervision and be ready to oppose all signs of autonomy. He must, therefore, be careful to assess the usefulness that various public bodies and institutions have for him, and to foresee the danger that their excessive independence may carry.

Louis XIV felt that, in any public body, any tendencies toward sovereign authority must be stifled, even at the price of changing the system of justice:

---

[1] Ch. Dreyss, ed., *Mémoires de Louis XIV pour l'instruction du Dauphin*, II (*Supplément aux Mémoires de 1661*), 441. Hereafter cited as Louis XIV, *Mémoires*.

[2] *Ibid.*, II (*Mémoires pour 1667*), 269.

Il fallait par mille raisons, même pour se préparer à la réformation de la justice qui en avait tant besoin, diminuer l'autorité excessive des principales compagnies qui, sous prétexte que leurs jugements étaient sans appel, et comme on parle, souverains et en dernier ressort, ayant pris peu à peu le nom de cours souveraines, se regardaient comme autant de souverainetés séparées et indépendantes. Je fis connaître que je ne souffrirais plus leurs entreprises.[3]

He practiced arbitrary jurisdiction by appointing special commissions. He earnestly believed that royal authority should not be limited in the smallest degree. Lest the parlements assume too much power, he let them act only as courts of justice. He required of them full acquiescence:

Je leur défendis à toutes en général ... d'en donner jamais de contraires à ceux de mon conseil, l'autorité que je leur avais confiée n'étant que pour faire justice à mes sujets, et non pas pour se faire justice elle-mêmes : qui est une partie de la souveraineté tellement essentielle à la royauté, et tellement propre au Roi seul, qu'elle ne peut être communiqué à nul autre.[4]

The doctrine of an indivisible sovereignty, resting entirely in the hands of the monarch, was best expressed in Louis XIV's attitude to the States-General. He distrusted the very idea of the States-General; he strongly disapproved of the previous constitutional practice : " ... c'est pervertir l'ordre des choses que d'attribuer les résolutions aux sujets et la déférence au souverain." [5] Consequently he never convoked the public assembly.

He argued that popular assemblies should be avoided as a great menace and as nests of unrest and revolution, because if they are left unhindered, their power can then be taken away only by extreme violence : "[le] pouvoir qu'un peuple assemblé s'attribue, plus vous lui accordez, plus il prétend; plus vous le caressez, plus il vous méprise; et ce dont il est une fois en possession est retenu par tant de bras, que l'on ne le peut arracher sans une extrême violence." [6]

Louis XIV insisted that the very existence of the States-General was a heavy burden on the monarch, whose efforts were spent in defending his position against popular usurpers. Inevitably, in those circumstances, the other interests of the crown must suffer.

---

[3] *Ibid.,* II (*Supplément aux Mémoires de 1661*), 438.

[4] *Ibid.,* p. 439.

[5] Grouvelle and de Grimoard, eds., *Oeuvres de Louis XIV,* II, 26. Hereafter cited as Louis XIV, *Oeuvres.*

[6] *Ibid.,* p. 28.

The conclusion which Louis XIV reached later was also inevitable: "Le Prince qui veut laisser une tranquillité durable à ses peuples et sa dignité toute entière à ses successeurs, ne sauroit trop soigneusement réprimer cette audace tumultueuse." [7]

From there, the next step was to assert the principle of absolutism. His unconditional rejection of the States-General entailed the suppression of all ideas pertaining to the theory of popular government. Louis XIV condemned the right to revolution, considering unconditional submission to the king a truly Christian principle.

> Il faut assurément demeurer d'accord que, quelque mauvais que puisse être un prince, la révolte de ses sujets est toujours infiniment criminelle. Celui qui a donné des rois aux hommes a voulu qu'on les respectât comme ses lieutenants, se réservant à lui seul le droit d'examiner leur conduite. Sa volonté est que, quiconque est né sujet, obéisse sans discernement.[8]

He praised submission not only as an ethical principle but as a practical necessity. He suffered directly from the Portuguese revolution, which upset his negotiations with that country and which led him to the following conclusion of the argument: " ... cette loi ... n'est pas faite en faveur des princes seuls, mais est salutaire aux peuples mêmes auxquels elle est imposée." He believed that the same spirit which turns the subjects against their superiors turns them against their kings: "La même humeur de sédition qui porte un subalterne à se commettre contre celui qui lui doit commander, le porterait assurément à cabaler contre nous-mêmes." [9] Further, forbidding all disobedience, he insisted on the necessity of passive obedience, which alone could ensure a reign undisturbed by irresponsible civil commotions.

The arguments of Louis XIV found a culminating point in the assertion of the principle of absolutism in questions relating to private property: "Les rois sont seigneurs absolus, et ont naturellement la disposition pleine et libre de tous les biens qui sont possédés aussi-bien par les gens d'église que par les séculiers." [10]

It was this statement that fully exposed the threat to religious liberty. As a ruler absolute in every sense, Louis XIV considered

---

[7] *Ibid.*

[8] Louis XIV, *Mémoires*, II (*Mémoires pour 1667*), 285; or Louis XIV, *Oeuvres*, II, 336.

[9] Louis XIV, *Mémoires*, II (*Supplément aux Mémoires de 1666*), 74.

[10] Louis XIV, *Oeuvres*, II, 121.

himself uncontested master of the consciences of his subjects. He
felt they were bound to follow his example and that opposition
was seditious and punishable. Unity of religion followed as a logical necessity. Violence was justified if it enforced obedience. In-
dulgence for heretics he regarded as tantamount to condoning injustice toward a great number of citizens.[11]

The danger for the Protestants grew as attacks on individual
freedom continued under the severe police regulations. In the eyes
of Louis XIV, the unconstrained use of individual freedom might
lead to seditious practices, and these he was resolved to suppress.

The political doctrine of Louis XIV, however, although sharply
defined and containing the basic tenets of absolutism, was not yet
fully formulated. It was the task of Bossuet to give final shape to
the theory of supreme authority of the king-in-state. Bossuet's absolutism was only less extreme. As his political system was erected
on unshakable religious assumptions, to which he referred for arguments and inspiration, the authority of the king was tempered by
the principles of divine justice. The absolutism of Bossuet was less
bluntly expressed, but it reached much deeper, leaving more room
for interpretation.

Like that of Louis XIV, the doctrine of Bossuet was related to
his time. Louis XIV formulated his concepts while he was giving
them concrete practical shape in political reality; Bossuet, interpreting the Holy Scriptures, claimed to find in them prescriptions
and doctrine related to contemporary government: " ... nous
tournerons dorénavant toutes les instructions que nous tirerons de
l'Ecriture au genre de gouvernement où nous vivons." [12]

Bossuet used it to reassert the sacredness of temporal authority
as derived from God: "Nous avons donc établi par les Ecritures
que la Royauté a son origine dans la Divinité même." [13]

Like Louis XIV, Bossuet claimed identity between the state and
the sovereign. To the prince, he claimed, and to the country, the
same services are due.

> Personne n'en peut douter, après que nous avons vu que tout l'Etat est
> en la personne du prince. En lui est la puissance. En lui est la volonté
> de tout le peuple. A lui seul appartient de faire tout conspirer au bien

---

[11] Cf. Louis XIV, *Mémoires*, II, 516.

[12] F. Lachat, ed., *Oeuvres complètes de Bossuet*, XXIII (*Politique tirée des propres paroles de l'Ecriture Sainte*), 532. Hereafter cited as Bossuet, *Oeuvres complètes*.

[13] *Ibid.*, p. 531. Cf. also "L'autorité royale est sacrée," *ibid.*, p. 533.

public. Il faut faire concourir ensemble le service qu'on doit au prince et
celui qu'on doit à l'Etat comme choses inséparables.[14]

Unlike Louis XIV, Bossuet distinguished between an absolute
and an arbitrary government. The first he thought legitimate, the
second contrary to divine law. An absolute government he defined
as one immune from human constraint.[15] He further claimed that,
under legitimate government, all persons are free,[16] but arbitrary
rule brings lawlessness and serfdom. The way the argument was
presented was new, but it was based on the same assumption as
that of Richelieu and Louis XIV; namely, that the good of the
state should come first.

This latter argument served Bossuet as a useful pretext for discarding the burden of popular institutions while denying to the
people the right to sovereignty. He admitted later that the prince
and the people have mutual interests. But while letting these interests curb the authority of the prince, he hastened to conclude that
for this reason there is no need for the people to make any claim
to sovereign rights.[17]

Bossuet maintained that no authority deriving from popular
institutions can ever equal that of the king. He was convinced that
royal authority cannot be opposed and resisted. He not only considered disobedience illegitimate, as an opposition against an established authority, but bluntly labeled the spirit of revolt as being
anti-Christian; for government must remain unchangeable, perpetu-
ating itself and rendering the state immortal.[18] Upholding the theory
of divine right, Bossuet saw the problem of obedience as a religious question: "On doit obéir au prince par principe de religion
et de conscience." [19]

For these reasons he considered the spirit of Protestant resistance both antireligious and politically revolutionary: "Il n'y a
rien de plus opposé à l'esprit du christianisme que la Réforme se
vantoit de rétablir que cet esprit de révolte." [20] All he allowed
the subjects to use against the violence of rulers, were "respectful

---

[14] *Ibid.*, XXIV, 1.
[15] Cf. *ibid.*, p. 105.
[16] Cf. *ibid.*, p. 106.
[17] Cf. *ibid.*, XV (*Cinquième avertissement*), 474.
[18] Cf. *ibid.*, XXIII (*Politique*), 425.
[19] *Ibid.*, p. 535.
[20] *Ibid.*, XV (*Cinquième avertissement*), 380.

remonstrances": "Les sujets n'ont à opposer à la violence des princes que des remonstrances respectueuses, sans mutinerie et sans murmure, et des prières pour leur conversion." [21] He regarded a state of servitude under the ruler as natural. He rejected the theory of social contract, founded all social relationship on naked power, and explained the various stages in social history as being the result of the periodic overthrow of existing forces by new victorious forces. Consequently his monarchism had a decided authoritarian flavor. The *force coactive,* or the power to enforce execution of legitimate orders, he permitted no one but the prince. "Il n'y a point de force coactive contre le prince ... Au prince seul apartient le commandement légitime; à lui seul apartient aussi la force coactive." [22]

As a perfect repository of power, the prince must be obeyed blindly. Absolute authority is a necessity, and the innocence of the subjects their only legitimate line of defense. "Sans cette autorité absolue, il ne peut ni faire le bien, ni réprimer le mal: il faut que sa puissance soit telle que personne ne puisse espérer de lui échapper: et enfin la seule défense des particuliers contre la puissance publique, doit être leur innocence." [23]

The vastness of such absolute power, detrimental to all civil liberty, was not the only danger for the Protestants; they were threatened in no less degree by certain limitations imposed on that power.

The limitations set on sovereign monarchism were the result of its divine origin. Among these natural restrictive duties was an over-all protection of religion and of the Church, as explained by Bossuet in 1662, in his *Sermon sur les devoirs des rois:*

> Votre Majesté saura bien soutenir de tout son pouvoir ce sacré dépôt de la foi, le plus précieux et le plus grand qu'elle ait reçu des rois, ses ancêtres. Elle éteindra dans tous ses Etats les nouvelles partialités.
>
> .   .   .   .
>
> L'Eglise a tant travaillé pour l'autorité des rois, qu'elle a sans doute bien mérité qu'ils se rendent les protecteurs de la sienne.[24]

There was equally a direct obligation placed on the king to abolish heresy: "Le prince doit employer son autorité pour detruire

[21] *Ibid.,* XXIV (*Politique*), 16.

[22] *Ibid.,* XXIII, 560.

[23] *Ibid.,* p. 559.

[24] Lebarcq, ed., *Oeuvres oratoires de Bossuet,* IV, 367–369. Hereafter cited as Bossuet, *Oeuvres oratoires.*

dans son Etat les fausses religions." [25] Such conduct was necessary to maintain the stability and solidity of the political system: "La véritable religion étant fondée sur des principes certains, rend la constitution des Etats plus stable et plus solide." [26] It was also needed for the prince's own protection. Since active religious persecution was thus integrated into the political system, liberty of conscience, strictly speaking, became an impossibility.

The hold which the doctrines expounded by Louis XIV and Bossuet had on people's minds is perhaps best reflected in the fact that they were completely accepted by a Huguenot pastor, Elie Merlat. His book *Traité sur les pouvoirs absolus des souverains* (1685) attested his subservience to the doctrine of his ruler. Writing a review of this book, in his *Nouvelles de la république des lettres,* in August, 1685, Bayle testified: "Il [Merlat] remarque que ceux qui ont le droit absolu & entierement illimité n'ont pas besoin de justifier leurs actions par des principes exterieurs, et qu'il suffit qu'ils alleguent que tel a été leur bon plaisir, d'où il resulta que leur puissance n'est point sujette à l'examen de leurs Sujets, & qu'elle est un droit d'impunité à l'égard des peuples." [27]

Merlat's book was significant, although its appearance did not cause any stir. It reflected the views of an important section of Protestant opinion, which was anxious to draw the King's attention to the Protestants' usefulness in the struggle of the monarchy against the temporal claims of the Pope. "Sa doctrine," said Bayle, "est fort commune parmi les Protestants, comme il paroît par un nombre infini de Livres qu'ils ont composez contre les prétensions de la Cour de Rome." [28]

The *Traité sur les pouvoirs absolus des souverains* reflected the dilemma in which the Huguenots found themselves: torn between the desire to give full support to the monarchy and a feeling of inner revolt against the subjugation entailed by the prohibition of all disobedience.

Merlat was a believer in the absolute authority of kings, but was careful not to leave the definition of absolutism unqualified. Like Bossuet, he made it accountable to divine justice. [29]

His conception of absolutism was in certain respects more ex-

[25] Bossuet, *Oeuvres complètes,* XXIV, 42.
[26] *Ibid.,* p. 31.
[27] Pierre Bayle, *Oeuvres diverses,* I, 353.
[28] *Ibid.,* p. 354.
[29] Cf. *ibid.,* p. 353.

treme than Bossuet's, in others more restricted. He wanted the prince to be directly responsible to God alone, and bound by no rules other than his own will: "Les souverains, à qui Dieu a permis de parvenir au pouvoir absolu n'ont aucune loi que les règles à l'égard de leurs sujets, leur seul volonté est leur loy et ce qui leur plaît leur est licite." [30]

Although Merlat was an extreme thinker, like Bossuet he allowed only passive disobedience when the law of God was broken by a temporal ruler. Passive or silent disobedience, according to Merlat, was allowed in things temporal related to religion.

> Mais que veut-il [Merlat] que l'on fasse, lors que le Souverain s'en prend à l'essenciel de la Religion? Il veut qu'on lui désobéisse sans aucun mouvement de revolte, quoi qu'il en vienne aux moiens les plus violens, & qu'on ne se porte jamais à la moindre resistance exterieure, autre que celle que pourroit produire le refus de blesser directement sa conscience par des actes de Religion contraire à la pieté qu'on professe.[31]

But in matters of conscience Merlat admitted the right of disobedience. He stressed, however, the important difference between refusal to obey the king against one's own conscience, and an open revolt under the pretext that conscience was threatened. It was this revolt that he called a crime.

The book betrays Merlat's awareness of the problem of disobedience, but he used the argument only as one of the proofs of unlimited monarchical power. "Il [Merlat] fait voir," wrote Bayle, "que la puissance illimitée qu'il donna aux Princes, ne peut jamais s'étendre sur les actes immédiates & interieurs de la Religion, qu'ainsi les Sujets n'ayant rien à craindre de ce côté-là, ne peuvent jamais en prendre occasion de se soulever." [32] Merlat assigns an absolute, indeed divine, finality to the power wielded by an absolute monarch—power which no human being is able to alter, least of all the subject.

The degree to which Merlat accepted divine right made his version of absolutism an extreme one. His conclusions were consistent with the assumption of the divine right of monarchy. He

---

[30] E. Merlat, *Traité sur les pouvoirs absolus des souverains* (Cologne, 1685), p. 59, as quoted in Frank Puaux, "L'Evolution des théories politiques du Protestantisme français pendant le règne de Louis XIV," *Bulletin de la Société de l'histoire du Protestantisme Français*, LXII, 398.

[31] Bayle, *Oeuvres diverses*, I, 353.

[32] *Ibid.*

succeeded in adding his share to the body of absolutist doctrines, but he failed in defending the Huguenot case. His book bears testimony to the difficulties encountered by advocates of the same cause and to the involved byways into which their thought wandered.

ABSOLUTISM IN PRACTICE

In order to eliminate heresy, the lay and ecclesiastical authorities maintained a remarkably uniform policy. Coöperation was assured by the clergy's constant pressure on the King. Although in their anti-Huguenot activity the clergy and the monarchy did not always move in harmony, ultimately their singleness of purpose became apparent. Motives for intolerance varied with each party, being of a more religious nature in the case of the clergy and more political in the case of the temporal authority; yet they merged as Louis XIV became a docile supporter of the clergy's will, with which he identified his own personal absolutist will.

Louis XIV was not the direct heir of the tradition of persecution. He was too much a pupil of Mazarin to initiate any drastic measures against the Huguenots. But he also possessed a strong autocratic sense, which he began to display soon after he came of age; his famous dictum "L'Etat c'est moi" was coined in 1655. His absolutism was expanding continuously and progressively with the growing number of his personal victories over his Court and his subjects, ensuring their complete subjugation. He formulated his ideas on the character of his rule and of his activities as a sovereign perhaps earlier than he was able to give to these theories of government any practical expression.

Thus he says in his *Mémoires,* which he started to write in 1661, that it was in that very year that he formed his plan regarding the Protestants: "Et quand à ce grand nombre de mes sujets de la R.P.R. qui étoit un mal que j'avais toujours regardé, et que je regarde encore avec douleur, je formai dès lors le plan de toute ma conduite envers eux." [33] It seems, however, that this was but an address to posterity, in particular to the Dauphin, for whose benefit he desired his own rule to appear more purposeful and consistent

[33] Louis XIV, *Oeuvres,* I, 84.

than it had actually been. A document regarded (unlike many of his writings) as authentic spoke of his desire to avoid any new form of pressure on the Huguenots and to keep them within the limits of existing edicts and declarations.

> ... je crus ... que le meilleur moyen pour réduire peu à peu les Huguenots de mon royaume, étoit, en premier lieu, de ne les point presser du tout par aucune rigueur nouvelle contre eux; de faire observer ce qu'ils avoient obtenu de mes prédécesseurs; mais de ne leur rien accorder au delà, et d'en renfermer même l'exécution dans les plus étroites bornes, que la justice et la bienséance le pouvoient permettre.[34]

If such was his "plan," it did not coincide with his later policy. Indeed, the very absence of stringent measures [35] for many years after may be used as an argument against the theory that at an early date a master plan already existed in his mind. Even in 1680, according to Rulhière, "il n'y avoit point encore de projet fixe, de plan déterminé." [36] Louis XIV's natural clemency and his sense of justice could hardly have been the sole reasons for the slow effect and for the delayed execution of the plan, had there been one.

The restrictive legislation after 1660 was not directed by a single mind. It was a series of events for which the King alone was not entirely responsible; it was the result of the general pressure from below, which found its way to the King's conscience from so many quarters that finally all his authority and power were subservient to influences mainly external to him. He had no plan for "his whole conduct" in respect to the Huguenots, although he later put one in operation. He was resolved that Protestants should live within the limits of the restrictive legislation. He also expressed a somewhat vague opinion that something must be done about the Protestants, but for a while he left that idea to mature under the tutorship of the clergy.

The moment when a decisive trend was started and a new policy declared was not far distant; 1665 was probably the beginning of

---

[34] *Ibid.,* pp. 86–87.

[35] A rare instance of rigorous measures was the ordinance of intendant Colbert du Terron, confirmed by the Council of State in 1661, as a result of which no Protestant could inhabit La Rochelle unless he proved that he had resided there prior to 1627. The order served as an excuse for the ruthless expulsion of 1,800 Huguenots from the town. Cf. J. B. E. Jourdan, *Ephémérides historiques de la Rochelle,* p. 348, as quoted in J. Viénot, *Histoire de la Réforme française,* II, 409; see also p. 457.

[36] C. C. de Rulhière, *Eclaircissemens historiques,* p. 183.

a period in which the Court became certain as to the general course of action against the Calvinists. The change was the consequence of external pressure resulting from the prevailing anxiety and the general feeling of hope that the new ruler would inaugurate an epoch of grandeur. "Il se remue pour Votre Majesté quelque chose d'illustre et de grand, et qui passe la destinée des rois vos prédécesseurs." [37] Behind it there was an imperative general desire for the uncompromising absoluteness of royal authority and a policy suited to such a regime. Also, together with the full support which the people were prepared to give, they showed readiness for future uncomplaining submission.

In that pursuit of absolutist aims rather vaguely comprehended by the public, the prevailing irrationalism made it possible for the waves of adulation to spread and mount to heights never known before. Ideal conditions were created for a striking and enduring practical example of the theory of divine right. Sweeping changes were in evidence, and on their eve the Huguenots could not overcome their misgivings that they might be submerged in the first tides of the new spirit. But they did nothing practical to escape the danger.[38] If they had realized how fatal the new trend in French politics was for their cause, they would have at least hesitated to give the wholehearted and uncritical support to the monarchy that they continued to give until the revocation of the Edict of Nantes. Their perseverance in that policy was blind, because they were unable to foresee its consequences; it was also suicidal, because they were only strengthening the system which one day was to find means for their extermination. They never gave enough attention to the simple truth that their attitude of worship toward all that pertained to the monarchical order could be viewed with nothing but suspicion by the Catholics, and most of all by the Jesuits.

The Jesuits defended the divine right of kings with great ardor, and by this very fact were compelled to think of the Protestants as enemies of the divine law, simply because they had had a "re-

---

[37] Bossuet, "Sermon sur les devoirs des rois" (April 2, 1662), in Bossuet, *Oeuvres oratoires*, IV, 375.

[38] In fact they could not have done much to change their fate appreciably. The only alternative to submission was open revolt, an unrealistic policy because the forces ranged against them were much stronger than during the wars of religion and in the 'twenties. Revolt would have only meant an earlier and shorter agony.

publican" tradition and could not be expected to have undergone a change of heart now. Hence the Huguenots could not be trusted. This ingenious sophistry was responsible for turning the theory of divine right into a poisoned weapon, striking the loyal Protestants, who did not suspect the vicious, casuistic interpretation given to the simple and unambiguous loyalty to the king which they tried so eagerly to display.

On the accession of Louis XIV to the throne, the Protestants renewed their assertions of their loyal belief in monarchism. In 1661 and 1662, Drelincourt preached the need for submission to the monarch, by whose grace religious liberty is maintained.[39] Drelincourt, like Amyraut, Bochart, and Daillé, belonged to the troop of famous pastors who, until their deaths in the first decade of the reign of Louis XIV, had identified the good of their brethren with that of the monarchy. Others continued on the same lines, affirming their faith in the monarchy. Du Bosc, preaching in 1674, insisted that a monarch in his kingdom is like God; he has neither superiors nor equals. The sermons of Du Bosc were flowery panegyrics filled with the ideas of absolutism,[40] with which he was toying as if unconscious of the future dangers which absolute rule carried for his coreligionists.

As before, the means used by the preachers and authors were either direct glorification of the king in sermons and writings, or flattering appraisal of the monarchist system with reference to the events in England, which they scrupulously followed and commented upon. Expressing his joy at the restoration of the English monarchy, in a book dedicated to Charles II, Louis Hérault made the point, typical of his coreligionists, of emphasizing his "particular inclination" to monarchy, which was preferable, he wrote, to all other governmental systems: " ... de tous les gouvernements politiques j'ay tousjours eu une inclination particulière pour le Monarchique, et l'ay tousjours preferé à tous autres, comme estant une image plus expresse de la puissance de Dieu souveraine et indépendante." [41] These assurances were needed all the more as

[39] Cf. Ch. Drelincourt, *Le Buisson d'Horab* (Charenton, 1662).

[40] Cf. Du Bosc, *Sermons sur divers textes de l'Ecriture*, IV, 89 ff., as quoted in A. Galland, "Les Pasteurs français Amyraut, Bochart, etc., et la royauté de droit divin, 1629–1685," *Bulletin de la Société de l'histoire du Protestantisme Français*, LXXVII, 415–416.

[41] Louys Hérault, *Le Pacifique royal en joye*, p. 5.

the Huguenot status appeared less secure; and although little was effected by them and although they failed to dispel the suspicions habitually held by Catholics about the Protestants, they were repeated again and again. Du Bosc, Claude, Jurieu, and Merlat all preached obedience to the king, right up to the fatal year 1685.

The attitude of the Catholics also provided justifiable ground for the Huguenot reaction of despairing indignation at the revocationary tendencies, felt soon after 1660, when the misgivings of the Huguenots increased rapidly. In 1665 the King promised the clergy that he would interpret in their favor all issues not quite clearly explained in the edicts,[42] and his relations with them became closer. There must have been apprehensions that this underlining of the new trend in policy meant that it was likely to be serious and permanent, because in 1666 the exodus of French refugees started on a large scale.[43]

On September 6 of that year, in his letter to the Elector of Brandenburg, Louis XIV argued that he was determined to preserve the religious status of his subjects.[44] The letter, like many other statements of the King, affirmed all Protestant privileges, but only in order to save appearances.[45] There could be no mistake about the real intentions of the Court in 1666, when the Catholic clergy converted into a general law all the particular *arrêts* which

---

[42] Cf. *Collection de procès verbaux des assemblées générales du clergé de France*, IV, 907, as quoted in Frank Puaux and Louis A. Sabatier, *Etudes sur la révocation de l'édit de Nantes*, pp. 42–43. Hereafter cited as Puaux and Sabatier, *Etudes sur la révocation*.

[43] The total number of refugees of that first emigration is not available, but compared with the later exodus, caused by the *dragonnades,* it was limited: its numbers ran only into thousands, and not yet tens of thousands. But the proportion of newcomers in the Protestant refugee communities abroad was considerable. Thus at Canterbury the number of Huguenots attending their church was 900 in 1634, increasing to 1,300 in 1665—a rise of 50 per cent in three decades. Then it nearly doubled in the next decade, rising steeply to 2,500 in 1676. Cf. Ch. Weiss, *Histoire des réfugiés protestants de France*, I, 265.

[44] "... l'une de mes principales applications est de faire religieusement garder à mes sujets de ladite Religion, en toutes affaires et en toutes rencontres, tout ce qui leur appartient par les concessions des Rois mes prédécesseurs et les miennes, en vertu de nos Edits sans souffrir qu'il y soit en rien contrevenu ...," as quoted in Jean Claude, *Les Plaintes des Protestans cruellement opprimez dans le royaume de France* (Pièces justificatives), ed. by Frank Puaux, p. 124. Hereafter cited as Claude, *Les Plaintes des Protestans*.

[45] Cf. Elie Benoit, *Histoire de l'edit de Nantes*, IV, 12.

they had requested separately and which had been passed by either the parlements or the intendants.[46] Emigration, which had developed so suddenly, stopped three years later, owing to two curiously incongruous measures. The first, adopted on February 1, 1669, which abolished the previous declaration of the clergy of 1666, had been largely due to Colbert's influence; the second, passed in August in the form of an edict signed by Colbert, forbade any Frenchman to settle abroad.[47] Both acts opposed the slogan of the Court, "politique d'abord," and revealed Colbert's conviction that economics should come first.[48] Thus certain tolerant tendencies of Colbert, manifest in the order of February, 1669, were obviously due to that conviction.[49] It gave rise to a feeling that toleration may profit if economics is not always to give way to politics—a conviction revealing the existing rift between the economic dictator and his sovereign prince. By annulling the declaration of 1666, the first measure helped to stress the division between the religious policy of the King and that of the clergy.

Although since 1666 the gap between the policies of Louis XIV and the clergy had narrowed, it was still wide enough to admit of discrepancies between their respective actions. This gap accounted for the bewildered state of the Huguenots, taken aback by apparently contradictory declarations and orders. The incoherence of the regulations marked the conflict between royal absolutism and the clergy. It can also be regarded as a proof that neither of these two was alone responsible for the new revocationary trends. Jurieu gave evidence of a general onslaught on Calvinism: "Et il estoit d'autant plus necessaire de travailler à la justification du Calvinisme qu'aujourd'hui il est attaqué avec une violence prodigieuse. Tout le monde se mêle de luy porter des coups ... C'est une affaire de concert." [50] It was the active participation of the clergy which decided the issue. The King followed suit. The clergy secured quick

---

[46] Cf. Eugène and Emile Haag, *La France Protestante*, I, lxxvi.

[47] Cf. *ibid.*, Pièce justificative No. XCII.

[48] Cf. A. Piettre, *Economie dirigée d'hier et d'aujourd'hui, du colbertisme à notre temps* (Paris, 1947), p. 26.

[49] Even the edict forbidding emigration was not symptomatic of intolerance, as it was not specifically directed against the Protestants; it affected all Frenchmen.

[50] Pierre Jurieu, *Histoire du calvinisme et celle du papisme, mises en parallèle*, préface [unnumbered pages].

success by an appeal to his ignorance in religious matters and to his piety as a true devotee. His education made him incapable of contradicting the churchmen.

It is true, however, that even without the marriage of the ecclesiastical with the lay and absolute elements, which subjected the Huguenots to a period of legal persecution lasting twenty years, conditions for the Protestants were unfavorable. The flame of irrational hatred toward the Calvinists, inconspicuous under Mazarin,[51] began to burn anew in Catholic hearts. The zeal for conversions loomed larger. The clergy were lucky to be thus provided with a natural ground for the exploitation of popular passions, to which they applied their forces not less readily than to the exploitation of the immense powers of the King. By steering public opinion on its natural course and by harassing and influencing the monarch, they were able to have religious policy under their control and to guide and accentuate still more that spirit of conversion which imbued Louis XIV with the sense of a holy mission.

The greatest success of the clergy consisted perhaps in convincing the King of the holiness and glory of the task of bringing the Calvinists back to the mother Church. Once this view was adopted, the King did not swerve, and the position of the Catholic ecclesiastics, who of necessity were patrons of the mission, became impregnable. Once this mission became a *raison d'état*, relinquishing all minor prey, it found its main scapegoat in the whole Calvinist church. Coördination was achieved in the Catholic camp. Lesser skirmishes, such as the conflict between the Jesuits and Port Royal, serving a less grandiose aim, were, at least in part, suspended.

Port Royal, anxious to take a leading part in the battle for purification of the Catholic doctrine, was equal to the occasion. In 1664 "the Great" Arnauld (1612–1694), supporting the Jansenists, though at the time officially not in their ranks, wrote a basic work in which for the sake of a general offensive against the Calvinist heretics he sought to compromise with the arguments and methods employed by the Jesuits, in particular by Cardinal

---

[51] "... une haine que le temps n'avoit pas encore assoupie. L'animosité avoit survécu aux troubles et dans beaucoup d'esprits, la crainte avoit survécu au danger." Rulhière, *Eclaircissemens historiques,* p. 33.

Bellarmin.[52] In 1668 he lent himself to the cause of the "peace of the church" concluded as the Peace of Clement IX.

The support of Arnauld helped the King to achieve this religious peace, later hailed as one of the most glorious achievements of his reign. It was a kind of truce, following a conflict which had started as a purely factional dispute within the Catholic camp, between the Jansenists and the Jesuits, and had only later assumed the form of a religious controversy—a fact which shows that the "Jansenist heresy" had never existed before the Jesuits started to interpret it.[53] Louis XIV wanted to avert at any price the danger of the impending schism, and so he aimed at concluding a truce in 1669, whereby the legal status of the Jansenists was reëstablished. The armistice was precarious. It was based on a distorted notion of the facts and was misleading in its consequences. The security of the Jansenists never became permanent, because the agreement was based on casuistic terminology which gave free scope to equivocal interpretations. The armistice conveyed to the public at large an erroneous belief in the possibility of bringing all the French to one creed.

Another unquestionable success of the clergy lay in preparing the ground for the revocation in such a way as to make a serious breach in the absolute power of Louis XIV while using him as a

---

[52] "C'est proprement ce que l'on a eu dessein de faire de cet argument de Bellarmin et que l'on pourra faire encore de quelques autres tant de luy que des autres Ecrivains Catholiques, en leur laissant de bon coeur la gloire de les avoir trouvez les premiers, en reconnoissant que l'on ne fait que marcher sur leurs pas et suivre leurs pensées, et en taschant seulement de les rendre plus utiles à l'Eglise, plus capables de faire impression sur les esprits, et plus incapables d'estre eludées par les deffaites des hérétiques." A. Arnauld and P. Nicole, *La Perpétuité de la Foy de l'Eglise catholique touchant l'eucharistie defendue contre le livre du Sieur Claude,* I, préface ("La Grande Perpétuité de la Foi"), [unnumbered pages]. *La Petite Perpétuité de la Foi,* published by Arnauld in 1664, provoked a theological controversy between Port Royal and the Huguenots. The Protestant answer came from Jean Claude in his *Réponse aux deux traités* (1665) and *Réponse au livre de M. Arnaud* (Quevilly and Rouen, 1670). Nicole retorted with *Les Préjugéz légitimes contre les calvinisme* (Paris, 1671) answering which Claude wrote *La Défense de la Réformation contre le livre intitulé: Préjugéz légitimes* (Paris, 1673). In this attempt to defend the legitimacy of the Reformation, Claude acquitted himself so well that Port Royal acclaimed him the most eloquent counsel of the Reformers. He soon became one of the leading spokesmen of the Calvinists.

[53] As in the case of the Five Propositions to which an ex-Jesuit, Nicolas Cornet, reduced the teachings of Jansen.

tool. They made the authority of the King serve their own ends. They ultimately lessened the autocratic power of the King, though in religious policy they wanted him to keep the authoritarian tradition and welcomed any strong action on his part against the heretics. It was through the clergy that Richelieu gained his further posthumous victories. Taking the lead in intolerance, the clergy found that by managing the King they could give to the spirit of intolerance a dynamic vitality. He was to find too late that what had been needed was the reform of the religious policy of the Catholic Church, and not his own obedience to the clergy in religious matters. The religious policy of the Catholic Church showed only too clearly that there were limits beyond which the King, in spite of his authority, could not go. The Huguenot issue was another factor which showed this, and he failed with it in somewhat the same way as did Richelieu. In both cases there were the same external appearances of glittering success. But whereas Richelieu knew when to stop, merely leaving directions and memoranda to posterity, Louis XIV pursued the policy of persecution to the bitter end. "Louis XIV trouva ainsi dans les deux Religions les bornes de sa puissance." [54]

The indebtedness of Louis XIV to Richelieu in the sphere of religious policy has never been described in the terms it deserves. The evidence of direct influence is certainly scanty, but even the available data seem to have attracted little attention. In the early years of his reign, Louis XIV received a memorandum [55] entitled "Considérations de Religion et d'Etat pour faire voir la nécessité et la possibilité, qu'il y a de réunir les Hérétiques de France à l'Eglise Catholique"—a plan for the revocation of the Edict of Nantes. The project was clearly the same as Richelieu's. It contained a proposal to convert fifty ministers, to convoke a synod at which the converts would vote for union with the Catholic Church, and then to revoke the Edict as useless. [56] The plan was not put into effect in the strict sense, but some of its spirit left a deep impression on subsequent history, especially with respect to the idea that revoca-

---

[54] Rulhière, *Eclaircissemens historiques*, p. 137. Rulhière seems to have understood the problem of the clash between the Catholic and Protestant churches and the will of the King, with a result fatal for the authority and power of the latter.

[55] Rulhière points out the attempts to carry out the plan contained in the memorandum inspired by Richelieu and backed by newly converted Turenne. Cf. *ibid.*, pp. 116-117.

[56] Cf. *ibid.*, pp. 105, 113–114.

tion must follow as a result of a *fait accompli,* when prolonged maintenance of a meaningless legal agreement became ludicrous.

Similarly, another, better-known document, styled Code Michault,[57] outlived Richelieu, who had been its chief prompter. Its author was Michel de Marillac, and its true object was to give legal sanction to some five hundred rules enslaving the nation by making it a real police state. All movements abroad would be checked by magistrates, to whom all citizens would have to report; all contact with foreign ambassadors would be forbidden; all popular assemblies would be ruled out; and passive obedience would be required of the nation. The code was rejected by the parlement; in any case its adoption was superfluous because of the rapidly expanding autocratic personal rule of the Cardinal. Its tradition was revived in 1669 by Colbert because Louis XIV chose to choke his subjects with legal restrictions which served to cover his own illegal action. The royal absolutism was different from that of Richelieu in that the former sought to fortify in a permanent fashion whatever terrain it gained and laboriously reduce to submission every aspect of national life by passing laws which concerned the whole nation. The absolutism of Richelieu was personal; it dealt with minute aspects of life and showed itself in his daily relations with his subordinates. He created a tradition on which Louis XIV could erect an edifice. The absolutism of the *roi-soleil* quickly became an all-embracing system; the King had an easier task with his subjects, whose initiation into the new way of life had been completed by the Cardinal.

The antiemigration Edict of 1669, which reflected certain clauses of the Code Michault, bore the character of a general measure affecting everybody in the state. It did not touch upon the Protestant question at all. It was as French subjects and not as Calvinists that the Huguenots were reduced to subservience to drastic rules. But it showed the powerful indirect impact of the absolutist thought of Richelieu on the destiny of the Huguenots under Louis XIV, since it was a prelude to countless further measures which no group in the state could withstand.

The main agents, who saw that the results of Richelieu's action in matters of religion were not wasted, and that his will was executed, were the clergy and the Jesuits. Their attitude determined the character and the extent of royal absolutism in religious issues.

---

[57] For the Code Michault, see *ibid.,* pp. 73–76.

The role of the Jesuits was crucial, because the order was responsible for providing the method for efficient persecution—a terrible legal weapon of casuistic argument. Given the method, the clergy could proceed with the anti-Huguenot policy which soon became the policy of the state. Soon the "peace of the church," an internal Catholic alliance, consolidated the camp and made it impregnable even against the King. Louis XIV seemed to follow no religious policy of his own. His behavior in this respect showed his serious weaknesses as a statesman. His policy was that of a weak though continuous defense against the Church, to which he constantly referred for counsel and to which he was constantly giving way. His revolt, belated and useless, came only on his deathbed. Surrounded by churchmen, whose authority he uncritically accepted, he allowed himself to listen to their extravagant praises. These, appealing to his immense vanity and inflating his royal ego, made him lose all sense of reality. By urging him to trample on any opposition, the clergy made him incapable of realizing that he sanctioned, protected, and increased a religious absolutism which he was unable to control.

To wrest from the King the power of decision in religious matters—to reduce his *de facto* absolute religious authority—was a task for which Jesuit thought could largely take the credit. Its refined and deadly dialectic served not only to provide a painless death for the Huguenots by legalistic means, but also to render the King insensible and to make him act as if in a deep trance. He kept repeating that it was his concern to maintain the status of the Calvinists, but he was unable to see that attempts to reduce it were relentlessly pursued in the legal field, and that he played no small role in helping the process. He became the first victim of the dialectic, much earlier than the Huguenots, and he realized only too late how misinformed he had been in religious affairs—particularly in relation to the number of conversions of Protestants—and how closely his policy had been guided by the Catholic clergy.

The first signs of that guidance were noticeable early. In 1651, Bishop de Comminges, addressing the child-monarch, expressed the wish that the "deplorable" liberty of conscience make no further progress.[58] The plan was exacting, and, although it was not

[58] " 'Nous ne demandons pas,' disait à Louis XIV enfant l'évêque de Comminges, 'que Votre Majesté bannisse à présent de son royaume cette malheureuse liberté de conscience que détruit la liberté des véritables enfans de Dieu, parce que nous ne

yet pushed too far, it made a lasting impression on the youthful
King by urging his submission and obedience. Once Louis XIV was
in the grip of the ecclesiastics, it was left to them to formulate
the most effective method by which the Edict of Nantes might
be destroyed and by which the King might be induced to hasten its
destruction.

The first formulation of this long-term policy was made in 1655
at the Assembly of the Clergy by Henry de Gondrin, the Archbishop of Reims. He denounced the declaration of Saint Germain
(1652) as the cause of the full reëstablishment not only of the
Edict of Nantes but also of a number of measures supplementary
to it.[59] Further, he proceeded to the formulation of principles aimed
at destroying the Edict, and urged the strict interpretation of the
clauses of the Edict by arbitrary action of lawyers, whenever necessary. By making a point of maintaining in their integrity all the
rules made in 1598, regardless of all changes since that time in the
custom and spirit of society, he forged a formidable anti-Huguenot
weapon for anyone who wished to use it. His policy, which Louis
XIV did not fail to adopt later, concealed brutal and ruthless
persecution behind an apparently strict legalism.

Meanwhile, from 1661 on, smaller vexatious measures were
undertaken by the King, showing, if not yet his complete concur-
rence in the clergy's action, at least his active support. In April of
that year he granted, at the request of the Assembly of the Clergy,
the right to put into effect the declaration of July, 1656, establishing a mixed commission to oversee the administration of the
Edict of Nantes. The intention of the clergy in making this request
was to show to the Calvinists that their religion was "just tolerated"; the commissions, where already in operation, served that
purpose; the choice of peculiar "Protestant" members, who often
acted against their coreligionists, assured the Catholic success.
Ultimately, mixed commissions became a natural breeding ground
for abuse,[60] encouraged anti-Huguenot chicanery, and left a per-

jugeons pas que l'exécution en soit facile, mais nous souhaitons au moins que ce mal ne
fit point de progrès, et que, si votre autorité ne le peut étouffer tout d'un coup, elle le
rendit languissant et le fît périr peu a peu par le retranchement et la diminution de
ses forces.'" *Remonstrances du clergé de France*, April 11, 1651, as quoted in Puaux
and Sabatier, *Etudes sur la révocation*, pp. 37–38.

[59] Cf. *Remonstrances du clergé de France*, April 2, 1656, as quoted in Puaux and
Sabatier, *Etudes sur la révocation*, p. 39.

[60] Cf. Puaux and Sabatier, *Etudes sur la révocation*, pp. 44–45.

manent memorial in the mass destruction of Protestant churches.[61]

The policy thus inaugurated by the clergy of France was not given exact form until the Jesuit Pierre Meynier published his *Exécution de l'Edit de Nantes* [62] (1662), an ingenious prescription for a perfidious interpretation of the clauses of the Edict of Nantes. The clergy profited enormously by this publication; the effectiveness of their policy was greatly enhanced by their immediate adoption of the casuistic pattern outlined by Meynier. A passage in Meynier relating to Protestant funerals was given immediate attention. His argument [63] that, because the Edict made no mention of day funerals, all Huguenot funerals had to take place at night was instantly submitted to the King, who in an order-in-council decided the issue against the Protestants.

The clergy began to see clearly that the only way to induce the Huguenots to change their religion was to limit all their liberties and privileges, then to forbid re-conversion, and finally at one blow to revoke all the edicts.[64] That policy was strictly connected with the plan to get complete spiritual control over the King, make him the dupe of his own piety, and have him sanction actions the true significance of which was hidden from him. He had to be involved in the gradual diminution of Calvinist liberties; he had to be persuaded that the policy was his own; yet he was not to think that it meant persecution, but simply a strict and just administration of the law.

Deceived by the clergy's gross misrepresentation of facts, Louis XIV did not guess that he would be bound to decide on revocation by the very process of drawing a logical conclusion from the action which had made the Edict of Nantes a dead letter. It was ignorance

---

[61] Cf. Haag, *La France Protestante, Pièces justificatives* [unnumbered volume], p. 368, Pièce justificative No. LXXXVIII.

[62] Meynier published a series of works all under the same title, *Exécution de l'Edit de Nantes,* each relating to a different province; e.g., Languedoc, Poitou, Dauphiné, etc. The first was *Exécution de l'Edit de Nantes dans le bas Languedoc* (Pézénas, 1662).

[63] "L'étude approfondie du texte du traité de 1598 ne porte nulle part que l'enterrement d'un prétendu réformé puisse estre fait du jour, il doit estre fait de nuit." Pierre Meynier, S.J., *Exécution de l'Edit de Nantes* (1662), p. 304, as quoted in Puaux and Sabatier, *Etudes sur la révocation,* p. 50.

[64] Cf. Pierre Jurieu, *La Politique du clergé de France,* pp. 21–23. Jurieu thus summed up the point of view of the clergy: "Il faut diminuer peu à peu leurs libertéz, et quand cela sera réduit à peu de chose et que leur nombre sera fort diminué, on révoquera tout d'un coup tous leurs édits." *Ibid.,* p. 23.

that he showed, rather naïvely, when he admitted that he would personally refrain from granting any favors to the R.P.R. because of his goodness and for the sake of the Calvinists, in order that they should not miss the opportunity to ponder on their disadvantageous position as a minority.[65] His good nature prompted him to dispense with any general plan for outright pressure on the Protestants; yet the clergy knew better than to let him freely exercise his good will. On several occasions he showed anxiety over the negligent way in which certain paragraphs of the Edict had been carried out. This desire for a genuine supervision of the legal situation, reflecting his good intentions,[66] the clergy used to their own advantage by reversing it to serve the cause of revocation.

These endeavors bore their first fruits in February, 1665, when Louis XIV publicly declared his intention to see all his subjects profess one creed.[67] The grip of the clergy over the King, stronger since 1660, increased, owing to the financing of the Court by the Church. The illness of the Queen Mother, when a wave of piety swept through the Court, was another important cause.

Nor was the new reign lacking in opportunities for the Catholic clergy to prevail over the Protestant. The disputes concerning the nomination of mixed commissions were made to serve this end, as was the inequality in the financial situation between the Catholic Church and the Calvinists, who requested the King for aid at every assembly.

There is no doubt that it was the clergy who initiated at that time all actions against the Protestants. Contemporary views, both Huguenot and Catholic, corroborate the opinion that the clergy had a leading role in persecution. All achievement in that field up

[65] "Mais quant aux grâces qui dépendoient de moi seul, je résolus, et j'ai assez ponctuellement observé depuis, de n'en faire aucune à ceux de cette Religion; et cela par bonté plus que par aigreur, pour les obliger par-là à considérer de temps en temps d'eux-mêmes, et sans violence, si c'étoit par quelque bonne raison qu'ils se privoient volontairement des avantages qui pouvoient leur être communs avec tous mes autres sujets." Louis XIV, *Oeuvres,* I (*Mémoires*), 87–88.

[66] "Ces surséances que le roi a accordées font voir que ce prince est bon et qu'il donnerait beaucoup plus de repos, s'il n'était continuellement sollicité par le clergé." Jurieu, *La Politique du clergé de France,* p. 20.

[67] Déclaration pour l'exécution de la Bulle d'Alexandre VI au sujet des Jansénists. Cf. H. Gélin, "Madame de Maintenon convertisseuse," *Bulletin de la Société de l'histoire du Protestantisme Français,* XLIX, 250. Hereafter cited as Gélin, "Madame de Maintenon," *Bull.*

to that time has been shown to be theirs.[68] A sign of this achievement was a declaration forwarded to the King expressing the design of the clergy in the form of twenty-two articles limiting
Protestant liberties.[69] The declaration claimed that the task of conversion ought to be made a national issue. Technical instructions
on how to deal with the Protestants were given in a timely publication by Pierre Bernard, a lawyer and judge at Béziers and author
of the legal treatise *Explication de l'Edit de Nantes* (1666). His
case provides one of the most remarkable examples of Jesuit penetration which, already appearing in Gallican and Jansenist doctrines, reached the councils of the King and controlled the high
clergy. The Court and most of the clergy, while deriding Jesuit
casiustry, were unable to stop the Jesuits from gaining spiritual
leadership. Bernard was not the inventor of the system he recommended: his book was a crafty legal comment on the work of
Meynier, *Exécution de l'Edit de Nantes,* which not only provided
him with the solid basis of authoritative theological argument,
but also taught him the dialectical art. Like Meynier, Bernard
wrote in the spirit of the Spanish theologian Escobar (1589–1669),
making subtle distinctions between shades of meaning, fencing off
every proposition with various reservations, and employing the principle of probability to show that every law, if properly tackled, can
be inverted.

Meynier had been so much contaminated by the principles of
Escobar, that, interpreting the principle that a sovereign is not answerable to his own laws,[70] he felt it necessary to explain why neither
Louis XIV nor his father had immediately abolished the Edict of
Nantes. His tone was nearly apologetic when he spoke of the clemency and sense of pity of both kings.[71] Escobar formulated many
straightforward questions, which he answered bluntly. Must a sovereign obey the laws of his predecessor? No, provided a scandal is

---

[68] "... ce qui a esté fait jusqu'à présent, est deu au zèle de quelques grands prélats
et au soin qu'ils ont pris de le faire réussir." Pierre Bernard, *Explication de l'Edit de
Nantes par les autres édits de pacification et arrêts de règlement,* préface. Hereafter
cited as Bernard, *Explication de l'Edit de Nantes.*

[69] "Articles concernant la religion, lesquels messieurs les archevesques, evesques et
autres ecclésiastiques, députez en l'assemblée géneralle du clergé supplient très humblement le Roy de leur accorder." Puaux and Sabatier, *Etudes sur la révocation,* p. 48.

[70] Cf. Antonius de Escobar y Mendoza, *Liber theologiae moralis,* p. 40.

[71] Cf. Louis A. Sabatier, "La Révocation et les Jésuites," in Puaux and Sabatier,
Etudes sur la révocation, pp. 133–134.

avoided.[72] Must a sovereign observe the laws he has made? No, because laws are for his subjects and not for him.[73] How can he evade laws? By finding evidence of their nonacceptance by the people, as, without acceptance, laws have no value;[74] or by extension or restriction of the meaning of words which may be used to interpret the legal rules as desired—in unfavorable matters by keeping to the natural meaning of words, in favorable circumstances by stretching the substance of words as far as possible.[75]

Meynier tinted the cold logic of Escobar's arguments with even stronger shades of dialectical sophistication, obscuring the status protecting the heretics with dialectic through which current ideas could not penetrate without change. Bernard borrowed heavily from the arguments of the two Jesuits, but he gave the final touches to their method and launched it in French public life. He provided a legal frame and presented a plan from the point of view of a practicing lawyer, referring dialectical rules to particular cases and describing the way in which those rules could withstand the impact of practice.

If the works of Escobar and Meynier had opened new vistas in unknown lands, Bernard devised practical ways of exploring them. His book marked an epoch. He helped to bring on persecution by giving full legal backing to a vicious interpretation of the clauses of the Edict of Nantes. Until his time, malicious interpretation had been carried out only on a small scale and no written prescriptions had been available except those of Filleau,[76] published in 1666. The merit accruing from such action had previously been of a strictly religious nature, and persecution had never acquired the full status of a recognized system in the civil sphere. Owing to the acceptance of the principles of Meynier and Bernard, religious persecution could henceforth be performed under the official guise of legal dis-

---

[72] "Tenetur Princeps suorum praedecessorum Leges observare? Proeciso scandalo non tenetur . . ." Escobar, *Liber theologiae moralis,* p. 40.

[73] ". . . lex obligat subditos, nullus autem sibi subditos est . . ." *Ibid.*

[74] Cf. *ibid.,* pp. 38–39.

[75] "Licet ne leges interpretari, non solum exponendo, verum etiam ampliendo & coarctando? Licet." *Ibid.,* p. 46. "Quonam modo humana lex interpretanda est? Lex quidam odiosa explicanda & extendanda iuxta naturalem verborum proprietatem: non vero strictius aut laxius. At in materia favorabili explicanda & extendenda est, quantum verba patiuntur." *Ibid.,* p. 47.

[76] *Decisions catholiques;* cf. A. J. Grant, *The Huguenots,* p. 149.

ciplinary measures, and no longer only for spiritual glory. The persecuted were reduced to a band of notorious lawbreakers, if not
criminals. The various means of oppression of the Huguenots after
1660 had a strong flavor of legalism. Of six ways of persecution
practiced at that time, as testified by Claude,[77] all but one or two
either belonged to the sphere of law or used legal means.

The effect of the dialectical method, however revolutionary,
would have been of little significance without the collaboration of
Louis XIV. He became intensely interested in it, pragmatically testing the utility of theoretical devices, yet not grasping the deep sense
of dialectic theory against which he was unable to protect himself.
He had no understanding of its implications, although his own ideas
were not far removed from it. He was essentially a man of action,
ready as a rule to take the obstacles at one bound, bursting with
indignation at any sign of opposition, and yet susceptible to the influence of men of experience and authority. The clergy, seizing their
opportunity, could not have acted more cunningly than they did, involving the King in a series of practical legal measures, all slowly
destroying the fabric of Protestant liberty without directly attacking the principle of toleration. In a conspiracy of silence about the
destruction of the Huguenots, the King had probably only a vague
notion of the intricate relationship between his own action and that
of the clergy, and of the methods involved. He lacked insight and
proved unable to find out for himself the true state of Huguenot
affairs. But his intolerance was not entirely due to his ignorance;
otherwise it could never have been seriously contended [78] that he
was the prime mover of the Revocation. His intolerance was rooted
in his doctrine of the state; from that doctrine, sooner or later, he
was bound to draw the logical conclusions.

Sometimes, in day-to-day legislation, the administration of Louis
XIV, responding to the pressure of the clergy and in conformity
with its spirit, was an important factor leading to the act of revocation. The latter followed only after more than four hundred [79] mi-

---

[77] (1) Judicial chicanery, (2) deprivation of employment, (3) infractions of the
Edict, (4) new legislation, (5) treachery, (6) inspiring general hatred of the Huguenots among the people. Cf. Claude, *Les Plaintes des Protestans*, p. 6.

[78] The Revocation, according to André, was his own work, ordered personally to
the people about him. Louis André, *Louis XIV et l'Europe*, p. 218.

[79] Cf. Claude, *Les Plaintes des Protestans*, p. 6.

nute decisions, in the form of orders, regulations, and acts which seemed unconnected with one another,[80] had grown to the height of a pyramid to which nothing could be added save the last pronouncement making the Edict of 1598 null and void.

Already on November 6, 1662, as has been noted, the Council had regulated the time of Protestant funerals, limiting it to the dawn and dusk hours [81]—an order satisfactory from the point of view of Meynier, whose perfidious interpretation of the clauses of the Edict had given rise to that decision.

Bernard's detailed instructions [82] on reducing the number of Protestant churches were permeated with the same Escobarian spirit which induced Louis XIV to explain to the Elector of Brandenburg that the only churches which had been razed were those constructed since 1598 and therefore illegally.[83]

The best way to limit the scope of Article XXXVII, one of the Edict's "particular" or secret articles, and to reduce the number of Protestant schools, consisted, according to Bernard, in regarding the word "school" as applying only to the primary stage.[84] Since

[80] "[Soon after 1660] ... on vit successivement paroître un grand nombre d'Edits, d'Arrêts, de Déclarations qui avoient également pour objet de restreindre les privilèges des Calvinistes, sans qu'on puisse inférer de leur apparente connexité, qu'ils soient émanés d'un même plan, d'un système déjà formé pour l'entière ruine de la Secte. Ils tenaient à l'esprit général de ce temps là, au zèle du Clergé qui ajoutoit ... des demandes toujours nouvelles, à la vigilance d'une Administration active." Rulhière, *Eclaircissemens historiques*, p. 50.

[81] F. A. Isambert, A. Jourdan, and others, *Recueil général des anciennes lois françaises: depuis l'an 420 jusqu'à la Révolution de 1789*, Vol. XVIII, No. 396, p. 20. Hereafter cited as Isambert, *Recueil général*. It is true, however, that the number of restrictions was soon to be decreased by the orders of 1663 and 1669.

[82] He suggested the following procedure: first, to let the Protestants prove, by using the Edict of Nantes, that they possess the right to exercise their religion, remembering that even if the right has been exercisd for long, this is no proof, since there can be no appeal against the perennial natural law of the Catholic Church; second, to deny the validity of proofs submitted either by rejecting oral testimonies or by questioning the legality of consistorial and other records; third, to abolish the churches until only 25 per cent of their total number are left. Cf. Sabatier, in Puaux and Sabatier, *Etudes sur la révocation*, pp. 139–140.

[83] "... on n'a abattu aucuns de leurs temples [des réformés] que ceux qui ont été bâtis depuis l'Edit de Nantes ... qu'ils n'ont jamais eu droit de faire construire." Louis XIV to the Elector of Brandenburg, September 10, 1666, as quoted in Claude, *Les Plaintes des Protestans*, Pièces justificatives, pp. 123–124.

[84] Cf. Bernard, *Explication des articles particuliers joints à l'Edit de Nantes*, pp. 276 ff., as quoted by Sabatier, in Puaux and Sabatier, *Etudes sur la révocation*, pp. 141–142.

1612 the Huguenots had enjoyed the privilege of setting up small schools. In 1671 the administration forbade more than one school and one teacher for each locality.[85]

Similarly, in order to get hold of the souls of Protestant children, it was necessary, in the opinion of Bernard, to distort Article XVIII of the Edict, making the word "children" applicable only up to the age of seven.[86] He agreed that Catholics were forbidden by Article XVIII to convert Protestant children by force and against the wish of their parents, but, he maintained, it was nowhere stated that older children could not choose their religion.[87] Here the response of the administration was slower, and the validity of the orders-in-council of 1662 and 1664 was maintained. These upheld [88] Article XVIII of the Edict, ordering the children to be brought up in the religion in which their father had died; in case of mixed marriages, children had to follow the father's faith. In 1669 it was enacted that no children, either Catholic or Protestant, were to be constrained to any religion [89]—a decision which caused furious indignation among the clergy. It was only in April, 1681, that the parlement of Rouen put into practice the seven-year age limit principle of Bernard.[90] The royal declaration of June, 1681, followed, giving to Protestant children the option of conversion at the age of seven, and thus abrogated the three previous orders-in-council.[91]

Certain incidents of quasi-collusion of Church and state against Protestants were not synonymous with the King's obedience to the clergy in all matters after 1666. Perhaps more often than not, the administration was reluctant to condone the too hasty decisions of the clergy, amending their precipitate declarations and rejecting all those measures which were excessively harsh in the treatment of the religious minority. The situation, which should have been eased after 1669 by the religious peace, showed that the clergy still

---

[85] Cf. Isambert, *Recueil général,* Vol. XVIII, No. 664, p. 442.

[86] Cf. Bernard, *Explication de l'Edit de Nantes,* p. 100.

[87] Cf. *ibid.*

[88] Cf. Isambert, *Recueil général,* XVIII, 23, as quoted in Ch. Benoist, *Condition juridique,* p. 216.

[89] Cf. Isambert, *Recueil général,* Vol. XVIII, No. 549, p. 199.

[90] Cf. *ibid.,* XIX, 267.

[91] Of May 19 and September 18, 1663, and of April 23, 1665, ordering that boys under fourteen and girls under twelve not be influenced in religious matters. Cf. *ibid.,* Vol. XIX, No. 968, p. 269.

needed to win over the King. Against the background of the con-
solidation of the Catholic camp, which was hailed as a great success for the monarchy, the lack of complete agreement between the
spiritual and temporal powers was conspicuous. The Church could
not precipitate revocationary trends by the arbitrary decisions to
which it occasionally resorted, but only by getting the King under
its domination during his not infrequent periods of acute piety, when
he was eager to repent of his sins at any price. Clearly, the attack
of the spiritual power sought the most vulnerable points in the
King's mentality. The armor of his absolutism could be pierced
through his extreme sensitivity to the idea of merit in helping the
cause of the Church and thus redeeming his soul, which was tainted
by mortal sin. As the clergy knew that he was well aware of his own
weaknesses, the only problem was how to use his repentance in the
cause against heresy. The right way was shown in the general tendencies of anti-Huguenot activities which, during the period when
the Church sought to gain control over the King, were confined to
religious matters—the protection of Catholics and the purchase of
Calvinist souls by gifts and bribery.

The notion that the protection of Catholics was one of the primary concerns of religious policy naturally emanated from ecclesiastical circles. Pressure was exerted in that direction, and declarations sanctioned by the administration were issued whenever
the King seemed undecided about his course of religious action, as
in 1663 and 1665 (declarations against re-conversion), or when
his policy of conversion, which he pursued in the second decade of
his reign, was not yielding the expected results, as in 1679 and
1680. In the last year, previous declarations against re-conversion
were combined into an edict. It seemed to be the policy of the clergy
to see that at least one of the two trends, protection of Catholics or
conversion of Huguenots, was pursued satisfactorily. Whenever the
King was more directly engaged in giving active support to anti-
Protestant policy, as in the second decade of his reign, the clergy
seemed to slacken in direct intervention, testing the new ground on
which the King would be induced to step later.

After 1670 the work of conversion found in him an enthusiastic
supporter. The method of buying consciences he had chosen from
the start, expressing in 1661 his resolution to give money pay-
ments to docile Huguenots and to convince and instruct them

through the persuasion of Catholic priests.[92] An early case of financing this trading in souls took place in 1663, when Colbert offered 3,000 livres to the Bishop of Uzès to aid a Huguenot lawyer by buying him an office, provided he made a sincere conversion.[93] It was only after 1669 that Louis XIV became subject to periodic attacks of piety, which were never permitted by the clergy to follow a haphazard course. He was affected in this way in 1670, probably in 1674, too, and still more severely in 1676.[94] The first attack had left permanent traces, since in 1673 the Elector of Brandenburg heard that the intention of the French King was to uproot the Protestant religion wherever he could find it.[95]

All that time, the spiritual guardianship assumed by the clergy over the King, became more close. The opposition of the King showed itself, until then, chiefly in his deliberately slow ways of dealing with the Huguenots. The best moment for the Church to gain an ascendancy over him was when, during a bout of piety, he felt he must expiate his amorous liaisons with an act of extreme devotion and when his supreme power was left open to exploitation for spiritual ends.

It was on such an occasion in 1674 that he gave a third of his revenue from *regale* to the cause of converting the heretics, creating a fund, known as *caisse de conversions,* the administration of which was given to Paul Pellisson-Fontanier. This institution, organized as a ministry, proved a heavy and awkward liability. It is true that it must have partly lessened the bitterness of the clergy caused by the right to *regale,* by which the King received all income from vacated bishoprics and nominated candidates to ecclesiastical benefices. The use to which the money was put by Pellisson provided a solution satisfactory for the clergy and even made

---

[92] "... je résolus aussi d'attirer, même par récompense, ceux qui se rendroient dociles; d'animer autant que je pourrois les évêques, afin qu'ils travaillassent à leur instruction, et leur ôtassent les scandales qui les éloignoient quelquefois de nous." Louis XIV, *Oeuvres,* I (*Mémoires*), 88.

[93] Cf. E. M. Guitard, *Colbert et Seignelay contre la Religion réformée* (Documents inédits), p. 32.

[94] Cf. Rulhière, *Eclaircissemens historiques,* pp. 118–119.

[95] "... l'intention du roi étoit de ruiner la religion protestante partout où il la trouvait ... la résolution en est prise." M. de Vaubrun to the Elector of Brandebourg, as quoted in Gélin, "Madame de Maintenon," *Bull.,* XLIX, 251.

it easier for the Jesuits to approve of that lucrative royal benefice.

But the purchase of conversions was costly. The results were meager, though the amounts expended were raised from year to year to increase the number of conversions.[96] Besides, the evil done was much more serious than a drain on financial resources. The "conversions" subsidized by the ministry of Pellisson created the wrong impression. They helped later to convince Louis XIV that the Huguenots were not truly devoted to their creed and that the willingness to abandon the R.P.R. was genuine and widely held. The speed with which conversions were obtained, in spite of the irreparable harm thus done to the Calvinist cause, was still unsatisfactory, as was suddenly realized in 1679. The Secretary of State, Phélypeaux de Châteauneuf, then started to study local conditions in the provinces to find a more efficient method. The inquiry did not put an end to the transactions, which were no more satisfactory after 1680 than before.[97] Louis XIV gained in this way [98] an erroneous opinion of the strength of the Protestants' attachment to their church. He thus felt that it was unstable and that many Protestants would be easily attracted by the bait of six livres per head, the price Pellisson at first paid every newly converted person.

This move of Châteauneuf gave rise to two memoranda,[99] one Jansenist and the other Molinist, presented to the King in response to the query of his minister. The report embodying the Jansenist views was based on the instructions issuing from the clergy. It was permeated with the austere piety characteristic of Port Royal. Yet, although it considered that the conversion of members of the erring religion was necessary, and that to enter the Church without a sincerely pious attitude was worse than to remain outside, it breathed a certain kind of philosophic, and essentially Christian, tolerance. The Molinist report was concerned with eradicating heresy by an

---

[96] Ten thousand in three years. Two years later the total number of conversions was 50,830. Cf. Viénot, *Histoire de la Réforme française*, II, 432.

[97] Data relating to Aunis and Saintonge illustrate the slow rate of conversions, which in 1682 were marked by a sudden drop in number and a corresponding rise of the average cost per head. In 1681 the number of conversions in Aunis and Saintonge was 1,503; the total outlay amounted to 11,659 livres, the average cost per head being 7 francs, 75 centimes (1 livre = 1 franc; cf. G. Zeller, *Les Institutions de la France au XVIe siècle*, p. 240). The first ten months in 1682 brought just over 600 converts, costing 8,000 livres or about 13 francs per head. Cf. Haag, *La France Protestante*, VIII, 177.

[98] Cf. Rulhière, *Eclaircissemens historiques*, pp. 148, 176.

[99] About the two memoranda, see *ibid.*, pp. 164–170.

appeal to royal authority. It suggested the passing of a series of
severe acts, one of which should be the suppression of the *Chambres
de l'Edit*. Taken together, the memoranda reflected the keen rivalry
between the Jansenists and the Jesuits—their conflict still continuing despite the officially recognized "peace of the church,"
which could not eliminate the deep doctrinal differences. The Jesuits,
who adopted the theory of one of their own members, Luis de
Molina (1535–1600), asserted the idea of unrestrained freedom
of the will and were concerned with the juxtaposition of grace and
free will. The emphasis, which they put on the element of freedom
of consent in the will, was disregarded by the Jansenists, who in
this respect followed the tradition of the early Protestants.

The two societies were both eager to get the credit for conversions, each one hoping that the other might be judged heretical.
Both reports achieved some measure of success, though neither of
the schemes was accepted by the King in its entirety. But the need
for more effective means against the Huguenots was acknowledged
by the Court. The urgency of such a need was stressed by an immediate suppression of the *Chambres de l'Edit* by the parlements
in the South, following the Molinist advice. In January, 1679, the
last remaining *Chambres* were closed [100]—an occurence which
signified for the Jesuits a victory, desired, it would seem, for
reasons predominantly, if not purely, religious. The King at that
time was guided by similar motives. His zeal for conversion was
outstanding, and he used his absolute authority to engender his own
zeal in others. In this he found a general response; indeed, those
at Court or in the administration who escaped its influence were
rare.[101]

For the clergy, the road lay open to an undivided success. By
assuming control over the conscience of Louis XIV, the clergy
achieved their long-sought aim. Their ascendancy formed a favorable basis for the final assault on Protestantism—an assault conceived as a joint move with the monarch. Owing to that alliance, the
rigid authority of the clergy found a safe niche under the monarchy
—a situation strengthened by the Gallican Articles in 1682.

A closer inquiry into the real authorship of the Revocation of the

---

[100] Cf. Benoist, *Condition juridique,* p. 273; already in 1669 the parlements of Paris
and Rouen had got rid of their *Chambres*. See also Rulhière, *Eclaircissemens historiques,*
p. 171.
[101] Cf. Rulhière, *Eclaircissemens historiques,* pp. 176–177.

Edict of Nantes focuses attention on Richelieu. The Revocation was in a double sense the work of the spirit of Richelieu: his autocratic will, his idea of state unity and of *raison d'état,* his hatred of all elements of opposition, and his absolutist doctrine were all inherited by Louis XIV; his proselytizing plans, on the other hand, developed by the persevering labors of Father Joseph, were preserved and revived by the clergy and the Jesuits. The fact that this influence of the Cardinal was not obvious can be seen not only in standard interpretations of Richelieu's "tolerant" policy but also in the division of opinion on the nature of the main reasons for the Revocation. The reasons given vary between two extremes: the predominantly political and the religious. Both the conflict between the monarchy and Rome, in which any rash treatment of heretics could be considered an asset for the temporal power, and Louis XIV's royal Gallicanism have been advanced as arguments in favor of the political alternative.[102] Yet it has been pointed out that pure devotion, derived from the divine nature of royal authority, provides the clue.[103] It has also been indicated that the intolerance shown in the revocationary measure was the mark of adherence to uncompromising and dogmatic religious convictions, an essentially Protestant attitude, which the Catholics for once adopted.[104] Although these contradictory statements are hard to refute as explanations, they do not reveal the whole truth. The opinion which assigns a relative predominance to the political factor sounds more plausible.[105] But how are the religious and political motives to be separated? Where did the pressure of the clergy on Louis XIV's pious nature end, and where did his absolutism and his royal Gallicanism begin?

It has often been said that whenever the Pope and the French King quarreled, the Protestants inevitably suffered. This generalization is still true in the case of the internal alliance between the

---

[102] Cf. G. H. Dodge, *The Political Theory of the Huguenots of the Dispersion,* p. 13.

[103] "La dévotion sincère provient du fait qu'il se fait considérer comme le représentant de la divinité sur la terre et responsable devant elle seule." André, *Louis XIV et l'Europe,* pp. 217–218.

[104] Cf. Lord Acton, "The Protestant Theory of Persecution," *Essays on Freedom and Power,* p. 109; quoted above, chap. ii, n. 59.

[105] "The Revocation of the Edict of Nantes," wrote Harold Laski, "has political unity rather than religious truth as its objective." H. J. Laski, *The Rise of European Liberalism,* p. 53.

monarchy and the Gallican clergy—a phase in the conflict between the temporal and the spiritual powers. This alliance between two supreme authorities who were able to muster all available material and spiritual resources was a decisive factor in the history of the Edict of Nantes. The role of various individuals in the Revocation either was subordinate to these authorities, or resembled that of their agents. This became quite clear in the five years preceding the Revocation itself. In 1680 the Assembly of the Clergy suddenly changed its usual tone of complaint over the ineffective religious policy and congratulated the King on his achievements.[106] It was already sure of success. There can be no doubt that the members of the Court, and in particular the councilors and the intendants, by their eager support of conversions, brought the drastic solution nearer. As early as 1680, Madame de Maintenon had started her private conversions in order to please the King. Later, in 1683, after her secret marriage to the King, she was anxious to establish her influence over him by displaying a religious zeal similar to that of the late Queen.[107]

It was also in 1680 that Louvois drifted into the revocationary current of public opinion; a ruthless careerist, he at least was frank enough to admit that Calvinism for him meant only a religion disliked by the King. In 1681, Marillac, the intendant of Poitou, exceeding the orders of Louvois, became a zealous leader of conversions by means of the *dragonnades*. Only those who were sympathetic to the idea of converting by force could make headway at the Court. Colbert did not lose his influence with the Council at once, and he was spared disgrace because of his great repute; yet he had no alternative but to acknowledge that victory lay with the clergy: "Quoi qu'il en soit la victoire que le Clergé remporta sur les Huguenots fut célèbre."[108]

A partisan of peaceful methods, Colbert, in 1682 and 1683, in two separate letters, advised bishops and intendants to organize bloodless conversions "avec tout ce raisonnement de la prudence et l'honnêteté chrétienne. Ce sont des âmes qu'il faut gagner à Dieu par la douceur de la charité ..."[109] But the *dragonnades* of

---

[106] Cf. Rulhière, *Eclaircissemens historiques*, p. 183.

[107] Cf. *ibid.*, p. 231.

[108] J. B. Colbert, *Testament politique*, p. 400.

[109] MS letter of Colbert, Fr. 7044, fol. 54, as quoted in Guitard, *Colbert et Seignelay contre la Religion réformée*, p. 37.

1681 convinced Louis XIV of the effectiveness of armed action, reducing to a matter of days the painstakingly slow work of Pellisson, which had lasted for months. The expedient of Marillac yielded 37,000 converts in Poitou, an unexpected result which was overwhelming for the Court.[110] Simultaneously the clergy intervened with their theoretical justification of *compelle intrare,* or converting by force. The *Avertissement pastoral de l'Eglise gallicane à ceux de la R.P.R. pour les porter à se convertir et à se réconcilier avec l'Eglise,* prepared by the clergy in 1682, contained threats of serious repercussions in cases of disobedience.

The clearest sign that the spirit of intolerance was becoming a serious threat can be seen in the wave of emigration, which in 1681 carried away 3,000 families.[111] Intolerance, of all shades and degrees, was spreading; it ranged from the passionate yet superficial persecution of members of the administration and the Court to the deep, silent intolerance which the clergy adopted at a later stage, and which had originated with La Chaise[112] and the Jesuits in 1682.

Responsibility for the Revocation rests to some degree on Le Tellier, Louvois, Châteauneuf, Seignelay, Madame de Maintenon, Father La Chaise, Harlay, the Archbishop of Paris, and the intendants Marillac, Bâville, Foucault, and de Muin. But those who must chiefly be held accountable are the King and the whole body of the clergy. Theirs was the idea, the policy, and the method of realization: the encouragement given to the executive officers, the incitement to organize conversions, the acceptance of brutality, and the disregard of persecutions. It is significant that the Protestant liberal attack of this period was directed against both the power of the clergy and that of the King. It contested the absolutist monarchical power by declaring it should serve the interests of the people; it also placed this power on a secular basis and thereby undermined the interests of the spiritual authorities.

Thus, when the liberal reaction came, it emphasized the fact that the anti-Huguenot movement reached its climax soon after the spiritual and temporal authorities had been welded together by the Articles of 1682; the Church and the state in close alliance continued to destroy heresy—their common enemy. It was not a coin-

[110] Cf. Viénot, *Histoire de la Réforme française,* II, 441.
[111] Cf. Haag, *La France Protestante,* I, lxxix.
[112] Cf. Rulhière, *Eclaircissemens historiques,* pp. 227–229.

cidence that the Revocation came soon after the official recognition of Gallicanism in France.

RATIONALIST AND SECULAR REACTION

The process by which the clergy molded the will and faith of Louis XIV has been dealt with at some length, because during that process the period of the legal life of the Edict of Nantes drew to its sudden close—following the second series of *dragonnades* in 1685. In the sphere of doctrine, the immediate result of the Revocation was that absolutism was attacked from abroad. The ensuing controversy, although it sprang from the events of 1685, had its deeper roots in the reaction which had already affected France for some fifteen years. This reaction, directed in the main against the clergy, reveals the true source of religious absolutism.

Coöperation with the King was of major importance for the clergy, because there was a general reaction against stiffening ecclesiastical authority. Significantly, it was not royal absolutism but the excessive authority of the clergy which invited the main opposition between 1670 and 1685. In 1681, Jurieu condemned the intolerance of the clergy, but was still far from criticizing his "glorious monarch," in whom he had high hopes regarding the future of toleration; indeed, Jurieu assured the King of the loyalty of his Protestant subjects:

> La diversité des Religions qui est encore en France, n'empêche pas que notre Glorieux Monarque ne soit l'admiration de tout l'Univers et la terreur de toute l'Europe. En un mot, il n'y aura jamais de trouble dans l'Estat par la diversité des Religions, pendant que l'on voudra bien protéger et tolerer les Protestans. Tant qu'il plaira au Roy, il aura en eux des sujets d'une fidelité inviolable.[113]

The aid extended by the monarchy to the clergy was timely. The latter, Jurieu maintained, were rigidly reactionary; their attitude condoned an inelastic, doctrinaire intolerance which was commended [114] as being for the good of the state. It was grossly behind the times; it had learned little from the Reformation, re-

---

[113] Jurieu, *La Politique du clergé de France,* p. 241.
[114] Cf. *ibid.,* p. 189.

maining narrowly dogmatic. This is not, of course, tantamount to saying that the average Protestant clergyman was of high standard. Jurieu's complaints in this respect were bitter.

The reaction which followed in the form of Socinianism was worthy of the Arminian tradition. One of the impulses was given by Isaac d'Huisseau with his *La Réunion du christianisme* (1670), in which he proposed to apply Cartesian logical rules to religious thought. He regarded the institution of the Church and all tradition as unnecessary and urged a belief in the universal, clear, and simple truths found in the Bible. His rationalist attitude led him straight to Irenism: he tried to save the position of the Protestants by preparing the way toward conciliation by a union between the Calvinists and the Lutherans within a wider union of all Christians. In his book *Remarques sur le livre de d'Huisseau* (1670), La Bastide described him as a Socinian, and his book as a highroad to Socinianism.[115] Huisseau was a Socinian at least in his refusal to accept anything he was unable to comprehend with clarity. Backed by the Protestant Academy of Saumur, he trod the highroad to modern rationalism, causing a profound reaction against the Scholastic system in theology. He acted as a severe critic of rigid Calvinist dogmas, earning the condemnation of the Synod of Saumur in 1670. He never wished to convert anybody; he merely laid stress on the essential features of all Christian churches, urging conciliation by recognizing a basis common to all and ignoring the nonessential differences.[116] He engendered in other Socinians the impression that the Reformation had been only half-performed, and now needed to be completed. He gave impetus to the Pajonist movement, aiming at the reconciliation of theology with liberty, which he promoted with Claude Pajon at the Academy of Saumur. After the Revocation of the Edict of Nantes, Pajonism was attacked by Jurieu; the discussion flared up into a heated controversy between Jurieu and Bayle [117]—symptomatic of the deep cleavage between the Protestant exiles on the problem of toleration.

Huisseau and the Pajonists represented the tide of new thought which had arisen as a reaction against the clergy's uncompromising opposition. This opposition took definite shape in 1682 with the adoption of the ruthless doctrine of *compelle intrare*. Bossuet, the

---

[115] Cf. Frank Puaux, *Les Précurseurs français de la tolérance au XVIIᵉ s.*, chap. iv.

[116] Cf. Isaac d'Huisseau, *La Réunion du christianisme*, pp. 151–160.

[117] Cf. below, chap. vi.

leading spokesman of the Catholic clergy, gave this doctrine his official approval: "Je suis et j'ai toujours été du sentiment: 1⁰ que les princes peuvent contraindre par des lois pénales tous les hérétiques à se conformer à la profession et aux pratiques de l'Eglise catholique; 2⁰ que cette doctrine doit passer pour constante dans l'Eglise, qui non seulement a suivi, mais encore a demandé de semblables ordonnances des princes." [118]

The spirit of the period was compressed in an almost symbolic event of dramatic brevity—the debate between Claude and Bossuet in 1678. Held at the request of Madame de Duras, who staged the debate at her house, it reflected, against the background of religion, the conflict between authority and liberty, of which the Bishop of Meaux and the Pastor of Charenton were the respective advocates. Claude earned in it a lasting reputation as a champion of freedom of thought and inquiry without restraint, and of the supremacy of individual conscience over arbitrary decisions. He warned that blind obedience to the authority of the Church had led the Catholics to idolatry. He urged that only what is clearly embodied in the Scriptures be accepted; what is not in the Scriptures does not belong to the revelation and therefore is not the object of faith. He devised ways of accepting the teaching of the Church: "Pour les autres poincts qui ne se peuvent regler ny par le silence, ny par les lumieres évidentes de l'Ecriture, avant que de les recevoir, ou de les condamner, ils doivent tâcher de s'en instruire, par les voyes que Dieu a ouvertes, & établies dans son Eglise, & cependant présumer bien des décisions des Assemblées." [119]

Bossuet defended collective against individual rights. He spoke of an authority which was necessitated by life, and which enjoined a discipline. This discipline would provide an avenue to the profound satisfaction which, he believed, individuals derive from obedience. He regarded submission to authority as a necessary feature of all churches:

> Ma premiere réflexion est sur la réponse que fait M. Claude aux Actes tirez de la Discipline de ses Eglises. Je me suis servi de ces Actes pour montrer qu'il estoit si necessaire à tous particuliers dans les questions de la Foy de se soumettre à l'autorité infaillible de l'Englise, que les Pré-

---

[118] Bossuet, *Oeuvres complètes,* LII, 234, as quoted in Puaux and Sabatier, *Etudes sur la révocation,* p. 88.

[119] Claude, *Réponse au livre de Monsieur l'evesque de Meaux intitulé Conference avec M. Claude.*

tendus Réformez, qui la rejettoient dans la speculation, se trouvoient forcez en meme temps à la reconaitre dans la pratique.[120]

Claude, sympathizing with Pajonism, was defending a losing cause against Bossuet. He gave further expression to his attitude at conferences with Pajon in 1676, the year in which Pajonism was condemned by the Synod of Paris. The point of view represented by Bossuet had a brighter future; the Counter Reformation was now victorious, and Huisseau's project for a new reformatory trend leading to a union of churches came at the wrong moment. Pajon argued in vain:

> Mais, à l'égard de nos consciences, ils [le clergé] ne sont plus rien; parce que nos consciences ne dependent que de Dieu ... les qualitez qu'ils s'attribuent, en se qualifiant Archevêques, & Evêques, no leur donnent aucune autorité sur nos consciences, jusqu'à ce qu'ils nous ayent fait voir que ce qu'ils enseignent, est autorisé par l'Evangile de Jesus Christ.[121]

The clergy sought to achieve religious unity by stamping out heresy and not by compromise and conciliation. It was Jurieu who made public his suspicions on this matter. "Si par le terme de réunion, on entend simplement un retour à l'Eglise Romaine, sans qu'elle se reforme & qu'elle se relâche en rien, il est clair que c'est abuser des termes, & cela ne s'appelle pas réunion." [122] The cause of the clergy, moreover, was particularly well served by the indisputable authority of the King; the powerful machinery of the absolute monarchy worked toward religious unity by excluding the dissenters rather than by winning them over. The freedom-seeking Socinian arguments were suppressed. Yet the influence of the philosophic rationalism which they introduced began to filter through to many minds. Its chief exponent, Spinoza, produced his *Tractatus Theologico-Politicus* (1670), in which he expressed his bold conviction that politics and religion belong to different spheres and that both should be established on a secular basis.

Spinoza distinguished between an outward and an inward aspect of religion. "I speak expressly of pious practices and outward religious observance, not of those sentiments of piety and veneration

---

[120] Bossuet, *Conference avec M. Claude Ministre de Charenton sur la matière de l'Eglise.*

[121] Claude Pajon, *Remarques sur l'Avertissement Pastoral, etc.,* p. 36.

[122] Jurieu, *Lettre de quelques Protestans pacifiques, au sujet de la réunion des Religions à l'assemblée de Messieurs du clergé de France, qui se doit tenir à Saint-Germain-en-Laye,* p. 10. Hereafter cited as Jurieu, *Lettre de quelques Protestans.*

towards the Supreme Being . . . For inward worship and pious contemplation are the inalienable right of all." [123]

Inner religious experience he considered to be the right of all individuals: ". . . inward worship and pious contemplation are the inalienable right of all." [124] External religious practices, "religious worship and pious practices," were to him a matter of public concern, to be determined and to acquire legal force through an act of the ruling authority. "Religion . . . only acquires the force of law by the decision of those who have the right of commanding, and . . . God has no kingdom among men save by those who hold the chief authority." [125] In the absence of a ruling power, religion, as Spinoza saw it, is secularized by a process of reasoning:

> . . . religion among the ancient Hebrews acquired the force of law from the fiat of the governing authority alone; and this authority destroyed, religion in itself could no longer be regarded as a system adapted to a single nation, but became a catholic or universal system of reason; I say of reason, for the truly catholic religion was not yet made known to man by revelation.[126]

The tendency to secularize politics appealed to Jurieu, who took the role of leader of the Protestant "liberal" reaction in the pre-Revocation days. Full of apparently contradictory traits, he shared some of them with the Socinians, whom he hated with the zeal of an Inquisitor and whose ideas he later ascribed to his opponent Bayle. His liberalism had a rationalist background shared indeed by the Socinians; a declared monarchist (also like the Socinians), he defended monarchy against the idea of popular rights on rational grounds, and on the same grounds spoke of toleration as a matter of expediency, though admitting the need of intolerance in certain circumstances.

> Il y a des occasions dans lesquelles un Prince peut employer la rigueur des Edits pour empêcher la diversité des Religions; c'est dans la première naissance des Schismes. Mais quand une fois un Schisme est fait; quand une Secte est devenue nombreuse & forte, c'est d'aller contre l'esprit de l'Evangile que d'employer ou la violence ou la mauvaise foy pour remedier à ce mal.[127]

[123] Benedict de Spinoza, *Tractatus Theologica-Politicus*, p. 328.
[124] *Ibid.*
[125] *Ibid.*, p. 328; see also pp. 327, 330.
[126] *Ibid.*, pp. 330–331.
[127] Jurieu, *La Politique du clergé de France*, p. 238.

His rational attitude led him from intolerance to toleration, the beneficent role of which he recognized, in spite of his deeply rooted belief that it does not agree with religious teachings. "Je n'examine point à present si cette tolerance si generale pour toutes sortes de Sectes est selon les principes de la Religion; je ne le croy pas trop. Mais je soûtiens hardiment, que, selon les regles de la Politique, cette tolerance generale est ce qui fait la force & la puissance de cette République [Hollandaise]." [128]

Toleration, in Jurieu's estimation, not only has a role definitely assigned in time (after the schism has been made) but also varies in relation to its objects:

> Les Princes Huguenots ne peuvent pas avoir la même tolerance pour les Catholiques dans leurs Estats, que les Princes Catholiques peuvent avoir pour les Huguenots; parce que les Princes Protestants ne peuvent estre assûrez de la fidelité de leurs sujets Catholiques, à cause qu'ils ont fait serment de fidelité à un autre Prince qu'ils considerent comme plus grand que tous les Rois; c'est le Pope.[129]

According to this relativity of standards of comparison applied to Catholics and Protestants, the intolerance of the Huguenots toward the Catholics is justified by the allegiance of the latter to a foreign power, the pope, while the intolerance of the Catholics is given no ground for defense.

Jurieu pleaded for toleration, defending the Huguenots, whom he felt to be seriously threatened after 1680. His appeal was directed to the clergy, whom he regarded as guilty of anti-Protestant policy: "Pour disposer les esprits à cette réunion, il faudrait messieurs que vous fissiez cesser ces rigueurs & les severitez que l'on exerce contre nous par tout le Royaume, sous vôtre direction & à vôtre sollicitation." [130]

His plea was partly formulated as an attack against the clergy—an attack expressed in 1682 in general but blunt terms and anticipating the subsequent events. "Le clergé," warned Jurieu, "a dessein de nous combler de miseres, & de nous rendre nôtre Religion odieuse par la multitude des calamitez qu'on y attachera." [131] As the policy of the clergy moved in the direction anticipated by Jurieu, in 1685, he accused them in an open statement of complicity

---

[128] *Ibid.*, p. 239.

[129] *Ibid.*, p. 121.

[130] Jurieu, *Lettre de quelques Protestans,* p. 78.

[131] Jurieu, *Les derniers efforts de l'innocence affligée,* p. 71.

in excesses: "On a déjà rasé nos Temples, dissipé nos Troupeaux, chassé la plupart de nos Ministres; la tentation & l'épouvante ont déjà fait succomber un grand nombre de gens à qui vous faites l'honneur de donner le nom de Convertis: Si par vos Conseils Sa Majesté continue cette conduite à l'égard des Sujets fideles ... "[132]

The defense of the Huguenot cause thus led Jurieu to anti-clericalism; he regarded the clergy as chiefly responsible for intolerance, and although he was aware of the responsibility of the King in this matter, he did not yet dare to attack him directly. Until the Revocation, he showed a definite preference for monarchy over the form of a popular state—the view stated in his *Les derniers efforts de l'innocence affligée* (1682). Through a Huguenot *jurisconsulte,* he said: "Y a-t-il quelqu'une de nos actions qui signifie que nous souhaiterons de changer la forme du Gouvernement present & d'une Monarchie en faire un Etat populaire? Qu'y gagnerions-nous, & ne serions nous pas bien plus en sureté, si nous estions exposez à l'autorité et à la fureur d'une beste aussi farouche & aussi peu raisonnable qu'est le peuple?"[133]

His rationalistic approach deterred him from laying down hard-and-fast rules. He refrained from vast generalizations and reached his conclusions pragmatically. Testing each case separately, he would register different rules for different circumstances. He had a modern legal mind, though it was obscured by gusts of violent fanaticism. He could with equal seriousness justify Huguenot intolerance and ask for Catholic toleration. He defended the monarchy against the pretensions of a popular state, but he admitted the right to religious self-determination as conscience dictates, and he supported the claim that the edicts, which the kings had treated as they pleased, were in fact irrevocable. He thought that "les Edits de pacification peuvent être considerez à cinq égards, & qu'en tous ils sont irrévocables."[134]

Jurieu tried to save the relationship between the Protestants and the monarchy by excluding the problem of resistance from the sphere of religion. "S'il faut que le Calvinisme meure," he advised, "il vaut mieux qu'il meure innocent."[135] In his *Histoire du calvinisme*

---

[132] Jurieu, *Lettre de quelques Protestans,* p. 11.

[133] Jurieu, *Les derniers efforts de l'innocence affligée,* pp. 26–27.

[134] Jurieu, *Avis aux protestans de l'Europe,* published with his *Préjugez legitimes contre le Papisme,* p. [10] (unnumbered).

[135] Jurieu, *Histoire du calvinisme et celle du papisme,* préface.

(1683), he praised obedience as an essentially Protestant virtue. He also defended the view that in the sixteenth-century wars, religion was only incidentally involved; admitting that some religious wars were legitimate, he advanced a concept secularizing the right to resistance. Yet the same belief in "secularization" preserved his mildly Monarchomach attitude, helping him to set moderate limits to monarchical power. His rejection of unlimited monarchy in the *Histoire du calvinisme* was typical: he did not argue in a philosophical vacuum; he referred to concrete examples, decribing the state not only as it should be, but as he saw it in practice. He viewed critically both extremes—unlimited rule and unrestrained radicalism:

> Les maximes de Buchanan & de Paraeus sont assurement fausses dans la generalité dans laquelle ces autheurs les proposent, car ils pretendent que c'est là le droit general des peuples & des Roys: ce qui n'est pas vray; mais la Theologie de l'Apologiste [Arnauld], qui met tous les souverains sans distinction au dessus des loix n'est pas moins fausse.[136]

Jurieu accounted for a variety of conditions necessitating different sets of institutions and principles on which government is based.

> On sçait que les droits des souverains sont aussi differents que les peuples & les nations. Chaque Royaume se gouverne selon ses loix & selon l'usage. Il y en a où les Roys sont absolument souverains, il y en a d'autres où leur authorité est borné par les privileges des sujets ... Je voudrois bien que notre orateur [Arnauld] allast debiter ses maximes outrées sur l'authorité des Roys, aux dietes de Ratisbonne & à celles de Varsovie, il verroit comme il seroit receu à prouver que l'Empereur & le Roy de Pologne sont en pouvoir de disposer des vies & de la fortune des particuliers comme de leur bien propre.[137]

There is a certain undogmatic vagueness in the assertions and a flexibility of prescription apparent in his further statement: "Il y a donc des lieux où les maximes de Buchanan & de Parée sont très veritables, & il y en a d'autres où elles sont très fausses. Il y a aussi des estats où la Theologie de l'Apologiste [Arnauld] doit estre suivie, & d'autres ou elle seroit un crime de leze Majesté contre l'estat." [138]

Jurieu explicitly allowed disobedience when freedom of con-

---

[136] *Ibid.*, II, 288; Jurieu refers to Arnauld, the author of *Apologie pour les catholiques* (Liège, 1681).

[137] Jurieu, *Histoire du calvinisme et celle du papisme*, II, 288–289.

[138] *Ibid.*, p. 289.

science is affected: " ... nous nous croyons dispensés d'obeir à nos Roys quand ils commandent quelque chose de contraire à nostre religion & à nostre conscience." [139]

In nonreligious matters he insisted that obedience is due to the princes. Though he objected to a boundless royal authority, he freed it from the shackles of natural law. He believed that the supreme authority depends on usage and customs; being different and residing in a different body in each country, it can be regulated only by positive law: "L'autorité Royale & monarchique est donc purement de droit positif, car si elle estoit de droit naturel il s'ensuivroit que les gouvernements democratiques & aristocratiques pecheroient contre le droit de la nature; ce qui est extravagant." [140]

This quasi-liberal secular monarchism, as represented by Jurieu, was nourished by the rational and expedient speculations which he was always cultivating. His writings prior to 1685 reveal a sober thinker of essentially sound argument. Though after the Revocation the quality of some of his polemic writings deteriorated, he did not change his ideas as much as is sometimes believed. He had never previously defended an unlimited monarchy—a fact which shows that even before 1685 he was at heart a Monarchomach. Though in principle a believer in passive obedience, he opposed the doctrine that kings are above the law; according to him, obedience is due to the prince, but subjects are no longer bound if their conscience is openly violated by the ruler's disregard for religious freedom.

---

[139] *Ibid.*, p. 291.
[140] *Ibid.*, p. 290.

VI

CONSEQUENCES OF THE REVOCATION

Salus populi suprema lex.

Suaderi debet religio, non cogi.

"Ma première divinité Louis XIV."—Pierre Bayle, *Oeuvres diverses, II* (*La Cabale chimérique, 1691*), 677.

"Est-ce donc que l'heureuse revolution d'Angleterre n'est pas un prelude de la notre un presage qui nous la fait esperer, & un moien qui nous y conduit?"—Isaac de Larrey, *Réponse à l'Avis aux réfugiez* (*1709*), p. 22.

THE ATTACK FROM ABROAD ON ABSOLUTISM

The Revocation brought about the full emergence of doctrines the origins of which are to be found in the earlier secular reaction, and which in the end acquired an antimonarchist twist. This accounts for Jurieu's sudden change of front after the Revocation. As in the days of the Monarchomachs, the political situation found immediate reflection in doctrines.

Since the Revocation scarcely changed the status of the Huguenots, who had already been deprived of their rights and liberties by scores of decrees and orders, it was not the Revocation itself which determined the nature of the response to it by Protestant political writers. All that the Revocation did was to draw attention to the person ultimately responsible for it—the monarch—and thereby evoke a furious reaction from Protestants abroad. When Jurieu began to write against Louis XIV, he had already waged a long anticlerical campaign. His *Lettres pastorales* (1686–1689) were written both as a challenge to the Catholic clergy and as an appeal to the Calvinists to revolt against the French King. But the radicalism of Jurieu was not extreme. He still believed monarchy to be the best type of government, and extreme popular rule impracticable; he wanted monarchy to take the responsibility of government, though monarchy should be checked from below by the people or their representatives. He made explicit the nature of his accusation: the King, by using force against his subjects' conscience, had become an outlaw; hence revolt against him was proper and legal.

Jurieu defended the rights of the people against those of the King not only because he was indignant at the Revocation and needed a weapon with which to combat the monarch, but also because he sought to transplant the success of England's Glorious Revolution onto French soil. He also encountered strong opposition from the clergy, who firmly sided with Louis XIV. In the ensuing conflict and in the heat of controversy, Jurieu's ideas on monarchy acquired a radical tint which they had not had originally. Similarly, in the heat of the controversy with Bayle, he gradually became extremely intolerant. The incongruity apparent in his simultaneous defense of popular sovereignty and rejection of toleration can be explained not only by his obsession with truth [1] but also by his inability to hold purely popular principles. He was originally a liberal monarchist—a fact which proved decisive, even when the Revocation uprooted his original opinions. In adopting popular views, he did not come round to the view that the monarch should be entirely deprived of his power; his new theory on governmental system recognized the possibility of coexistence of royal responsibility with popular representation. But the shock of the persecutions and the bitterness inspired by the Revocation in 1685 led him ultimately to reject his earlier liberalism.

The decade following the Revocation was marked by two outstanding controversies: the discussion between Jurieu and Bossuet, and the protracted dispute in which Jurieu and Bayle were the main opponents. While the former discussion was in the main related to the problem of sovereignty, the latter centered around toleration.

Jurieu's views on sovereignty are found in his *Lettres pastorales*, in which he challenged the *Histoire des variations* of Bossuet.

---

[1] As Professor Dodge sees it: cf. G. H. Dodge, *The Political Theory of the Huguenots of the Dispersion*, p. 334. Hereafter cited as Dodge, *The Political Theory of the Huguenots*.

Jurieu still upheld some of his old views: his secularism, reflected in his belief that no government is of divine origin; his belief in monarchy as the best type of government; and his advocacy of obedience to sovereign power. At the same time, the *Lettres pastorales* embodied a budding "revolutionary" doctrine. It was in this work that Jurieu established his position as leader of the "zealous" and uncompromising Huguenot majority in exile. His vivid writings, together with his fervent political temperament, had a large share in the renascence abroad of the Huguenot political party.

It is true that conditions were then extremely favorable to the revival of political activity, especially among the numerous zealot colonies in London, Rotterdam, The Hague, Geneva, Zurich, and Berne, which were eager to manifest their indignant fury. But, despite this favorable atmosphere, the immense influence of Jurieu on Huguenot *émigré* politics must not be underestimated. It was he who reversed the traditionally loyalist Protestant policy by arguing forcefully in favor of revolutionary views, on which, he urged, all future relationship with the king should be founded.

The direction of the new attack was revealed in the dispute with Bossuet, when Jurieu displayed many of his merits, but also betrayed his weaknesses. Although Jurieu succeeded in becoming the chief spokesman for the Huguenot majority, from the start he overstepped the limits of conventional behavior. Under his leadership, the Huguenot community in exile was involved in an intricate tangle of slanderous intrigues, and he was the last man to be able to show the way out of the predicament. At the height of the controversy, he was led from insult to injury; in spite of the sharpness of his tongue, his reasoning could not always stand a critical test. Careful scrutiny shows that his argument was often shallow, the way in which he presented the principle of popular sovereignty doubtful, and his discussion with Bossuet futile. Had the terms used in the dispute been precisely and clearly defined, the futility of the controversy would have been obvious. Yet, if account be taken of Jurieu's irreconcilability of temperament, it seems clear that any compromise was impossible; he had to fight a political as well as a theological battle. The need to restate the principle of sovereignty served as a good occasion; it helped Jurieu to comment on conditions in England and in particular to justify the English people's revolutionary action. Jurieu's radicalism thus had an immediate influence by stimulating the somewhat barren political convictions of the Huguenots, who, because of their long loyalist tradition, had been unable to develop any fruitful theories.

For all its boldness and vision, the doctrine had the defects of its merits. It might appeal to contemporaries as relevant to the issues of the day; yet it was clearly designed to meet the needs of the moment only. Jurieu made no effort to veil this and made no attempt to discuss the origins of political society; he had no interest in, and did not discuss the idea of, a first social contract by which society had been made. It was the second contract, the agreement between the people and the king, that attracted him, because the principle of revolt could be built on its basis. Jurieu's theory was not without shortcomings, which Bossuet was very ready to point out. The Bishop of Meaux quoted Jurieu's proof that sovereignty is in the people. The people, according to Jurieu, give sovereignty; therefore they must possess it. Bossuet asserted the contrary: "Ce seroit plutôt le contraire qu'il faudroit conclure, puisque si le peuple l'a cédée, il ne l'a plus." [2] Yet, for all his logic, Bossuet was unaware that his dispute with Jurieu was a misunderstanding, that its continuation was possible because neither adversary made his statement sufficiently clear, and that, from the start, the argument was unduly emphatic and the cleavage between the two theologians so deep as to eliminate the possibility of reaching an agreement. Besides, the two writers used the concept of sovereignty as a medium for trying to reach opposing objectives. The goal of Jurieu was to justify revolt; that of Bossuet, to assert the need of obedience to authority. Although occasionally the opponents confessed adherence to what amounts to the same principle of sovereignty, inevitably their conclusions were different.

Jurieu introduced the idea of sovereignty together with that of contract. The latter, he maintained, determines the powers given to the monarch by the people. Unlimited power is illegitimate. Complete sovereignty does not reside in the monarch; monarchy is not its source. "La souveraineté appartient radicalement et originalement au peuple." [3] The people are the controlling and supervising factor; from them the stream of sovereign power flows, and they

---

[2] F. Lachat, ed., *Oeuvres complètes de Bossuet,* XV (*Cinquième Avertissement*), 464. Hereafter cited as Bossuet, *Oeuvres complètes.*

[3] Pierre Jurieu, *Lettres pastorales adressées aux fidèles de France qui gémissent sous la captivité de Babylone,* XVIIIᵉ lettre, 3ᵉ Année, p. 416.

can dispense or withhold that power, should the need arise. "Le peuple est la source de l'autorité des Souverains, le peuple est le premier sujet où réside la souveraineté: le peuple rentre en possession de la souveraineté aussitost que les personnes ou les familles à qui il l'avoit donnée viennent à manquer, le peuple enfin est celuy qui fait les Rois." [4] The people grant sovereignty only conditionally, always keeping in their hands the power of controlling the monarch. "Les peuples ne donnent jamais aux Souverains et ne peuvent donner l'administration des affaires publiques sans se réserver ou expressément ou tacitement le droit de pouvoir aux désordres que les souverains pourraient causer à la Société par une mauvaise administration." [5] The sovereignty of the people is of the highest order, and from it the sovereignty of the monarch is derived. "Il est clair que c'est parce que les Peuples sont en pouvoir de se choisir des maîtres où ils veulent, qu'ils font leurs Souverains, et qu'ils leur donnent la Souveraineté pour autant de temps que le salut de l'Etat le demande." [6]

The special character of the duty of obedience follows from this: the obedience of the subject lies within the limits of the contract; outside the contract the subjects are absolved from obedience. Yet, disobedience should be rare. Only an extraordinary action of the monarch demands it; it must be guided by the rule *salus populi suprema lex*. The public good demands that in extreme cases of flagrant violation of law by the prince, the restraining power of the people over their ruler should take the form of a revolt. "Monsieur de Meaux is to know, that . . . according to us," Jurieu wrote, "it is not always forbidden to make use of Arms in favour of Religion." [7] He distinguished between establishing religion by force, which he rejected, and defending it by the same method, which he justified by the right of self-preservation and by the law of nature.

The Glory of Planting Christianity by Arms has been due to Popery, and its Princes. But to Defend Religion by Arms is another thing, and there is neither Reason nor Authority by which it can be proved to be a Crime. All the World is agreed that Defense is lawful and allowed by the Laws

---

[4] *Ibid.*, XVIIᵉ lettre, p. 390.

[5] *Ibid.*, p. 389.

[6] *Ibid.*, p. 396.

[7] Jurieu, *Judgment upon the Question of Defending our Religion by Arms with Reflections upon the Affairs of England in his Ninth Pastoral Letter of the Third Year*, p. 4.

of Nature, to which the positive Laws of God never made any Contradiction.[8]

The theories of Jurieu met with strong opposition from Bossuet. He branded them seditious and devoted his *Cinquième Avertissement aux Protestans sur les lettres du ministre Jurieu contre l'histoire des variations* (1690) to their condemnation.

Bossuet attempted to destroy the theory of popular sovereignty by undermining that of contract. He dismissed the latter with contempt; to him, only the force emanating from a high authority could create that binding force which holds together a political community; contract was not only meaningless, but dangerous. He accused Jurieu of contradiction in terms: "S'imaginer maintenant avec M. Jurieu, dans le peuple considéré en cet état, une souveraineté qu'est déjà une espèce de gouvernement, c'est mettre un gouvernement avant tout gouvernement et se contredire soi même." [9] He accused him further of seditious and destructive influences: "Voilà jusqu'où M. Jurieu poussa les choses par ses séditieux raisonnemens. Il renversa toutes les puissances, et autant celles qu'il défend que celles qu'il attaque." [10] He warned that in propagating the theory of popular sovereignty, Jurieu was in danger of unleashing forces that might produce devastating consequences. "Il est odieux ... par principes ... d'établir, comme fait encore M. Jurieu, des maximes séditieuses qui tendent à la subversion de tous les empires et à la dégradation de toutes les puissances établies de Dieu." [11] To him, popular sovereignty meant license and not true liberty; it was anarchy ending in tyranny. Jurieu, who believed that liberty could be found in a people's state, had, in Bossuet's opinion, hopelessly confused the issue, degrading the idea of liberty to a position of precarious independence amid chaos and anarchy.

S'il plaît à M. Jurieu d'appeler souveraineté cette liberté indocile qu'on peut céder à la loi et au magistrat, il le peut; mais c'est tout confondre: c'est confondre l'indépendance de chaque homme dans l'anarchie avec la souveraineté. Mais c'est là tout au contraire, ce qui la détruit. Où tout est indépendant, il n'y a rien de souverain: car le souverain domine le droit.[12]

---

[8] *Ibid.*, p. 6.
[9] Bossuet, *Oeuvres complètes*, XV (*Cinquième Avertissement*), 465.
[10] *Ibid.*, p. 439.
[11] *Ibid.*, p. 380.
[12] *Ibid.*, p. 466.

By exposing "anarchistic freedom" in a popular state, Bossuet prepared the ground for an authoritarian rule. He considered complete submission to powerful rulers a civic virtue: "Ce n'est pas toujours abandonnement ou foiblesse de se donner des maîtres puissans: c'est souvent, selon le génie des peuples et la constitution des Etats, plus de sagesse et plus de profondeur dans ses vues." [13] He thought it erroneous to superimpose, as did Jurieu, a higher authority over the existing sovereign power. Such a usurping authority, he pointed out, almost invariably flatters the people, and the consequences for the latter are always bad: the people are given promises, are soon exploited, and are bound to end in subjugation. "C'est toujours ou leur liberté qu'on leur veut rendre, ou leur bien qu'on leur veut assurer, ou leur religion qu'on veut rétablir. Le peuple se laisse flatter et reçoit le joug. C'est à quoi aboutit la souveraine puissance dont on le flatte." [14] As a means to social stability, Bossuet sought to deprive individuals of their right to self-defense against legitimate power: "Le seul principe qui puisse fonder la stabilité des Etats, c'est ... qu'aucun particulier ou aucun sujet ... n'a droit de défense contre la puissance légitime ... pour un autre principe, c'est avec M. Jurieu ébranler le fondement des Etats et se déclarer ennemi de la tranquillité publique." [15]

Opposing both the system of popular government and the idea of individual freedom, Bossuet focused attention on the connection between the two. He believed that both have their roots in anarchy; but while the former is subsequently transformed, the latter must eventually be discarded. At one time, Bossuet seems to have expressed the view held by his opponent: " ... toutes sortes de magistratures ou de puissances légitimes venoient originairement de la multitude ou du peuple." [16] He immediately qualified this statement, however, making clear where his disagreement with Jurieu lay. To him, the "popular" phase of sovereign power is only transitory. Sovereignty is not firmly placed at some point and attached to some body; it is a changing principle. "Il ne faut non plus s'imaginer que la souveraineté ou la puissance publique soit une chose comme subsistante, qu'il faille avoir pour la donner; elle se forme et résulte de la cessation des particuliers." [17] Sovereignty, in the doctrine of

---

[13] *Ibid.,* p. 474.
[14] *Ibid.,* pp. 480–481.
[15] *Ibid.,* p. 441.
[16] *Ibid.,* p. 465.
[17] *Ibid.*

Bossuet, is flexible, subject to variation and shifting from master to master. It is a confusing concept, and Bossuet recommends that it be renounced, together with "cette liberté qui fait tout craindre."[18]

A new attack on absolutism was launched in 1689 by the author of *Les Soupirs de la France esclave qui aspire après la liberté*. He bade defiance to Bossuet, while continuing in the spirit of certain ideas contained in the *Lettres pastorales*. Though the book differed from the famous epistles, it breathed similar righteous indignation over oppression, and it continued in the tradition of advocating the *salus populi* principle. Although it cannot definitely be proved, Jurieu is given the credit of being its author.

The attack on royal authority was perhaps equally direct in the *Lettres pastorales,* but in the *Soupirs* it was more violent; the hatred of tyranny was stated here more sharply. The book gives an historical survey of the French monarchical system. It exposes the false notion that, merely because of ancient usage,[19] the people should bear the burden of absolute power. It seeks to destroy the opinion that the French monarchy originated as an arbitrary power.[20] It indicates the main trend in political life, poignantly describing the growth of royal power and its effects. It makes it clear that the king has replaced the state in its traditional role: "Le Roi a pris la place de l'Etat ... le Roi est tout & l'Etat n'est plus rien. Et ce ne sont pas seulement des paroles & des termes, ce sont des réalités."[21] Royal authority has become so elevated that all social distinctions appear negligible; the whole machinery serves only the aggrandizement of the king—"tout doit tendre uniquement à la grandeur du Roy."[22] Power has shifted in the direction of despotism, which the author of the *Soupirs* did not hesitate to call by name:

C'est la Puissance Despotique & le Pouvoir Arbitraire, absolu & sans limites que les Rois de France s'attribuent, & que Louis XIV a exercé & exerce d'une maniere à faire trembler tous les Païs qui ont des Rois. Le Roy de France ne se croit lié par aucunes loix, sa volonté est la regle du bon & du droit. Il croit n'être obligé à rendre conte de la conduite qu'à Dieu seul, il se persuade qu'il est le maître absolu de la vie, de la

---

[18] *Ibid.,* p. 466.
[19] Cf. *Les Soupirs de la France esclave qui aspire après la liberté,* p. 171.
[20] Cf. *ibid.,* p. 79.
[21] *Ibid.,* p. 23.
[22] *Ibid.,* p. 26.

liberté, des personnes, des biens, de la Religion & de la Conscience de ses Sujets.[23]

This state of affairs is opposed to the principles of reason, humanity, and Christianity: "Ce Pouvoir Despotique est si opposé à la raison qu'on le peut appeller insensé, si opposé à l'humanité qu'on le peut appeller brutal, & inhumain, si opposé même à l'esprit du Christianisme qu'on le peut appeller Anti-Chrêtien." [24] The distortion of the original aims of kingship is then pointed out:

> ... les Peuples ont établi des Rois pour conserver les personnes, la vie, la liberté & les biens des particuliers. Mais ce gouvernement de France est monté à cet excès de tyrannie qu'aujourd'hui le Prince regarde tout comme luy appartenent en propre. Il impose des tributs & tels qu'il luy plaist sans consulter ni Peuples, ni Grands, ni Etats, ni Parlements.[25]

The *Soupirs* made it clear that political institutions such as the States-General and the parlements have been relegated to insignificance, while royal power has vastly expanded. These institutions no longer guard the nation against tyranny, because they are not equal partners with the king and do not share sovereignty with him; they are no more than instruments in his policy. Their role has been reversed, burying all vestiges of the people's liberty. "Aujourd'hui le Roy est Maître Absolu des biens, de la vie & de la liberté de tous ses Sujets, de quelque qualité & condition qu'ils soyent." [26] This arbitrary incursion into private rights extends to the sphere of conscience: " ... le Roy est maître ... aussi de l'exterieur de la Religion; tellement qu'il n'est permis à personne de faire profession d'aucune Religion que de celle qu'il plait au Roy. ... le Roy ne veut qu'une Religion dans son Royaume, il en est le maître, il faut obeir, ... dit-on." [27] The author of the *Soupirs* condemns persecutions and the Revocation, and stresses that the royal policy in matters of conscience helps to justify these measures of intolerance.

The panacea for such ills is to be found, according to the *Soupirs,* in setting definite limits to royal power,[28] restoring the States-General and the parlements to their previous position, recognizing

---

[23] *Ibid.,* pp. 29–30.
[24] *Ibid.,* p. 30.
[25] *Ibid.,* p. 19.
[26] *Ibid.,* p. 173.
[27] *Ibid.,* p. 44.
[28] Cf. *ibid.,* p. 53.

the privileges once granted to the people, accepting the rules of justice and equity, and remembering that "les Rois ont les armes en main uniquement pour l'interêt & pour la conservation des Peuples." [29]

The *Soupirs* was more than an incitement to action on the English pattern, which its author planned should be carried out in France in the interest of the Reformed religion as a whole. Its importance was greater than that of Hotman's *Franco-Gallia*, to which it bore close resemblance by its historical construction. Attacking absolutism, it urged that "la vie & la liberté des hommes ne peuvent être justement soûmis à des peines capitales pour des choses en elle même indifferentes." [30] Thus it gave a glimpse of a philosophical approach, until then so seldom chosen by writers on the problems of persecution and toleration. It reached out toward the issues which were more fully discussed during the main toleration controversy between Bayle and Jurieu, and with which the majority of Protestants in exile were more or less actively concerned.

THE TOLERATION CONTROVERSY

The appearance in 1686 of Bayle's *Commentaire philosophique sur les paroles de Jesus-Christ, Contrains-les d'entrer* ushered in a new phase in the battle for toleration. Although the direct attack on absolutism remained of paramount importance for some time— since it was by a successful challenge to royal authority that the Huguenots might hope to win back their civil rights—yet the long-term effects of the ideas contained in the *Commentaire* were revolutionary. The gulf between the two Huguenot parties in exile, the moderates and the zealots, was widened still more; the line defended by Jurieu was challenged, and the impact of his violence lessened; a certain skepticism in both his followers and his opponents was a harbinger of hope that a harmonious and smooth relationship might be one day established among members of different religions. The dispute also had a more direct effect by arousing a deep antagonism between the main opponents, Jurieu and Bayle;

[29] *Ibid.,* p. 43.
[30] *Ibid.,* p. 41.

the conflict which flared up later around *L'Avis important aux réfugiez* (1690) turned these two outstanding Huguenots into mortal enemies.

When grappling with the problem of constraint, Bayle, the "philosopher of Rotterdam," was struck by the immense difficulties involved, and his doubts were awakened. In his philosophical system, he left room for formidable complexities and contemplated solutions which were neither easy nor strictly predictable. He built his theory of history on the principle of accidental causes determining later events, and, in his *Dictionnaire* (1697), he endeavored laboriously to describe separate and entirely isolated facts. A profound skeptic, he was moved neither by Jurieu's exuberant enthusiasm bordering on fanaticism, nor by his readiness to oversimplify. Bayle accepted the existence of innumerable factors which finally determined every issue, and arrived at the conception of a highly intricate mechanism of cause and effect in history. His was not the easy way of the doctrinaire, who unthinkingly follows a straight path. It was in the nature of his genius to detect the presence of complications in every issue, rather than to seek for some generalized formula.

Bayle's argument on tolerance lay in the realm of philosophy, and had Jurieu been prepared to join battle on his opponent's ground, the dispute would have become a purely philosophical one. Jurieu, however, for all the secularism he had shown earlier, clung to the theological side of the problem, and the controversy between the two men became one between religion and philosophy. Although the dispute clearly demonstrated the superiority of Bayle's logic over his opponent's, it failed to liberate the idea of tolerance from the shackles of theology. Each of the two opponents, moreover, usually preferred to argue from his own point of view, and Jurieu was not entirely beaten on theological grounds. On the other hand, Jurieu persistently refused to take up the philosophical challenge of Bayle.

Bayle wrote in his *Supplément du Commentaire philosophique* (1688) that he was dealing with "une doctrine qui est une notion du sens commun." [31] That is to say, the idea of tolerance, though not a commonly accepted doctrine, could, in the light of the nature of reality arrived at by the Baylian method of reasoned investigation, be shown to be nothing more or less than common sense.

[31] Pierre Bayle, *Oeuvres diverses*, II (*Supplément du Commentaire philosophique*), 497.

Truth, according to Bayle, can be apprehended through reason—
that "supreme tribunal"—and is not something objective, external
to the human mind, or given by grace. If one accepts his premise,
the argument of Bayle appears perfectly consistent.

In putting his case for tolerance, Bayle used arguments based on
both reason and law. "La non-tolérance est contraire au droit & à
la Raison, ... les hommes qui font des loix par raport à la conscience
excedent manifestement leur pouvoir, & les font sans autorité." [32]
Man-made regulations affecting conscience have no validity, because
lawmakers are not entitled to enter this sphere. Refuting the words
of St. Augustine, "Compel them to come in," Bayle did not intend
to deny the right of oppression by sovereigns for legitimate causes.
"Je n'ai pas prétendu," he explained, "trouver mauvais que le Roi
& la République de Pologne se tiennent en garde contre l'audace des
Cosaques." [33] But he insisted that power over conscience does not
belong to the sovereign and gave two alternative reasons: sovereign
power comes either directly from God, or from the people. If it
is derived from God, then the sovereign can impose no laws which
will compel the subjects to act against their consciences, for "autrement il s'ensuivroit que Dieu pourroit conférer à l'homme le pouvoir d'ordonner la haine de Dieu, ce qui est absurde & nécessaire-
ment impossible." [34] If, on the other hand, a sovereign is established
by popular will, he has no power over his subjects' consciences, because no individual would accept an order to hate his God. "Les
Rois n'ont ni de Dieu, ni des hommes, le pouvoir de commander à
leurs Sujets qu'ils agissent contre leur conscience, il est manifeste que
tous les Edits qu'ils publient sur cela sont nuls de droit, & une pure
usurpation, & ainsi les peines qu'ils y opposent pour les contrevenans
sont injustes." [35]

Addressing Bossuet, Bayle said that heretics should not be pe-
nalized for their religious convictions. Bringing legal arguments to
his aid, he pointed out that the legal system puts stress on leniency
rather than severity. He urged that heretics are not by nature male-
factors, as Bossuet thought, and he objected to the idea that they
are punishable. Bayle remarked that in the system of Bossuet special
"conscience tribunals" would be needed, with judges as conversant

[32] *Ibid.* (*Commentaire philosophique*), p. 412.
[33] *Ibid.*
[34] *Ibid.*, p. 384.
[35] *Ibid.*, pp. 384–385.

with the nature of the causes of heresy as they are with the civil and criminal codes.[36]

Though Bayle advanced this religious liberalism on the philosophical plane, Jurieu exposed what he called Bayle's religious indifference. "Il [Jurieu] m'accuse aussi d'introduire l'indifférence des Religions," admitted Bayle.[37] The Baylian theory of noninterference by the sovereign in matters of conscience Jurieu regarded as a gross exaggeration, a kind of religious anarchy. "Selon lui [Bayle] les Souverains ne se doivent point mêler des affaires de la religion que pour abandonner chacuɲ à son caprice."[38] According to Bayle, Jurieu's arguments were meaningless because they did not deal directly with the ideas of his opponent, and so were mostly irrelevant to the dispute. "Il [Jurieu] a continuellement comis le Sophisme de ne point prouver ce qu'il faloit," accused Bayle.[39]

Bayle probably meant to imply that Jurieu not only had condemned his arguments without answering them, but also had completely failed to understand the meaning of the central conception with which any discussion on toleration must deal—the conception of "heresy," "le terme ... merveilleusement equivoque," to use Bayle's own words.[40] Perhaps it was the equivocal nature of this term that accounted for the obscurity which often characterized the controversies of that time—an obscurity which Bayle himself did not fail to notice. "[Les] juges désinteressez," he wrote, "comme des Philosophes Chinois, trouveroient mes controverses plus embrouillées qu'un procès civil ou criminel."[41] He at least was aware of the growing confusion to which the controversy gave rise. To Jurieu, the problem did not present itself in the same light.

The difference between the two men was that whereas Jurieu was convinced he knew the truth, Bayle was critical enough to see that reality was not quite so simple. Bayle held that man is capable of knowing only partial truth—"Il [l'homme] ne connoît gueres la vérité qu'imparfaitement"[42]—and considered that to unearth

---

[36] Cf. *ibid.* (*Supplément du Commentaire philosophique*), p. 540.

[37] "Lettre de l'auteur a son Librairien sur la troisième partie [du *Commentaire philosophique*], Mai 1687," *ibid.*, p. 444.

[38] Jurieu, *Des droits des deux souverains en matière de religion, la conscience et le prince*, p. 274. Hereafter cited as Jurieu, *Des droits des deux souverains.*

[39] Bayle, *Oeuvres diverses*, II (*Commentaire philosophique*), 444.

[40] *Ibid.* (*Supplément du Commentaire philosophique*), p. 535.

[41] *Ibid.*, p. 520.

[42] *Ibid.* (*Commentaire philosophique*), p. 415.

truth in the case of heresy is a far more complicated affair than to solve a criminal problem. He distinguished between two kinds of heresy: nonseditious, which should be tolerated; and seditious, which ought to be suppressed.[43] At the same time he stressed the impossibility of finding a definition for the term under dispute: "Il est impossible de définir L'Hérésie." [44] He provided no ready-made solutions or universal formulae. Constantly aware of the complexities of the problem, he exasperated his opponents by the intricacy of his reasoning; little wonder that Jurieu shied away from an open philosophical contest.

> Pour réfuter l'Apologie que S. Augustin a faite des loix pénales en matiere de Religion, je n'avois besoin que de faire voir, que toutes ses raisons pouvoient être rétorquées sur les Orthodoxes persécutez par les Hérétiques. ... chaque parti a un égal droit de se servir des mêmes armes ... que les Hérétiques & les Orthodoxes l'auroient à l'égard des persécutions, s'il étoit vrai que Jésus-Christ eût ordonné d'user de main mise, & de faire entrer les gens par force dans son bercail.[45]

Bayle dealt extensively with the problem of compulsion in matters of conscience, making copious use of his own characteristic method of reasoning. Although in principle Bayle rejected compulsion, he admitted the need for it in special conditions of political emergency. Then, in order to preserve the state and the community from the seditious enemies of public security, sovereigns, he maintained, are entitled to legislate against conscience.[46] "S'ils peuvent faire cela," wrote Bayle, "ce n'est nullement en vertu de la parabole [Contrains-les-d'entrer]; c'est par de raisons de politique, lors qu'une secte leur est justement odieuse, par raport au bien public." [47] Although compulsion in matters of conscience may on occasion be a political necessity, religion cannot be used by sovereigns either as a pretext for creating stringent political laws or for penalizing their subjects. Bayle explicitly emphasized that "les Souverains ne peuvent pas faire présentement de leur Religion une loi politique." [48] Compulsion used by the sovereign cannot, according to Bayle, be accepted by religion—"la lumière naturelle, regle primitive & ori-

---

[43] Cf. *ibid.,* p. 416.
[44] *Ibid.* (*Supplément du Commentaire philosophique*), p. 519.
[45] *Ibid.,* pp. 538–539.
[46] Cf. *ibid.* (*Commentaire philosophique*), p. 412.
[47] *Ibid.,* p. 385.
[48] *Ibid.,* p. 410.

ginale de l'équité, ne reconnoîtra jamais pour divine une contrainte qui ne lui est pas conforme" [49]—unless this compulsion is a result of some divinely ordained rule. But because no rule of this kind had been known, "il faut donc conclure ... que Jésus-Christ n'a pas ordonné la contrainte." [50] To think that the persecution of heretics calls for God's benediction is preposterous, "car si cela étoit, le sort des Orthodoxes persécutez ne seroit pas semblable à celui des Hérétiques persécutez." [51] Referring to the recent persecution in France, Bayle said that the enforcement of the doctrine *Contrains-les-d'entrer* breaks all the bonds and obligations between men.[52] The forcible conversion ·of those outside the ranks of the Church favors irregularities which may change the meaning of sin, opening new ways for its interpretation. The state of authorized compulsion releases forces which are outside the control of those who order persecution, because it is impossible, once oppressive measures have been adopted, to draw the line and decide where to stop them. "Dès qu'on autorise la contrainte quelle qu'elle soit, il n'y a pas de point fixe pour s'arrêter, & que les mêmes raisons qui prouvent qu'on peut mettre un homme en prison pour fait d'Hérésie, prouvent encore mieux qu'on peut le pendre." [53]

Persecution and justice are flagrantly incompatible; the further persecutions go, the more absurd they become. By using the *reductio ad absurdum* method, Bayle shows the inconsistency of the principle of intolerance.

> Votre sentiment, me dira-t-on, est plus pernicieux que celui que vous réfutez; car en disculpant les Hérétiques, vous tâchez de prouver que leurs persécutions seroient justes ... Je réponds que ma preuve est une de ces manieres de raisonner qu'on appelle reductionem ad absurdum, & qui a toûjours été estimée souverainement efficace, pour désabuser les gens qui s'étoient laissez prévenir d'un faux principe.[54]

Bayle proceeded to demonstrate the paradox of intolerance: " ... Si Dieu avoit ordonné la contrainte de conscience, il s'ensuivroit que les Hérétiques pourroient contraindre légitimement & pieusement

---

[49] *Ibid.*
[50] *Ibid.*
[51] *Ibid.*, p. 400.
[52] Cf. *ibid.* (*Supplément du Commentaire philosophique*), p. 550.
[53] *Ibid.* (*Commentaire philosophique*), p. 383.
[54] *Ibid.* (*Supplément du Commentaire philosophique*), p. 539.

les Orthodoxes." [55] In reality, Bayle observed, contemporary Catholic intolerance was acute; whereas in Protestant-dominated countries, such as Holland, Catholics who were law-abiding were well treated.[56] Adherence to the principle of constraint, however, should be condemned irrespective of whether its partisans come from the orthodox or the heretical camp. "Le sens littéral de ces paroles Contrain les d'entrer," stressed Bayle, "sert contre les Orthodoxes de même que contre les Hérétiques." [57] He argued that to investigate the problems of the authority of the Church and of the faith also lead to the concept of tolerance. The point is illustrated by Bayle's remark that Catholics may also fall back on the ancient authority of the Roman Church and that reference to authority cannot be taken as the exclusive right of Protestants.

> Les Protestans seroient tout-à-fait injustes de contraindre les Catholiques ... quand ceux-ci leur représenteroient qu'ils ne peuvent se départir de l'appui de leur Foi qu'ils trouvent dans l'autorité d'un Concile, à moins qu'on ne leur fournisse un appui encore meilleur, & qu'ils ne peuvent croire, que ce soit un appui meilleur de se fier à l'interprétation qu'on donne soi-même à l'Ecriture, que de se fier à celle que lui ont donné pendant plusieurs siècles ceux qui ont gouverné le vaste corps de la Communion Romaine.[58]

Bayle contended that literal acceptance of the principle of constraint would be contrary to equity and humanity and would, in fact, be criminal behavior. He agreed with the view, expressed in Jurieu's *Le Vray Système de l'église* (1686), that one should secede from the Church if one believes its doctrines to be false, because one should follow the dictates of conscience, which prompt the choosing of a lesser evil.[59] But from this Bayle deduced a logical conclusion: "On ne peut nier la contrainte au sens littéral, sans introduire une tolérance générale." [60] In the problem of tolerance there should be no middle way and no compromise: " ... en cette rencontre on ne sauroit trouver de juste milieu; il faut tout ou rien; on ne peut pas avoir de bonnes raisons pour tolérer une Secte, si elles ne sont pas bonnes pour en tolérer une autre." [61]

---

[55] *Ibid.*
[56] Cf. *ibid.* (*Commentaire philosophique*), p. 413.
[57] *Ibid.* (*Supplément du Commentaire philosophique*), p. 538.
[58] *Ibid.*, p. 504.
[59] *Ibid.*, p. 499.
[60] *Ibid.* (*Commentaire philosophique*), p. 419.
[61] *Ibid.*

That seemed to him the only solution. The way of violence only postpones the settling of religious matters and the establishment of harmony and order. The way of persuasion, if it means persuading members of a religious sect to renounce their convictions, is an impossibility. There is no hope except in the adoption of communal laws and of moral codes forbidding violence. "C'est donc une chose manifestement opposée au bon sens, à la lumière naturelle, aux principes généraux de la Raison, en un mot à la regle primitive & originale du discernement du vrai & du faux, du bon & du mauvais, que d'emploier la violence à inspirer une Religion à ceux qui ne la professent pas." [62]

The arguments against his point of view, Bayle considered, provided at best no remedy and no solution to the problems of conscience: "L'opinion contraire à la mienne," he says, "ne sauroit remédier à nul de ces inconvéniens." [63] Indeed, in his opinion, they might be both dangerous and politically harmful: "Si la diversité des Religions cause quelque mal politique c'est à cause de l'intolérance." [64] On several occasions [65] he recommended "la voie de l'instruction," an education in reason, which would teach people to desire and create conditions of order and liberty, in which freedom of belief and freedom of the individual could be respected and maintained. Tolerance is the condition of order, and without it there could be no enduring peace: " ... c'est donc la tolérance qui est la force de la paix." [66] Conversely, intolerance is the source of "confusion & conflict"; indeed, "c'est la non-tolérance qui cause tous les désordres qu'on impute faussement à la tolérance." [67]

It was with this point that Jurieu fundamentally disagreed; in his book *Des droits des deux souverains,* which appeared in 1687, he described the attitude of Bayle as extreme beyond measure, vicious, and foolish, and his views as contrary to law. He maintained that everyone should comply with the law, which urges search for truth, work for the glory of God, and preservation of the purity of religion.[68] He laid special emphasis on what he considered to be

---

[62] *Ibid.,* p. 371.
[63] *Ibid.* (*Supplément du Commentaire philosophique*), préface, p. 501.
[64] *Ibid.* (*Commentaire philosophique*), p. 415.
[65] Cf. *ibid.,* p. 414; see also *ibid.* (*Supplément du Commentaire philosophique*), p. 555.
[66] *Ibid.* (*Commentaire philosophique*), préface, p. 364.
[67] *Ibid.*
[68] Cf. Jurieu, *Des droits des deux souverains,* p. 275.

God's commands to sovereigns. First, he saw the importance of preserving purity of religion; otherwise religion will be in peril: " ... si les Princes ne doivent pas emploier leur autorité pour ramener les gens à leur devoir & au vrai culte de la religion ... la voilà perdue sans retour & sans remede." [69] Second, he saw the hand of God in all that is done to establish true religion and destroy the false. But the authority of sovereigns, in his view, is limited; he quotes the principle *suaderi debet religio, non cogi,* and defines the limits within which the sovereign authority can act in matters of conscience: "L'autorité ne peut tuer, contraindre à un culte que l'on croit contre la conscience, dire à un homme, je veux tout à l'heure que tu adores Jesus-Christ, & que tu croies les dogmes de la religion chrétienne, ou tu mourras ... C'est à cet égard que vaut la maxime, *religio suaderi debet, non cogi.*" [70]

Within those limits, and since human beings, in his view, can do nothing against truth, it can be taken as an immanent and unchanging principle that "les Princes se peuvent servir de leur autorité pour supprimer l'idolatrie." [71] Even earlier (1685), when Jurieu's temper was more mellow and he was able to assert, "Il ne faut jamais forcer la bouche à une confession, qui seroit contredite par le cœur: il faut tolerer ses erreurs, et travailler doucement à instruire les personnes," [72] he had a deeply ingrained notion of "truth." When he used the word "toleration," he meant only toleration of error, and he refused to tolerate any betrayal of "truth." It was primarily for the sake of truth, which ought not to be scorned, that he insisted on recognition of personal religious convictions. The sentence "On peut bien tolerer une erreur, mais jamais on ne doit trahir la verité," [73] clearly reveals the peculiarly dogmatic and rigid attitude which he preserved unchanged throughout his life, and which helped him to defend partial toleration at first, and then intolerance.

Summing up the discussion in his *La Cabale chimérique* (1691), Bayle drew attention to the fact that those who are intolerant never

---

[69] *Ibid.,* p. 278.

[70] *Ibid.,* p. 286.

[71] *Ibid.*

[72] Jurieu, *Lettre de quelques Protestans pacifiques, au sujet de la réunion des Religions à l'assemblée de Messieurs du clergé de France, qui se doit tenir à Saint-Germain-en-Laye,* p. 28.

[73] *Ibid.,* p. 69.

change their opinion, regardless of the arguments they hear.[74] His spirit of tolerance was so genuine and so profound that he desired to leave everyone to his own opinions, rather than argue and arouse passions by disputes. He held that those who are tolerant should be moved by deep charity, probably meaning that by their non-interference with the consciences of others they would show the worthlessness of the dogma of persecution. For, indeed, Bayle was persuaded that "le dogme qui autorise les persécutions des Hérétiques ne vaut rien." [75]

Subsequently Bayle seemed to act according to principles self-imposed in *La Cabale chimérique,* in which he admitted that he was being urged by his spirit of tolerance to abstain from argument even in conversation, in order not to embitter religious opponents. He was so careful not to overstep the limits defined by his own words, "qu'il faloit combatre les hérésies avec douceur, & avec de bonnes raisons," [76] that for the sake of tolerance he even ended by not insisting on toleration. He shifted the emphasis from tolerance to religion; [77] contrasting them to each other, he came to regard the former as a remedy for ills arising from the latter. Instead of preaching the need for tolerance, he exposed some of the ill effects of the diversity of religions.

> Les effets de ces divisions de Religion ne nuisent pas peu à l'Etat: chaque secte se passionne contre les autres; c'est une source d'animositez qui gate le coeur; cela fait une grande diversion des soins que chaque particulier doit prendre du repos, & de la prospérité de la République, & ne permet pas qu'un Souverain donne toute son application aux principales affaires de l'Etat.[78]

Bayle laid down a distinction between religious conscience and rational conscience.[79] He held that religious conscience is by its nature intolerant and leads to persecution and revolt; persecution is dictated by it and is an act of good faith; religious bias therefore makes conscience truly erring. Earlier, when writing his *Commen-*

---

[74] Cf. Bayle, *Oeuvres diverses,* II (*La Cabale chimérique*), 676.

[75] *Ibid.*

[76] *Ibid.*

[77] On this and on the principle of erring conscience, see Jean Delvolvé, *Religion critique et philosophie positive chez Pierre Bayle,* pp. 410–414.

[78] Bayle, *Oeuvres diverses,* III (*Réponse aux Questions d'un provincial,* Troisième partie), 953.

[79] Cf. *ibid.,* p. 955.

taire, Bayle, although his argument for tolerance was then also based on the erring conscience, had denied that persecution can be prompted by sincerity. Jurieu, in his *Des droits des deux souverains,* pointed out the incompatibility of the two concepts, tolerance and erring conscience.[80] This objection was awkward for Bayle, because as long as a persecution can be effected in a sincere spirit, Jurieu's argument was hardly refutable. Bayle solved the dilemma later by inventing the two types of conscience, religious and rational, and putting the blame on religion.

The controversy over toleration, although extended into the eighteenth century, had lost its main impetus by 1692, not only because the chief interest had shifted and was centered around the anonymous and highly libelous *L'Avis important aux réfugiez* but also for other reasons, the responsibility for which rested with Bayle. The skeptical mind of the "philosopher of Rotterdam" doubted the existence of "fundamentals." It was thinkers like Jurieu who sought to establish certain fundamental principles of religion and who were even more anxious to ask others to accept those fundamentals as dogmas. Bayle, instead, taught the value of doubting, of thinking, and of reasoning, and his influence spread. There had grown up a group of people, mainly his friends and followers, some of whom took part in the controversy around the *Avis* and all of whom expressed views on tolerance similar to his. But none had ideas so profound as his, nor spoke with his force of conviction.

Isaac Papin, the author of the *Essais de theologie,* expressed his understanding of toleration in a veiled manner, when critically examining a text (ascribed to Jurieu) which lacked any spirit of toleration. "Un Theologien," Papin registered his surprise, "ne devoit il avoir aucune tolerance pour les moyens & les motifs qui portent a la sainteté?"[81] Papin showed some of the Baylian method of thinking in his arguments, such as *omne simile dissimile* or "il n'y a point de comparaison qui ne peche,"[82] and in his findings and conclusions: "Que chacun demeure dans la condition dans laquelle il étoit quand il a été appellé au Christianisme."[83]

Both Basnage de Beauval and Leclerc spoke, as did Bayle, of the need for charity—the basis of all tolerance. Leclerc tried to give

---

[80] Cf. Jurieu, *Des droits des deux souverains,* chap. iv.

[81] Isaac Papin, *Essais de theologie, etc.,* p. 9.

[82] *Ibid.,* p. 3.

[83] Papin, *La Vanité des sciences, etc.,* p. 82.

a wide base to his investigation of the problem of tolerance: he spoke of the divine design to make men free;[84] he regarded religious indifference with horror, and condemned hypocrisy; he found it necessary to appeal to conscience and to the "impulse of conviction"; and he believed that reason alone is sufficient to reach the right conclusions, which would find confirmation in religion.[85] But Bayle warned against the false impression that might arise from Leclerc's treatment of the problem. Opposing the view that this doctrine of tolerance had been treated in a spirit of broad understanding, he indicated its limitations:

> Il [Leclerc] exclut du bénéfice de la tolérance tous les sectateurs du systeme de Dordrecht, & tous ceux qu'on nomme Augustiniens ... Il ne trouveroit donc aucune société chretienne digne de sa tolérance, il se croiroit obligé de livrer au bras seculier si cela dépendoit de lui, tous ceux qui voudroit pas signer le formulaire qu'il dresseroit, & qui condamneroit nettement l'article de l'éternité des peines.[86]

It was perhaps Bayle alone who desired tolerance to be full and indivisible. His only modification was in urging restraint in the sphere of practical measures for furthering tolerance. The fact that he criticized all deviation from full acceptance of the principle, yet refrained from forcing his beliefs on others, shows the value he attached to that principle, the all-important role he assigned to it, and the attitude of devotion to it that he felt should take first place over merely practical considerations.

WIDER CONSEQUENCES OF THE REVOCATION

The controversies which took place after the Revocation of the Edict of Nantes became more and more confused. New groups of personalities took part, for whom the division into two broad groups, moderates and zealots, is too general and inaccurate a distinction. But on some occasions, a problem presented itself with such

---

[84] Cf. J. Leclerc, *Concerning the Choice of our opinion amongst the different Sects of Christians* (published with Hugo Grotius' *The Truth of the Christian Religion*), p. 312.

[85] Cf. Leclerc, *Supplementary Book II* to Hugo Grotius' *Truth of Christianity*, p. 253.

[86] Bayle, *Oeuvres diverses*, IV (*Entretien de Maxime et de Themiste*, Premiére partie), 31.

force and such lack of ambiguity that the dispute about it can be distinctly separated from the rest of the contemporary controversies. The most striking was the cleavage of public opinion caused by *L'Avis important aux réfugiez*—a cleavage which offers some justification for the conventional division of the Huguenots in exile into two camps.

The toleration controversy was still in progress when this exposure of the antiroyalist convictions of some of the Huguenot exiles appeared. It soon became clear that the crisis caused by the pamphlet was extremely serious. The pamphlet was, however, only vaguely and indirectly connected with the controversy over toleration; it did not give rise to any open discussion of that issue. It was an attempt made by the moderates to check the folly of the zealots; its ultimate aim was to solve the problem facing the Huguenots, not by opposing the King, as the zealots desired, but by insisting on dutiful obedience to Louis XIV. Whatever the goal of the author of the *Avis* might have been, the fact remains that he could have provided a remedy for the Protestant *émigrés* if he had succeeded in reducing the zealot majority. As it was, he only caused further discord and factionalism.

The character of the work betrayed an author who belonged to, or at least sympathized with, the moderate Huguenots. This, together with the cool objectivity of the book and its philosophic, almost cruel, impartiality, may suggest that Bayle was the author, as indeed Jurieu openly claimed. Bayle himself never openly denied that the book was written by him; the statement he made, in a letter written in January, 1691, was enigmatic: he explained that he did not want to criticize and refute the *Avis*, because such a criticism would entail the condemnation of some of Jurieu's pastoral letters, and this would give a weapon to the enemies of the Protestants in France.[87] This answer threw no further light on the problem of the authorship of the *Avis*. Bayle's sophistry was ingenious; any less adroit letter might easily have compromised him. As it was, his letter could be interpreted either as a successful attempt to steer clear of dangerous waters or as evidence of his reluctance to act in

---

[87] "... cette aprobation [par le synode de la réponse à *L'Avis aux réfugiez*] seroit une condamnation formelle de 4 ou 5 lettres pastorales de M. Jurieu ... Il me parait ... que c'est un terrible inconvenience, et que nous ne devons pas fournir des armes à nos Adversaires." Bayle's letter of January 29, 1691 [addressee unknown], *Lettres de Pierre Bayle, 1670–1706*, British Museum, Birch Coll. Additional MS 4226, fols. 56–57.

a way of which his spirit of philosophic detachment disapproved.

The philosophic atmosphere of the book was akin to Bayle's mentality, although the book possessed some features not always discernible in his writings. The *Avis* was conspicuous not only for its maturity of form, wealth of information, and careful presentation of arguments, but also for its virulence, pitiless irony, and sarcastic wisdom. Audacious, blunt, and merciless, it had no pity for the bickering exiles and exposed all their illusions by revealing the internal discord so seldom avoided by political refugees. It had a shattering, if sobering, effect. Its criticism was both destructive and, though in a dangerous way, salutary; for it discouraged the spirit of complacency that the Huguenot community, in the artificial conditions in which it lived abroad, had until then been unable to shake off. The writings of Jurieu had been provocative but too partisan to produce a similar effect; they had flattered the opinion of the exiles, whereas the *Avis* aroused general indignation. The *Avis* caused large-scale confusion by hitting the majority group of the exiles; by opposing popular theories, it worked for the benefit of the traditionalist tendencies.

The importance of the *Avis* lay both in its doctrinal content and in its practical instructions as to the course of policy the Protestants should pursue. The popular theory of the state was criticized unequivocally. Attention was drawn to the inconsistency of the attitude of the Protestants who, while professing to believe in the rights of the people, were responsible for publications against the pope; for the author of the *Avis* believed that to oppose the pope and to be a zealous royalist were necessarily concomitant attitudes. "Il n'y a rien de plus merveilleux que le zele que vos Ecrivains ont témoigné pour les Rois, quand il s'est agi de déclamer contre les Papes ... Alors il n'y avoit rien, selon vous, de plus sacré, ni de plus indépendent, que le caractère des Monarques." [88]

Referring to Jurieu's *La Politique du clergé de France,* which had dealt broadly with the loyalty of the Protestants to their monarch, the *Avis* stressed that such an attitude must be sincere and that monarchs should be sure of Protestant fidelity, and it refused to accept any Protestant claim to genuine antiroyalist and popular views [89] in the changed circumstances.

The *Avis* proceeded then to refute the theory of popular sover-

---

[88] Bayle, *Oeuvres diverses,* II (*Avis important aux réfugiez*), 592.
[89] Cf. *ibid.,* p. 593.

eigny. The concept of popular sovereignty was described in disparaging terms as "chimere favorite" and as a pernicious dogma. "Où est donc cette prétendue Souveraineté du peuple?"[90] asked the *Avis*. The validity of this dogma was undermined by making it sound absurd; its implications were brought to public notice. "Si une fois on établit pour principe, que la souveraineté émane du peuple, on conçoit chaque membre de la Société comme un Souverain absolu."[91] This type of quasi-absolute sovereignty which is vested in each individual "autorise chaque Particulier à s'opposer à tout le corps";[92] it fosters division and rules out the enforcement of obedience: "... si tous les hommes sont nez également souverains & indépendans ... il est clair qu'on ne peut contraindre a l'obeissance ceux qui trouvent les ordres injustes."[93] Finally, the doctrine contained in the numerous pamphlets published by the exiles was considered seditious from two points of view: first, because Protestant authors since the Revocation of the Edict of Nantes had urged the use of enemy powers for the restitution of their own rights;[94] and second, because it follows from the doctrine of popular sovereignty "que les Monarques ne sont que les premiers Officiers du peuple, & que tous les Magistrats subalternes ne sont que ses officiers inférieurs."[95] If the concept were valid, it would follow that everyone, from the king downward, was subject to supervision by those below him in the hierarchy: "Si vous voulez que vos dogmes se soûtiennent, il faut que les Grands Officiers de la Couronne veillent sur la conduite des Rois; que les Magistrats inférieurs veillent sur la conduite des Grands Officers, etc., ..."[96]

The author of the *Avis* predicted a sad future for all those who disobey their own rulers; he foretold that they would be committed to a state of confusion greater than under tyranny, because they would be subject to the whims of a "thousand tyrants." This confusion, however, would be well-deserved because "le peuple est toujours la dupe de ses pretendus libérateurs."[97]

He condemned all authors who incited the people to rebellion:

[90] *Ibid.*, p. 595.
[91] *Ibid.*, p. 594.
[92] *Ibid.*, p. 596.
[93] *Ibid.*, p. 598.
[94] Cf. *ibid.*, p. 592.
[95] *Ibid.*, p. 603.
[96] *Ibid.*
[97] *Ibid.*, p. 605.

"Ce ne sont donc pas de petits péchez ... que tous ces Libelles qui tendent au soulevement des peuples. Ce sont de vrais pillages & de vrais meurtres conseillez. Or en toute bonne justice, celui qui pousse les autres à dérober & à tuer, ne vaut pas mieux que celui qui dérobe & qui tue." [98]

At this juncture he advised the Protestants to disavow all indiscretions committed by satirists [99] and to recant and expiate publicly the harm which had been done: "Si vous m'en croiez, vous témoignerez publiquement vos regrets de ce que tant de personnes refugiées ... ont emploié ou à composer des Libelles, ou à traduier ceux des Anglois ..." [100]

Of the English pamphlets written by the Presbyterians, he spoke with equal displeasure; [101] he also stressed that English Catholic refugees behaved better than the Huguenots, though they had more reason for resentment.[102] He was disturbed, however, by the Huguenot approval of the Glorious Revolution.[103] The right to choose between obedience and disobedience and the freedom to criticize, "le droit d'examen," should, according to him, be withheld for the benefit of public peace. Such restrictions are fully justified by two outstanding achievements: the power of contemporary France, and the preëminence and glory of her monarch. Indeed, the *Avis,* full of pride in these achievements, was not free from servility toward the monarchy: "... cette grande puissance où elle [la nation] est montée, est le fruit des grands qualitez du Roi, & de son habileté dans l'art de régner." [104]

Jurieu's reply to the *Avis,* which he gave in his *Examen d'un libelle* (1691), was an apology for popular rights. Commenting on the remarks in the *Avis* that under popular sovereignty every individual has the right to rise against the ruler, he explained that the right to maintain order and safety belongs to the community as a whole, but that individuals are expected to play their part in maintaining public safety. The rights of the people may be involved, not

---

[98] *Ibid.,* p. 619.

[99] Cf. *ibid.,* p. 633.

[100] *Ibid.,* p. 609.

[101] "... on ait eu l'audace d'y publier un autre Libelle ... *L'irrévocabilité du Test & des Loix Pénales prouvée par la mort tragique de Charles Stuart* ... dans lequel on étale le procès & le supplice de Charles I avec des airs triomphans." *Ibid.*

[102] Cf. *ibid.,* p. 590.

[103] Cf. *ibid.,* pp. 600 ff.

[104] *Ibid.,* p. 625.

merely to bring about a revolution, but also as a delicate instrument to be applied whenever the state or religion is in danger. Jurieu refrained from assigning the respective shares of power to the people and the ruler; he held that too great an awareness on either side as to where real authority lay might be highly undesirable and dangerous. Neither is it desirable to inquire too closely into the problems of punishing rulers.

The important theory that Jurieu enunciated was that the people cannot act as judges of their sovereigns; indeed, they cannot be regarded as having sovereign power over the king.[105] But they may resist any form of tyranny and injustice, especially the unjust decisions of the majority. In opposing the views expressed in the *Avis,* Jurieu was critical of the unreserved acceptance of the majority principle. He contended that a minority had the right to contest majority decisions which it found unfair,[106] and used political examples to illustrate this, defending the minority rights of the Vaudois Protestants who had been led by desperation to start public disturbances and justifying the revolutionary Protestant movement in the Cévennes.

In his argument against the *Avis,* Jurieu was concerned with some of the practical issues it raised. He maintained that Bayle, whom he considered its author, had several reasons for publishing it.[107] For one thing, the author of the *Avis* obviously desired to separate the Catholic and the Protestant members of the anti-French League by widening the rift due to religious differences and by suggesting that the Protestants had definite interests in bringing about the ruin of France. Having thus "proved" that the Protestants were by nature seditious, he followed up his argument in the passage in the *Avis* attacking seditious movements by declaring that all seditions had always found supporters among the French Protestants. The next reason for writing the *Avis* was, according to Jurieu, to discourage the allied foreign powers from fostering hopes of stirring up internal troubles in France. In Jurieu's opinion, Bayle would have liked to see the potential revolutionary elements in France subjected to unlimited royal power and so cut off from making foreign al-

---

[105] Cf. *Examen d'un libelle* (The Hague, 1691), pp. 141, 146, as quoted in Dodge, *The Political Theory of the Hugenots,* pp. 107, 112–113.

[106] Cf. *Examen d'un libelle,* pp. 171 ff.

[107] His reasons, summarized below, are given by Dodge, *The Political Theory of the Huguenots,* p. 102.

liances. Jurieu thought that for Bayle the only hope for the Huguenots lay in winning over the King by adopting the policy of obedience and rejecting antiroyalist theories. Bayle could envisage no other remedy, Jurieu explained, because he considered that any aid given to the Huguenots by foreign allies could have only temporary effects, and that no external pressure of this kind would ultimately bind the decisions of the French King; moreover, it seemed to him that little indeed could be expected by the Huguenots from any policy which would humiliate France and overlook her *raison d'état.*

It should be noted that Jurieu, criticizing the theory of the author of the *Avis,* never derided his patriotism or his declarations of loyalty to the King. He himself professed loyalty to Louis XIV, and neither his doctrine of popular rights, which he openly advocated, nor his clandestine activity as an English agent was able to shake his lifelong reputation for loyalty to France. But he opposed excessive glorification of the King whenever this interfered with civil liberties or hindered the free manifestation of "truth." He believed that by struggling for liberty, he was rendering France a service.[108]

A similar plea for civic liberty was made by Abbadie, who, in his *Défense de la nation Britannique* (1692), following the example of Jurieu, continued to argue against the *Avis.* He dismissed the contention of the *Avis* that in order to keep public peace, freedom to criticize ("le droit d'examen") and the right of disobedience must be under control. "Comment le peuple n'auroit il point un droit qu'on ne peut ôter au moindre particulier, à moins que de lui ravir le privilege le plus essentiel de la creature raisonable? ... il n'y a que les betes & les creatures insensibles qui obeissent sans examen." [109]

Abbadie adopted a form of attack less violent than that of Jurieu; his arguments were not so aggressive and his tone was quieter; he tackled the problem on the basis of first principles and dwelt especially on the question of the nature of sovereign power. Trying to prove that sovereignty cannot be unlimited, he went back to its origins. Irrespective of the method by which sovereigns are established—patriarchy, conquest, the choice of the people, or the choice of God—according to Abbadie, "cela ne sera pas qu'ils [les

---

[108] Cf. *Examen d'un libelle,* p. 217, as quoted in Dodge, *The Political Theory of the Huguenots,* p. 103.

[109] Jacques Abbadie, *Défense de la nation Britannique,* p. 162.

Rois] ayent un droit illimité sur leurs sujets." [110] The authority of kings has two sources: the popular and the divine. "Il est vrai que l'authorité des Roys vient des peuples, mais il faut ajoûter qu'elle vient aussi de Dieu lequel se sert du consentement des peuples comme d'un moyen très legitime pour le communiquer aux Roys." [111] Abbadie showed that royal power is limited by the multitude of these sources. Kings are merely God's lieutenants: "... c'en seroit un autre [excès] d'impieté & d'idolatrie que de leur attribuer des droits qui sont propres à la Divinité. Tel est le pouvoir de sauver & de detruire sans faire injustice à personne, en quoi consiste proprement le pouvoir arbitraire." [112] This arbitrary power is not in accord with nature, with any legal system, or with human society in general, and it is not given to kings: "Ainsi il nous paroît que les Roys n'ont point un pouvoir arbitraire sur leurs sujets, puis que ce n'est ni la nature, ni la fortune, ni la loi, ni la religion qui le leur donne." [113] To bestow such a power on anyone would be equivalent to confounding law with force,[114] and to conferring upon kings the power of destruction. In fact—"Dieu n'a point communiqué le droit de destruction aux Roys. Ils portent l'épée de sa part, non simplement pour detruire, mais pour faire justice ... Lors donc qu'un Souverain devient le destructeur notoire de son peuple, il se revet des droits de Dieu; & lui applaudir c'est proprement disputer à Dieu sa souveraineté." [115]

Neither could the other source of the king's power, the people, have given him absolute power, because they had never possessed it: "Il est evident que le peuple n'a peu ni voulu conferer le droit absolu au souverain Magistrat. Il ne l'a peu, parce qu'il est impossible de donner ce qu'on n'a point, car le droit du peuple n'est que le droit qu'ont cedé les particuliers pour leur avantage commun." [116]

Abbadie strongly emphasized that even the legal power that individuals have with regard to property, children, life, reputation, liberty, conscience, and suchlike, is not absolute: "Qui ne sait que nous ne sommes que les seconds proprietaires de nos biens, Dieu

---

[110] *Ibid.*, p. 109.
[111] *Ibid.*, p. 212.
[112] *Ibid.*, p. 108.
[113] *Ibid.*, p. 136.
[114] Cf. *ibid.*, p. 131.
[115] *Ibid.*, p. 250.
[116] *Ibid.*, p. 117.

étant le premier, & qu'ainsi nous n'en pouvons point de droit disposer absolument." [117] Power over the conscience, for instance, is the exclusive prerogative of God: "Pour le droit que Dieu a sur la conscience, il est incontestable qu'il est tellement propre à Dieu qu'il est incommunicable à tout autre." [118]

In the name of freedom of conscience, Abbadie demanded the right to profess the Reformed religion. Since no one in the state is permitted to be without religion, he argued, the state should recognize a religion which the conscience of an individual desires. Abbadie insisted that conscience should be relied upon and taken as a decisive agent in religious matters: "Nous demanderons la liberté de professer celle-ci [la religion Reformée], parce que c'est celle qui s'accorde avec les mouvemens de notre conscience." [119] He was convinced that the voice of conscience should not be gainsaid: "Il ne nous appartient pas de juger de la conduite du Souverain; mais ne m'appartient-t-il point de juger que cette religion qu'on veut me faire embrasser est contraire aux mouvemens de ma conscience?" [120] Because it is imperative to follow conscience, he held that it is a crime to persecute and to punish the innocent,[121] and that constraint in the hands of government is a weapon which defeats its user, for it is fantastic to claim obedience from those who have been deprived of all liberties. "Y a t-il une pretention plus extraordinaire que celle de pretendre que ceux la vous doivent obeissance à qui vous ôtés jusqu'à la liberté de respirer & de vivre?" [122]

The principle of arbitrary rule is shaken even further by Abbadie's demonstration that arbitrary power is incompatible with three kinds of law: of royalty, of succession, and of contract.[123] All these laws are based on contractual or semicontractual agreements—a fact which implies limited authority of the contracting parties—and are concerned with the maintenance of the liberty, the rights, and the privileges of the subject.[124] Another brake on the authoritarian propensities of kings is put by religion. "La con-

---

[117] *Ibid.*, p. 114.
[118] *Ibid.*, p. 250.
[119] *Ibid.*, p. 177.
[120] *Ibid.*, p. 182.
[121] Cf. *ibid.*, p. 180.
[122] *Ibid.*, p. 187.
[123] Cf. *ibid.*, p. 120.
[124] Cf. *ibid.*

science," wrote Abbadie, "ne le leur enseigne pas moins que la nature. Car d'ou viennent les remors si communs à ceux qui abusent de
leur pouvoir." [125] It is God who has the sole authority over conscience.[126] The king can be lawfully resisted, and on some occasions
even deposed; but it is God, and not the people, who withdraws
the trust placed on the monarch.[127]

Plainly, Abbadie's case against the *Avis* was worded in milder
terms than Jurieu's; the right to revolt, as he saw it, has ultimately
the sanction of religion, and is under the control of God.

The authority of the king in dealing with matters of conscience is
determined by the fact that he is subordinate to God: "... les Roys
sont à l'égard du Dieu, ce que les Magistrats subalternes sont à
l'égard du Roy auquel ils obeissent." [128] By revoking the edicts, the
king forfeits his control over his subjects, who thereby lose their
membership in the community and become entitled to act according
to natural law.[129] Abbadie insisted, however, that by denying absolute
rights to kings, he was in no sense putting limitations on the royal
authority: "On se trompe beaucoup si l'on s'imagine qu'en sou-
tenant que les Roys n'ont point un droit absolu sur leur sujets, nous
revalons la dignité royale. Est ce la revaler, que de ne pas la confondre avec la majesté du Dieu? Et ne pourrons nous eviter le
reproche de sedition si nous ne tombons dans l'idolatrie?" [130]

The point of view stated by the *Défense de la nation Britannique*
not only represented a milder variety of opposition to the *Avis*
but brought into the dispute the pure element of religion—a factor
which worked imperceptibly toward making the government revise
its attitude toward intolerance. Since the Revocation, the goal of
the Court and that of the clergy had been the same: to ensure a large
number of conversions and thus bring the Huguenot problem to its
final conclusion by the elimination of the religious minority. Yet
their courses of action had not entirely coincided, for while the
government insisted on haste, judging results by the number of new
converts, the clergy stressed that all acts of abjuration must be sincere—an attitude which eliminated constraint as a method of con-

[125] *Ibid.,* p. 127.
[126] Cf. *ibid.,* p. 250.
[127] Cf. *ibid.,* pp. 192, 215.
[128] *Ibid.,* p. 134.
[129] Cf. *ibid.,* p. 188.
[130] *Ibid.,* p. 107.

verting. Baron de Breteuil, in his *Mémoire ou Rapport général sur la toleration des Calvinistes en France* (1786), wrote that "c'étoit la Religion elle-même qui avoit ramené le Gouvernement à la tolérance." [131] What he had in mind must have been the slight easing in oppression which ensued soon after the Peace of Ryswick (1697), though the treaty itself did not bring toleration. Near the end of the seventeenth century, there was, however, on the whole, still no visible change of policy toward the Protestants. Yet the lull in controversy in the period immediately preceding the Ryswick treaty was not groundless; the Huguenots saw that their interests were bound up with peace negotiations between Louis XIV and the allied countries, and hoped that, with the intervention of the Protestant powers, the peace would bring them full civil rights.

Harsh persecution, which involved the use of troops and frequent massacres of the Protestant clandestine gatherings "du desert," continued after the Revocation. Abbadie proclaimed that "personne n'est dragonné en Angleterre pour sa religion. Qu'on nous montre les Catholiques Romains soumis au gouvernement qui soient traités comme nous l'avons été en France." [132] These persecutions were in evidence right up until 1698, when, following special regulations to that effect, they subsided until the Camisard war broke out in 1702. All the protests of the Huguenots had not changed the course set by the government. Yet the failure of the conversions sponsored by the Court and the Church was so grave that toward 1698, as Breteuil says, "on étoit réduit à convenir qu'il restoit un grand nombre de Calvinistes, & que la plûpart de ceux qu'on avoit cru convertis n'avoient, en apparence, aucune Religion commune." [133] It was partly disillusion about the system so far practiced that made Louis XIV, in 1698, revise his religious policy, which up to then had been guided by the Jesuit schemes propounded before the Revocation, in favor of the Jansenist views, which opposed the policy of constraint.[134] Although at the close of the century a new scheme for general conversion was being considered,[135] like its

[131] Baron de Breteuil, *Mémoire*, as quoted in C. C. de Rulhière, *Eclaircissements historiques sur les causes de la révocation de l'édit de Nantes et sur l'état des Protestants en France*, Part 2, p. 32. Hereafter cited as Rulhière, *Eclaircissemens historiques*.

[132] Abbadie, *Défense de la nation Britannique*, p. 47.

[133] Breteuil, *Mémoire*, as quoted in Rulhière, *Eclaircissemens historiques*, Part 2, p. 24.

[134] Cf. *ibid.*, p. 82.

[135] Cf. *ibid.*

predecessor of the days of Richelieu, it was not put into practice.

There was a good deal of indecision in the royal policy; Louis XIV needed to take many arguments into consideration before he reduced the severity of his policy, even to so limited an extent as was done in 1698. He ignored some factors, such as the long-term economic consequences of the Revocation, in his policy. Otherwise persecution would have been stopped long before 1698, and there would have been no need for the ardent plea which Jurieu made to Protestant foreign powers during the peace talks:

> Nous les priâmes de considerer, qu'en ajoûtant la ruine de l'Eglise de France à toutes les pertes precedentes, il étoit clair que la veritable Religion se trouvoit dans le danger le plus évident où elle ait jamais été. Nous leur dîmes qu'il étoit temps de penser aux moyens d'arrêter ce torrent de prosperitez de Papisme, & de mettre des dogmes à la fureur de la persecution.[136]

The answer of Louis XIV was to give a new spur to the persecutions, coinciding with the visit of foreign envoys in France. "On a redouble les persecutions," wrote Jurieu [137] in his *Relation de tout ce qui s'est fait dans les affaires de la Religion Réformée*, a report which dealt with the Huguenot problem in relation to the peace negotiations. In the same report he stated the extent of the policy of oppression since 1686: "... nos freres ont souffert des maux qui ne se peuvent exprimer, des massacres, des supplices, des emprisonnemens, des condamnations aux galeres, des confiscations de biens, & toute autre espece de maux." [138]

In writing this account of atrocities in France and of the prolonged and useless negotiations of the Huguenots abroad, Jurieu adopted an attitude of resignation. He said with bitterness that "on nous faisoit esperer que le Roy de France de luy-même, apporteroit quelque adoucissement." [139] He made no direct attacks on the King. He even recalled the current opinion that all that was needed was patience, for the King's good nature would prevail. He described poignantly the feeling of depression widespread among the destitute Huguenots who had spent from ten to twelve years in exile, and

---

[136] Jurieu, *Relation de tout ce qui s'est fait dans les affaires de la Religion Réformée, & pour ses intérêts, depuis le commencement des Negociations de la Paix de Reswik*, p. 8.

[137] *Ibid.*, p. 39.

[138] *Ibid.*, p. 19.

[139] *Ibid.*

whom the Peace of Ryswick had now deprived of all hope: "Aujourd'hui ils ont tout consumé, & ils n'ont pas même conservé l'esperance." [140] He appealed to the charity of foreign countries, which had already extended their help to the *émigrés* of 1686, stressing that by further help they might lessen the wrong done at Ryswick. He urged the Huguenots to cultivate Christian virtues and comforted them by saying that the cause of the Reformation in France was not yet lost: "... la ruine totale de la Reformation en France ... n'arrivera pas; Dieu achevera son grand ouvrage, & le Roy Louys XIV n'achevera jamais le sien." [141]

However acute the state of depression into which the Huguenots sank, the debate over the *Avis* had not lost its freshness by the beginning of the eighteenth century. The century opened with a new civil war, the war of the Camisards, which had a limited theater of operation, a limited number of participants, and practically no theoretical background. It was indeed a spontaneous peasant uprising, owing its success to the leadership of Jean Cavalier. It was severe, and it was to last three years, long enough to stir up Huguenot feelings by its violence and cruelty. Then, in 1709, a long-delayed offshoot of the previous century's debate appeared in the form of Larrey's *Réponse à l'Avis aux réfugiez.* Though belated as an answer to the *Avis,* the work inevitably drew attention to the more permanent features in the controversy over the *Avis,* broadly following the line of Jurieu and Abbadie (especially of the latter), but breathing a new hope. In a strange way, it combined popular ideas with a certain faith in monarchy.

Larrey contended that the concept of the sovereignty of the people was not accepted by the Reformers in the form that the author of the *Avis* imputed to them. According to the *Avis,* sovereignty of the people meant the splitting up of authority among all individuals. This, insisted Larrey, not only gave a false picture of the doctrines accepted by the Reformers, for they believed that "la Souveraineté ne peut resider que dans la communauté, & non dans chaque particulier," [142] but imputed anarchistic views to the Huguenots: "A quoi se reduit enfin tout ce vacarme de l'Auteur de l'Avis sur le droit du peuple? A nous faire passer pour des partisans de

---

[140] *Ibid.,* p. 44.
[141] *Ibid.,* p. 66.
[142] Isaac de Larrey, *Réponse à l'Avis aux réfugiez,* p. 189.

l'Anarchie." [143] According to Larrey,[144] this way of presenting the doctrine allowed the author of the *Avis* to justify the *dragonnades* and the Revocation: "La Souveraineté du peuple une fois posée," Larrey quoted from the *Avis,* "... il s'ensuit encore, que si on usoit de la force pour la reduire à l'obeissance, comme le logement des gens de guerre, la punition des chefs des mutins, ce seroit une procedure criminelle, & une manifeste oppression." Larrey hastened to add that "il n'est pas difficile de reconnaître dans ces dernieres paroles la Dragonnade de la France." [145]

Larrey carefully defined the civil rights of the people; he regarded these rights as being equivalent to natural rights. Following Grotius and Abbadie, he used this term to mean the instinct of self-defense. The people receive their rights by birth; they make kings what they are and do not exist merely to serve the king's interests. Kings, on the other hand, though independent, are made for the people.

"Quelqu' independans que soient les Rois, ils ont été faits pour les peuples, & non les peuples pour les Rois." [146] The people give up their power to the king, but only under conditions, and they can take it back if the terms of contract are not kept by the ruler.[147] Larrey never opposed the rights of the people to those of the sovereign, but rather amplified one by the other. "Celui qui se declare ennemi de tout le peuple," he quoted from Grotius, "se depouille de sa Roiauté. C'est la maxime de Grotius, c'est la nôtre ..." [148]

Larrey preserved a warm feeling toward monarchy as personified in Louis XIV, "un Roi, dont nous avons été aussi idolâtres que les autres." [149] Speaking of the Revocation, he preferred to blame the clergy—"nous aimons mieux rejetter ce mystere d'iniquité sur un Clergé bigot & malin" [150]—rather than the glorious monarch. He could harbor no hatred toward the King, appealing rather to

---

[143] *Ibid.,* p. 191.

[144] Dodge came to the same conclusion. *The Political Theory of the Huguenots,* p. 136.

[145] Larrey, *Réponse à l'Avis aux réfugiez,* p. 189.

[146] *Ibid.,* p. 173.

[147] Cf. *ibid.,* p. 174.

[148] *Ibid.*

[149] *Ibid.,* p. 278.

[150] *Ibid.*

the King's generosity—"Revenez à vous, puissant Monarque" [151] —and he hoped that the Edict of Nantes would yet be restored by Louis XIV himself or by his successor.[152]

Although Larrey's hopes were left unfulfilled, his analysis of the situation was just. He saw that the consequences of the Revocation were detrimental to the State—"prejudiciable à l'interêt de l'Etat" —and he pleaded for the reëstablishment of the Edict and for the recall of the exiles. "C'est le seul moien de guerir les plaies, & d'effacer la honte qu'impriment la violation de la foi publique & les conversions forcées à l'honneur du Monarque & de la Monarchie: c'est l'unique voie dont on se puisse utilement servir pour empêcher la desolation d'un si beau Roiaume ... & inevitable, si la persecution continue." [153] He had been disquieted by the statistics of the numbers who emigrated, quoting 200,000,[154] or 10 per cent of the Huguenot population, as the number of those who had left France as a result of the Act of 1685.[155] The economic problem inherent in the emigration was brought up later by Breteuil, who, referring to the great number of emigrants, reported:

> Les Défenseurs de l'Intolérance sont embarassés eux-mêmes à ne pas avouer que cette mort civile, d'un si grand nombre de sujets du Roi, préjudice à tous les interêts de son Royaume, à l'honneur de son Gouvernement, aux progrès de la population, des manufactures & du Commerce, à la sécurité de l'Etat, à l'ordre des successions, à tout l'ordre civil.[156]

Emigration spelled loss to French industry and trade, an end to further colonial expansion, and the depletion of personnel in the army and navy. Some 20,000,000 livres in specie passed abroad, and some 12,000 first-class soldiers and sailors left the country. A striking feature of France after this emigration was the disappearance of the major part of the middle class.[157] The Revocation provoked the formation of the League of Augsburg and the war between 1688 and 1697. The Peace of Ryswick meant the end of the

---

[151] *Ibid.*

[152] Cf. *ibid.*, p. 442.

[153] *Ibid.*, p. 436.

[154] Cf. *ibid.*, p. 346.

[155] The total number of Huguenot refugees between 1600 and 1720 is given by Lavisse as approximately one million. Cf. E. Lavisse, *Histoire de France*, VIII, 343.

[156] Breteuil, *Mémoire*, as quoted in Rulhière, *Eclaircissemens historiques*, Part 2, p. 30.

[157] Cf. Sir J. A. R. Marriott, "The Edict of Nantes—Masterpiece or Blunder?" *Proceedings of the Huguenot Society of London*, XV, 405.

expansionist policy of France; Louis XIV was defending his gains, and, with all Europe allied against him and the country economically weak, he could only retreat and capitulate. The dispersion of the Huguenots had serious consequences, the implications of which were understood by the government, as was shown at the Peace of Utrecht, which reëstablished both freedom and commerce and the ordinance against emigration.[158] But the proper conclusions had not yet been reached, nor had account been taken of the tremendous price France was paying for intolerance. Some of her highly specialized industries were directly crippled by the emigration of the Protestants, who, alone in Europe, possessed the special skills needed to man them. France's loss was her opponents' gain, for the Huguenots settled down happily to their trade abroad, particularly in England and Holland. As an indirect result of the Revocation, France suffered a severe setback as a maritime power, because the war which ended at Utrecht eliminated her as a serious competitor in trade and overseas colonization.

After the Revocation, France fought her economic battles under a severe handicap. Economic reconstruction began only in the middle of the eighteenth century, in Poitou, where the manufacture of textiles, suspended for over fifty years, started anew.[159]

The spirit of toleration finally found recognition; but although it "followed trade," it cannot be explained by purely economic causes. Such an explanation would be as untenable as Weber's thesis that the Protestant ethic was the cause of capitalism. Both views are in the nature of historical "cribs": they supply all the answers, their assumptions are partial, their choice of illustrations arbitrary, their findings attractive but facile. Weber singled out one feature, the spiritual element in Calvinism, and brilliantly expounded the problem of its influence on economic life. The picture was strikingly simplified; he dealt with the ethical and religious side of Calvinism in complete isolation. "Weber looked upon Calvinism as something of an intrusive force from the outside, developed by its own inner dialectic, not simply a part of the socio-economic system that was producing capitalism." [160]

Tawney, accepting Weber's theory as one of the possible aspects of the relationship between capitalism and Calvinism, accuses Weber

---

[158] Cf. Rulhière, *Eclaircissemens historiques*, Part 2, p. 141.

[159] Cf. *Bulletin de la Société de l'histoire du Protestantisme Français*, LXXIX, 315.

[160] J. Milton Yinger, *Religion in the Struggle for Power*, p. 123.

of oversimplifying Calvinism itself.[161] Robertson says that "the spirit of capitalism has arisen rather from the natural condition of civilisation than from some religious impulse." [162]

Weber sinned heavily against semantic precision. He underlined certain nonfundamental traits of Calvinism as fundamental,[163] and he mistook the spirit of later Protestant communities, developing side by side with capitalism, for the original spirit of Calvinism. "Original Calvinism, however, found individualism abhorrent. The economic implications of the Reformation were not apparent until later and consequently were not understood as such by the reformers themselves." [164]

Apart from religion, what made the Huguenots the natural recipients of the "spirit of capitalism" were such circumstances as their long tradition as a minority group. Since the time of Richelieu they had been given little opportunity for any but economic activities. As a community of exiles, they were further forced by harsh conditions to cultivate those abilities and virtues which helped them in their existence.

The radical and liberal character of the ideas engendered by the Calvinists also sprang from contemporary conditions. One of the consequences of the diffusion of Calvinist thought was to help rescue the idea of toleration from oblivion, and to contribute to its adoption as a practical policy. It was certainly not only the cause of the Glorious Revolution that the Revocation had helped. In fact the success of the revolution, according to the Count d'Avaux, was due to 696 Huguenot officers who had joined the army of the Prince of Orange.[165] The Huguenot group in Holland acted for years as a bulwark against tyranny, and although claims that Jurieu was a father of the French Revolution are farfetched, the group of exiles created such a teeming center of intellectual and religious freedom that Locke felt quite at home while living in Holland, and his ideas ripened and matured from the stimulus he received there.[166] His lifework was to show that religious freedom lies at the root of political and social freedom.

---

[161] R. H. Tawney, *Religion and the Rise of Capitalism*, p. 320.

[162] H. M. Robertson, *Aspects of the Rise of Economic Individualism*, p. xvi.

[163] Yinger draws attention to this fact stressed by Brentano, Pirenne, and Robertson. Yinger, *Religion in the Struggle for Power*, p. 126.

[164] Ch. D. Cremeans, *The Reception of Calvinistic Thought in England*, p. 23.

[165] Cf. *Bulletin de la Société de l'histoire du Protestantisme Français*, LXII, 406.

[166] Cf. P. Fonbrune Berbinau, "Locke et la Tolérance," *Bulletin de la Société de l'histoire du Protestantisme Français*, LVIII, 573.

POSTSCRIPT

To end with a note on Locke may seem particularly fitting. His genius distilled the essence of a century of thought and struggle, spanning the period from Castellion to Bayle, and inspired him with conclusions that are occasionally reminiscent of Huguenot writings and that suggest workable solutions. He was Castellionist in his "irrationalism," in his insistence that faith and reason are not antithetical and that experience and revelation are the source of knowledge.[1] He moved away from Castellion in the sense that his argument for toleration rested on the plea for order and not for truth—a significant point of difference from the sixteenth-century way of thinking. His affinity with Bayle, on the other hand, was marked by his reasoned argumentation, his scorn for dogmatism—the greatest foe of tolerance—his conviction that there is nothing absolute about conscience, and his proverbial spirit of compromise, which was yet to triumph in political life in his own country.

It was ultimately Bayle's rationalism and skepticism which helped to elucidate the problem of conscience, around which the debate over toleration revolved. A new basis was established—which the sixteenth century would have regarded with horror—through recognition of the need for tolerance of erring conscience and not solely of a right conscience (implying the possession of truth). Bayle gave his support to the Cartesian tenet that erring conscience has all the rights of right conscience. He insisted that genuine truth (*vérité réelle*) and assumed truth (*vérité putative*) must be given equal treatment. Provided that the motives for action are honest, to persecute truth, according to Bayle, would be as correct as to persecute error. Hence his conclusion that all persecution for religious reasons is nonsensical, and his advocacy of a general attitude of tolerance.

Bayle's argument touched on the problem of conflict not only within the individual conscience but also between the individual and the state. Bayle saw enormous difficulties inherent in the latter conflict, and argued—as has been pointed out—that conscience cannot be regarded by the state as an absolute. The clash of two con-

---

[1] Cf. R. H. Bainton, *The Travail of Religious Liberty*, pp. 247, 248.

sciences leads to a stalemate: if the "true believer" must persecute and kill, the magistrate is bound to prosecute and punish him. Zealotry, proselytism, and tyrannicide must show the utter futility of mutual destruction and the ultimate need for compromise—for reciprocal recognition of some practical code of behavior.

Bayle's treatment of the problem has wide applicability: his arguments for tolerance can be used as a commentary on the modern political predicament. They touch on the ever-present problem of the peril of subversives and on the validity of the reasons given by vigilantes intent on suppressing dangerous elements. The passing of the era of intense religious persecution does not mean that human nature has changed significantly and that the mores have become milder, but simply that the emphasis has been shifted from the religious to the political sphere. Yet how thin is the rational crust of the modern man is shown in the fact that politics has its heretics and its martyrs, while the persistent failure of the powers of persuasion in imparting to opponents one's own creed or opinion can give rise to cynicism or despair. Men forever remain harassed by doubts and prone to be swayed by the forces of irrationalism. Modern behavioral sciences have devised complicated analytical tools but have failed to enable men to gain control over themselves. Men's failure as rational beings can be illustrated in the belief, begotten of fanaticism and doctrinaire politics, that to kill ideological opponents is justifiable. The logic of such an action is similar to that which lay behind the actions of both Reformers and Counter Reformers: the modern political "true believer" is after all not much different from the sixteenth-century religious zealot. History has thus completed a full circle, bringing no solution to the perennial problem of how rational control over men can be achieved.

Nor has the interplay of religious and political influences ceased. Future hope lies perhaps in man's becoming less vulnerable to the impacts of any ideology, religious or political. This would not imply a mere disbelief—a trend noticeable in the sphere of politics—but a certain amount of detachment from the tumult of the market place full of the antics of prophets and politicians. In this respect it is Richelieu who can serve as an outstanding example of ideological immunity. He provides a perfect case study of the relation between theology and politics. Philosopher, theologian, statesman, he had an ability to translate his philosophy into the language of action. He moved easily from the realm of theory to that of practice, applying expedient policies with Machiavellian cunning. In his day, the struggle for religious toleration became an essentially political issue, but it is not the substitution of politics for religion which is in question. A pure substitution would have involved political intolerance in lieu of religious intolerance and political fanaticism in place of religious fanaticism. However, the change which subsequently occurred did not result from the separation of two spheres but from a shift of emphasis. The theological, dogmatic elements in politics were yet to show themselves under a new guise.

By concentrating on his goals and on the mechanics of action, while not allowing himself to be affected by doctrinal considerations, Richelieu demonstrated that a certain interchangeability of religious and political means as instruments of control over men was possible. He thus arranged alliances with Protestant states to foster his international political ends, and used political means to suppress the Huguenot minority. His *tolerationism* had a rational basis. His rationality contributed to his success, confusing his opponents and impressing his successors, and helped him to avoid pitfalls into which theocratic states had fallen in the past, and into which the secularization of politics has subsequently led modern totalitarian states. For both the fanatics and the prophets who have ruled in such states have stood or fallen according as they observed or failed to observe Richelieu's guiding principle—avoidance of an appeal to the irrational.

SELECTED BIBLIOGRAPHY

Abbreviations used: *Bull.*—*Bulletin de la Société de l'histoire du Protestantisme Français*
Proceedings—*Proceedings of the Huguenot Society of London*

GENERAL SOURCES

Arnaud, E. *Histoire des protestants de Provence, du comtat venaissin et de la principauté d'Orange.* Paris, 1884.

Bainton, R. H. *The Travail of Religious Liberty.* Philadelphia, 1951.

Baird, H. M. *The Huguenots and the Revocation of the Edict of Nantes.* New York, 1895. 2 vols.

Benoit, Elie. *Histoire de l'edit de Nantes.* Delft, 1693–1695. 5 vols.

——— Eng. version: *The History of the Famous Edict of Nantes.* London, 1694. 4 vols.

Bonet-Maury, G. "Le Protestantisme français et la République, 1598–1685." *Bull.,* Vol. LIII.

Bouchez, F. *Le Mouvement libéral en France en XVII° s. (1610–1700).* Lille, 1908.

Buckle, H. T. *History of Civilization in England.* London, 1891. Vols. II, III.

Bury, J. B. *A History of Freedom of Thought.* Oxford University Press, 1952.

Cremeans, Ch. D. *The Reception of Calvinistic Thought in England.* University of Illinois, 1949.

Faurey, J. *L'Edit de Nantes et la question de la tolérance.* Paris, 1929.

Figgis, J. N. *Churches in Modern State.* London, 1913.

——— *Theory of the Divine Right of Kings.* 2d ed. Cambridge University Press, 1914.

Galland, A. "Les Pasteurs français Amyraut, Bochart, etc., et la royauté de droit divin, 1629–1685." *Bull.,* Vol. LXXVII.

Gooch, G. P. *English Democratic Ideas in the Seventeenth Century.* Cambridge, 1927.

Grant, A. J. *The Huguenots*. London, 1934.

Haag, Eugène and Emile. *La France Protestante ou Vies des Protestants français qui se sont fait un nom dans l'histoire*. Paris, 1846–1859. 9 vols. + *Pièces justificatives*.

Harsin, P. *Credit public et Banque d'Etat en France du XVIᵉ au XVIIIᵉ s.* Paris, 1933.

—— *Les Doctrines monétaires et financières en France du XVIᵉ au XVIIIᵉ siècle*. Paris, 1928.

Laski, H. J. *The Rise of European Liberalism*. London, 1936. 1947 ed. used.

Lavisse, E. *Histoire de France*. *Paris,* 1905–1908. Vols. VI, VII, VIII.

Leonard, E. G. *Le Protestant français*. Paris, 1953.

Pagès, G. *Naissance du Grand Siècle*. Paris, 1948.

Paquier, J.-B. *Histoire de l'unité politique et territoriale de la France*. Paris, 1880. 2 vols.

Persecution and Liberty: Essays in honor of George Lincoln Burr. New York, 1931.

Pintard, R. *Le Libertinage érudit dans la première moitié du XVIIᵉ siècle*. Paris, 1943. 2 vols.

Robertson, H. M. *Aspects of the Rise of Economic Individualism*. Cambridge, 1933.

Ruffini, F. *La libertà religiosa*. Torino, 1901.

Sagnac, P. H., and A. de Saint Leger. *La Prépondérance française*. Tome X de la collection L. Halphen et P. H. Sagnac. Paris, 1942.

Sée, H. *Les Idées politiques en France au dix-septième siècle*. Paris, 1923.

Sée, H., and R. Schnerb. *Histoire économique de la France*. Paris, 1939–1942. 2 vols.

Stéphan, R. *L'Epopée huguenote*. Paris, 1945.

Tabaraud, M. M. *Histoire critique des projets formés depuis trois cents ans pour la réunion des communions chrétiennes*. Paris, 1824.

Tawney, R. H. *Religion and the Rise of Capitalism*. London, 1926. 1944 ed. used.

Troeltsch, E. *The Social Teaching of the Christian Churches*. London, 1950. 2 vols.

Viénot, J. *Histoire de la Réforme française*. Vol. I. *Des origines à l'Edit de Nantes*. Paris, 1926. Vol. II. *De l'édit de Nantes à sa révocation*. Paris, 1934.

Viollet, Paul. *Histoire des institutions politiques et administratives de la France*. Paris, 1898. 4 vols.

Weber, Max. *The Protestant Ethic and the Spirit of Capitalism*. London, 1930. Eng. trans. of *Die protestantische Ethik und der Geist des Kapitalismus*. 1904–1905.

Yinger, J. Milton. *Religion in the Struggle for Power*. Duke University Press, 1946.

INTRODUCTORY

Primary Sources

Barclay, William. *De Potestate papae* . . . *eiusdem de regno et regali potestate*. 1600. Hanoviae, 1617, ed. used.

Bellius, Martinus (Sébastien Castellion). *De Haereticis; an sint persequendi*. Magdeburg, 1554.

Belloy, Pierre du. *Apologie Catholique contre les libelles declarations, etc., publiée par les Liguez*. 1585.

——— *De l'authorité du Roy et crimes de leze majesté*. 1587.

Beza, Th. (Théodore de Bèze). *Du droit des magistrats sur leur sujets*. 1575. In Simon Goulart, ed., *Mémoires de l'Estat de France sous Charles IX*.

——— *Epistolarum theologicarum liber unus*. Genevae, 1573.

——— *Icones, id est verae imagines virorum doctrina simul et pietate illustrium* . . . *additis eorundem vitae et operae descriptionibus*. Genevae, 1580.

——— *Traité de l'authorité du Magistrat en la punition des hérétiques*. 1560. N.B. Latin version: *De Haereticis a civili magistratu puniendis libellus*. Geneva, 1554.

Bodin, Jean. *Les Six livres de la République*. 1576. Lyon, 1579, ed. used.

Calvin, Jean. *Institution de la Religion Chrestienne*. Genève, 1560.

Coquille, Guy. *Oeuvres*. Bordeaux, 1703.

A Defence of Liberty Against Tyrants. London, 1924. Eng. trans. of *Vindiciae contra tyrannos*, by Junius Brutus (pseud.), with an introd. by H. J. Laski.

Goulart, Simon, ed. *Mémoires de l'Estat de France sous Charles IX*. 1576. Meidelbourg, 1578, ed. used.

——— *Recueil contenant les choses mémorables advenus sous la Ligue*. (*Mémoires de la Ligue*.) Amsterdam, 1758.

Henri IV. *Recueil des lettres missives* . . . Ed. by Berger de Xivrey. Paris, 1848.

Hotman, F. *Brutum Fulmen Papae Sixtii V, adversus Henricum Serenissimum Regem Navarrae, & illustrissimum Henricum Borbonium, Principem Condaeum*. Lugduni Batavorum, 1586.

—— *La Gaule Françoise.* Cologne, 1574.

Hurault, Michel. *Quatre excellens discours sur l'estat present de la France.* 1593. 1595 ed. used.

L'Hôpital, Michel de. *Oeuvres complètes.* Ed. by P. J. S. Dufey. Paris, 1824.

Mornay, Philippe de (Sieur du Plessis). Mémoires. Eng. trans. entitled *A Huguenot Family in the XVI Century.* Broadway Translations. London, 1925.

Ramus, Petrus. *The Three Partes of Commentaries, containing the whole and perfect discourse of the civill warres of Fraunce.* London, 1574–1576.

Rossaeus, G. G. *De Justa reipublicae christianae in reges impios et haereticos authoritate.* Antverpiae, 1592.

Valois, Marguerite de. *Mémoires.* Paris, 1853.

Secondary Sources

Acton, J. E., Lord. "The Protestant Theory of Persecution," *Essays on Freedom and Power.* Boston, 1948.

Allen, J. W. *A History of Political Thought in the Sixteenth Century.* London, 1941.

Armstrong, E. "The Political Theory of the Huguenots," *English Historical Review,* Vol. IV (1889).

Aubarède, G. d'. *La Revolution des Saints.* Paris, 1947.

Bainton, R. H. *The Reformation in the Sixteenth Century.* Boston, 1952.

Bainton, R. H., ed. *Concerning heretics: . . . an anonymous work attributed to Sebastian Castellio, now first done into English.* New York, 1935.

Bainton, R. H., and others. *Castellioniana.* Leiden, 1951.

Bossert, A. *Calvin.* Paris, 1906.

Buisson, F. E. *Sébastion Castellion.* Paris, 1892.

Choisy, E. *La Théocratie à Genève au temps de Calvin.* Genève, 1897.

Church, W. F. *Constitutional Thought in Sixteenth Century France.* Harvard University Press, 1941.

Dainville, Oudot de. "Contribution à la biographie de Jean de Saint Chamond," *Annales de l'Université de Montpellier.* Vol. III, No. 1. 1945.

Figgis, J. N. *Studies of Political Thought from Gerson to Grotius: 1414–1625.* Cambridge, 1931.

Grant, A. J. "The Problem of Religious Toleration in XVIth Century France," *Proceedings,* Vol. XIII (1923–1929).

Kingdom, R. M. *Geneva and the Coming of the Wars of Religion in France.* Geneva, 1956.

Labitte, Ch. *De la démocratie chez les prédicateurs de la Ligue.* Paris, 1866.

Lecler, J. *Histoire de la Tolérance au siècle de la Réforme.* Paris, 1955. 2 vols.

Lefèvre, L. R. *Le Tumulte d'Amboise.* Paris, 1949.

McIlwain, C. H. *Constitutionalism and the Changing World.* Cambridge, 1939.

Mesnard, P. *L'Essor de la philosophie politique au XVI° siècle.* Paris, 1936.

Murray, R. H. *The Political Consequences of the Reformation.* London, 1926.

Neale, J. E. *The Age of Catherine de Medici.* London, 1947.

Palm, F. C. *Politics and Religion in Sixteenth Century France: A Study of the Career of Montmorency-Damville.* Boston, 1927.

Raveau, P. *L'Agriculture et les classes paysannes: La Transformation de la propriété dans le Haut Poitou au XVI° s.* Paris, 1926.

—— *Essai sur la situation économique et l'état social en Poitou au XVI° s.* Paris, 1931.

—— *La Vie économique en Poitou au XVI° s. d'après les minutes de notaire de l'époque.* 1917.

Savory, D. L. "Broadcast on 27th July 1950," *Proceedings.* Supplement to Vol. XVIII, No. 4 (1950).

—— "Pope Gregory XIII and the Massacre of St. Bartholomew," *Proceedings,* Vol. XVII, No. 2.

Seitte, T. *Un Apôtre de la Tolérance au XVI° siècle: Michel de l'Hospital, Chancelier de France, 1506–1573.* Montauban, 1891.

Thompson, J. W. *The Wars of Religion in France.* Chicago, 1909.

Weill, Georges. *Les Théories sur le pouvoir royal en France pendant les guerres de religion.* Paris, 1892.

Wilkinson, M. *A History of the League or Sainte-Union: 1576–1595.* Glasgow, 1929.

Zeller, G. *Les Institutions de la France au XVI° siècle.* Paris, 1948.

FROM THE ISSUE OF THE EDICT OF NANTES
TO RICHELIEU

Primary Sources

Bellarminus, Robertus. *Opera omnia.* Neapoli, 1872. 8 vols.

Bignon, Hierôme. *De l'excellence des roys et du royaume de France.* Paris, 1610.

Bouffard-Madiane, J. de. *Mémoires sur les guerres civiles du duc de Rohan (1610–1629).* Arch. hist. de l'Albigeois. Fasc. 5. 1898.

Duchesne, André. *Les Antiquitez et recherches de la grandeur & maiesté des Roys de France.* Paris, 1609.

Henri IV. *Oeuvres (Lettres et harangues).* Ed. by Plon. Paris, 1941.

Loyseau, Charles. *Oeuvres.* Lyon, 1701.

Montchrétien, Antoine de. *L'Economie politique patronale: Traicté de l'oeconomie politique, dedié en 1615 au roy ...* Ed. by Th. Funck-Brentano. Paris, 1889.

Rohan, Henri de. *Mémoires historiques et discours politiques 1611–1629.* Amsterdam, 1756. 2 vols.

Rulmann, Anne. *L'Histoire secrète des affaires du temps depuis le Siège de Montpellier jusqu'à la Paix dernière* (1620–1627). MS, Nîmes, Bibliothèque municipale.

Savaron, Jean. *Premier traicté de la souveraineté du roy et de son royaume.* 1615. Collection des meilleurs dissertations, notices et traités particuliers relatifs à l'histoire de France. Paris, 1826, ed., ed. by Leber, Salgues, and Cohen, used.

Secondary Sources

Benoist, Ch. *Condition juridique des Protestants sous le régime de l'Edit de Nantes et après sa révocation.* Paris, 1910.

Dainville, Oudot de, ed. *Archives de la ville de Montpellier.* Tome VII.

Inventaire de Joffre. Archives du greffe de la maison consulaire. Armoire C.
Montpellier, 1939.

───── *Inventaire Sommaire des Archives Départementales de l'Hérault.* Série
13. *Comptabilités relatives aux gens de guerre des XVIᵉ et XVIIᵉ siècles.*
Tome VI. Montpellier, 1951.

De La Garde, H. *Le Duc de Rohan et les protestants sous Louis XIII.* Paris,
1884.

Isambert, F. A., A. Jourdan, and others. *Recueil général des anciennes lois
françaises: depuis l'an 420 jusqu'à la Révolution de 1789.* Paris [1822]–
1833. 30 vols.

Laugel, A. *Henri de Rohan, son rôle politique et militaire sous Louis XIII:
1579–1638.* Paris, 1889.

Schybergson, M. G. *Le Duc de Rohan et la chute du parti protestant en France.*
Paris, 1880.

Thomas, Eug., ed. *Inventaire & Sommaire des Archives Départmentales an-
térieures à 1790.* Hérault. Archives Civiles. Série C. Tome II. Montpellier,
1865.

POLITICAL THOUGHT OF RICHELIEU

Primary Sources

Dupuy, Pierre. *Commentaire sur le traité des Libertez de l'Eglise Gallicane de
Pierre Pithou.* [n.p.], 1639. 1652 ed. used.

Gallus, Optatus. *De Cavendo Schismate, ad illustrissimos ac reverendissimos
Ecclesiae Gallicanae Primates, Archiepiscopos, Episcopos, liber paroeniticus.*
Lugduni, 1640.

Griselle, E., ed. *Louis XIII et Richelieu, lettres et pièces diplomatiques.* Paris,
1911.

Lebret, Cardinal. *De la souveraineté du Roy.* Paris, 1632.

Lherminier. *Supplement à l'histoire de France 1624–1638.* British Museum,
Bibl. Egerton, MS 1673.

Marca, Petro de. *De Concordia sacerdotii et imperii, seu de libertatibus ecclesiae gallicanae.* Parisiis, 1641.

Le Mercure Jésuite. Vol. I. Genève, 1631.

Montigni, du Moulin, Durand, and Mestrezat (Quatre Ministres de Charenton). *Défense de la confession des Eglises réformées de France contre les accusations du Sieur Arnould ...*

Naudé, Gabriel. *Considérations politiques sur les coups d'Etat.* 1639. 1679 ed. used.

Richelieu, Cardinal, Duc de (Armand Jean du Plessis). *Lettres, instructions diplomatiques et papiers d'état.* Ed. by Avenel. Collections de documents inédits, etc. 1835, etc. 8 vols.

—— *Maximes d'Etat et fragments politiques ...* Ed. by G. Hanotaux. Collection de documents inédits sur l'histoire de France, Mélanges historiques. Vol. III. Paris, 1880.

—— *Mémoires ... depuis 1610 jusqu'à 1620.* Ed. by Petitot. Collection complète des mémoires relatifs à l'histoire de France, etc. 2ᵉ série, tomes X, XI. Paris, 1819, etc.

—— *Mémoires ... depuis 1610 jusqu'à 1638.* Ed. by Michaud and Poujoulat. Nouvelle collection des mémoires, etc. 2ᵉ série, tomes VII–IX. Paris, 1836, etc.

—— *Mémoires ...* Publiés d'après les manuscrits originaux pour la Société de l'histoire de France sous les auspices de l'Académie française. Paris, 1908–1932. 10 vols.

—— *Principaux points de la Foy de l'Eglise catholique défendus contre les quatre Ministres de Charenton.* Eng. version: *The Principal Points of Faith of the Catholike Church.* Paris, 1635.

—— *Testament politique.* Ed. by André. Paris, 1947.

—— *Traitté qui contient la méthode la plus facile et la plus asseurée pour convertir ceux qui se sont séparez de l'Eglise.* Paris, 1651.

Sanctarellus, Antonio. *Tractatus de haeresi, schismate, apostasi sollicitatione in sacramento poenitentiae, et de potestate Romani Pontificis.* Romae, 1625.

Secondary Sources

Albertini, Rudolf von. *Das politische Denken in Frankreich zur Zeit Richelieus.* Marburg, 1951.

Avenel, le vicomte G. d'. *Richelieu et la monarchie absolue.* Paris, 1884–1890. 4 vols.

Bridges, J. H. *France under Richelieu and Colbert.* London, 1924.

Burckhardt, C. J. *Richelieu: His Rise to Power.* London, 1940.

Deloche, M. *Autour de la plume du cardinal de Richelieu.* Paris, 1920.

Fagniez, Gustave. *Le Père Joseph et Richelieu.* Paris, 1894. Vols. I, II.

Gaquère, F. *Pierre de Marca (1594–1662)*. Paris, 1932.

Hauser, H. *La Pensée et l'action économiques du cardinal de Richelieu*. Paris, 1944.

Richard, Abbé. *Le Véritable Père Josef, capucin nommé au Cardinalat*. Saint Jean de Mauriene, 1704.

POLITICAL THOUGHT OF MAZARIN

Primary Sources

Amyraut, Moïse. *Discours de la souveraineté des Roys*. [n.p.], 1650.

———— *Du Regne de mille ans ou de la prospérité de l'Eglise*. Saumur, 1654.

Dumoulin, Pierre (the Younger). *Clamor regii sanguinis adversus parricides anglicanos*. La Haye, 1652.

———— *Défense de la Religion Reformée et de la Monarchie et Eglise Anglicane*. La Haye, 1650.

Joly, Claude. *Lettre apologétique pour le Recueil de Maximes véritables*. 1663.

———— *Recueil de Maximes véritables ... pour l'institution du roy*. 1653.

Mazarin, Cardinal de. *Lettres*. Ed. by P. A. Chéruel and G. d'Avenel. Collection de documents inédits sur l'histoire de France. Paris, 1872–1906. 9 vols.

Moreau, C., ed. *Choix de Mazarinades*. Paris, 1853. 2 vols.

Retz, Cardinal de (Jean François Paul de Gondi). *Mémoires*. Ed. by Maurice Allem. Paris, 1849.

———— *Oeuvres*. Ed. by Feillet, Gourdault, and Chantelauze. Paris, 1870–1896. 10 vols.

Rivet, André. *Jesuita vapulans*. Lugduni Batavorum, 1635.

Saumaise, Claude. *Defensio regia pro Carolo I*. Amsterdam, 1649.

Secondary Sources

Brette, A. *La France au milieu du XVIIᵉ s. d'après la correspondance de Gui Patin*. Paris, 1901.

Cousin, Victor. *Madame de Longueville pendant la Fronde*. Paris, 1859. 2 vols.

Denis, J. *Littérature politique de la Fronde.* Caen, 1892.

Doolin, P. R. *La Fronde.* Harvard University Press, 1935.

Pic, Pierre. *Guy Patin.* Paris, 1911.

POLITICAL THOUGHT OF LOUIS XIV

Primary Sources

Abbadie, Jacques. *Défense de la nation Britannique.* [n.p.], 1692.

Arnauld, A., and P. Nicole. *La Perpétuité de la Foy de l'Eglise catholique touchant l'eucharistie défendue contre le livre du Sieur Claude.* Paris, 1669–1672.

Avis important aux réfugiez sur leur prochain retour en France. Amsterdam, 1690.

Bayle, Pierre. *Dictionnaire historique et critique.* Rotterdam, 1720.

———— *Lettres de Pierre Bayle 1670–1706.* British Museum, Birch Coll. Additional MS 4226.

———— *Oeuvres diverses.* La Haye and Rotterdam, 1727–1731. 4 vols.

 La Cabale chimérique. 1691.

 Commentaire philosophique sur les paroles de Jesus-Christ, Contrains-les d'entrer. 1686.

 Nouvelles de la république des lettres. 1684–1687.

 Réponse aux Questions d'un provincial. 1706.

 Supplément du Commentaire philosophique. 1688.

Bernard, Pierre. *Explication de l'Edit de Nantes par les autres édits de pacification et arrêts de règlement.* Paris, 1666.

Bossuet, Jacques Bénigne. *Conference avec M. Claude Ministre de Charenton sur la matière de l'Eglise.* Paris, 1682.

———— *L'Exposition de la foy de l'Eglise catholique sur les matières de controverse.* Paris, 1671.

———— *Oeuvres complètes.* Ed. by F. Lachat. Paris, 1862–1866. 31 vols.

———— *Oeuvres oratoires.* Ed. by Lebarcq. Paris, 1914–1926. 7 vols.

Claude, Jean. *Les Plaintes des Protestans cruellement opprimez dans le royaume de France.* 1686. Paris, 1885, ed., ed. by Frank Puaux, used.

———— *Réponse au livre de Monsieur l'evesque de Meaux intitulé Conference avec M. Claude.* Quevilly, 1683.

Colbert, J. B. *Testament politique.* La Haye, 1693.

Escobar y Mendoza, Antonius de. *Liber theologiae moralis.* 1643. Lugduni, 1659, ed. used.

Hérault, Louys. *Le Pacifique royal en joye.* Amsterdam, 1665.

Huisseau, Isaac d'. *La Réunion du christianisme.* Saumur, 1670.

Jurieu, Pierre. *Avis aux protestans de l'Europe.* 1685. Printed with *Préjugez légitimes contre le Papisme.*

—————— *Des droits des deux souverains en matière de religion, la conscience et le prince. Pour détruire le dogme de l'indifference des religions et de la tolerance universelle. Contre un livre intitulé Commentaire philosophique sur les paroles de la parabole: Contrains les d'entrer.* Rotterdam, 1687.

—————— *Les derniers efforts de l'innocence affligée.* Villefranche, 1682.

—————— *Histoire du calvinisme et celle du papisme, mises en parallèle.* Rotterdam, 1683.

—————— *Judgment upon the Question of Defending our Religion by Arms with Reflections upon the Affairs of England in his Ninth Pastoral Letter of the Third Year.* London, 1689.

—————— *Lettre de quelques Protestans pacifiques, au sujet de la réunion des Religions à l'assemblée de Messieurs du clergé de France, qui se doit tenir à Saint-Germain-en-Laye.* 1685.

—————— *Lettres pastorales adressées aux fidèles de France qui gémissent sous la captivité de Babylone.* Rotterdam, 1686–1689.

—————— *Pastoral Letters* (1st year). London, 1691.

—————— *La Politique du clergé de France.* La Haye, 1681.

—————— *Préjugez légitimes contre le Papisme.* Amsterdam, 1685.

—————— *Relation de tout ce qui s'est fait dans les affaires de la Religion Réformée, & pour ses intérêts, depuis le commencement des Negociacions de la Paix de Reswik.* Rotterdam, 1698.

Larrey, Isaac de. *Réponse à l'Avis aux réfugiez.* Rotterdam, 1709.

Leclerc, J. *Concerning the Choice of our opinion amongst the different Sects of Christians.* Publ. with Grotius' *The Truth of the Christian Religion.* London, 1719.

—————— *Supplementary Book II* to Hugo Grotius' *Truth of Christianity.* London, 1814.

Louis XIV. *Mémoires ... pour l'instruction du Dauphin.* Ed. by Ch. Dreyss. Paris, 1860. 2 vols.

—————— *Oeuvres.* Ed. by Grouvelle and de Grimoard. Paris, 1806. 6 vols.

Pajon, Claude. *Remarques sur l'Avertissement Pastoral, etc.* Amsterdam, 1685.

Papin, Isaac. *Essais de theologie, etc.* Francfort, 1687.

—————— *La Vanité des sciences, etc.* [n.p.], 1688.

Les Soupirs de la France esclave qui aspire après la liberté. Amsterdam, 1689.

Spinoza, Benedict de. *Tractatus Theologico-Politicus.* 1670. London, 1862, Eng. ed. used.

Secondary Sources

André, Louis. *Louis XIV et l'Europe.* Paris, 1950.

Dedieu, Joseph. *Le Role politique des protestans français (1689–1715).* Paris, 1920.

Delvolvé, Jean. *Religion critique et philosophie positive chez Pierre Bayle.* Paris, 1906.

Dodge, G. H. *The Political Theory of the Huguenots of the Dispersion.* New York, 1947.

Gélin, H. "Madame de Maintenon convertisseuse," *Bull.,* Vol. XLIX.

Guitard, E. M. *Colbert et Seignelay contre la Religion réformée.* Documents inédits. Paris, 1912.

Hazard, P. *La Crise de la conscience Européenne (1660–1715).* Paris, 1935.

Lacour-Gayet, G. *L'Education politique de Louis XIV.* 2d ed. Paris, 1923.

Lureau, R. *Les Doctrines politiques de Jurieu, 1637–1713.* Bordeaux, 1904.

Marriott, Sir J. A. R. "The Edict of Nantes—Masterpiece or Blunder?" *Proceedings,* Vol. XV (1933–1937).

Nourrisson, J. F. *La Politique de Bossuet.* Paris, 1807.

Orcibal, J. *Louis XIV et les Protestants.* Paris, 1951.

Puaux, Frank. *Les Précurseurs français de la tolérance au XVII° s.* Paris, 1881.

———— "L'Evolution des théories politiques du Protestantisme français pendant le règne de Louis XIV," *Bull.,* Vol. LXII (1913, 1914). Published separately as *Les Défenseurs de la souveraineté du peuple sous le règne de Louis XIV.* Paris, 1917.

Puaux, Frank, and Louis A. Sabatier. *Etudes sur la révocation de l'édit de Nantes.* Paris, 1886.

Rebelliau, A. *Bossuet.* Paris, 1909.

Robinson, Howard. *Bayle the Skeptic.* New York, 1931.

Rousset, C. F. M. *Histoire de Louvois et son administration politique et militaire.* Paris, 1862–1863. 4 vols.

Rulhière, Claude Carloman de. *Eclaircissemens historiques sur les causes de la révocation de l'édit de Nantes et sur l'état des Protestants en France, depuis le commencement du Règne de Louis XIV, jusqu'à nos jours.* [n.p.], 1788.

Weiss, Ch. *Histoire des réfugiés protestants de France.* Paris, 1853. 2 vols.

INDEX